DR. BADER'S PEST

NATURAL SOLUTIONS
To
THINGS THAT BUG YOU

BY

DR. MYLES H. BADER

IF THEY ARE FLYING, CRAWLING, BURROWING OR SNEAKING IN, THIS BOOK HAS THE ALL-NATURAL SOLUTION

THIS BOOK WILL PROVIDE THE METHOD OF ELIMINATING ALMOST ANY INSECT or BUG PROBLEM NATURALLY!

NATURAL SOLUTIONS TO THINGS THAT BUG YOU

By
Dr. Myles H. Bader

NOTE:
Some substances in this book can be harmful if not used with caution. Please avoid disregarding precautions or breathing in or ingesting the ingredients. When working with any chemical it is always advisable to wear a protective mask and/or rubber gloves. Many, but not all, of the solutions in this book are harmless to humans and pets. The information provided in this book is for educational and entertainment use only. You accept full responsibility for any use of this information, which is provided "as is" without any representations or warranties whatsoever. Telebrands Corp. ("Publisher") is not responsible for any errors or omissions. Publisher shall not be liable, in contract, tort, or otherwise, to the reader or any other entity or individual for any personal or property injury, loss of profits, direct, indirect, special, punitive, consequential, special or incidental loss or damage, of any nature whatsoever.

TELEBrands **PRESS**

Fairfield, NJ 07004

A WORD ABOUT THE AUTHOR

Dr. Myles H. Bader known as the "Wizard of Food" as well as the "Buggy Professor" has been a prolific writer of kitchen reference, household hint and cooking secret books for over 17 years. Dr. Bader is also a recognized leader in the field of preventive care, weight management, nutrition and wellness and has been a guest on over 6,000 radio talk shows and 135 television shows including Oprah, The Discovery Channel, America's Talking, HGTV, QVC, Trinity Broadcasting, Fox & Friends, NBC and Help at Home.

Dr. Bader received his Professional Medical Degree from Loma Linda University and is board certified as a Preventive Care Practitioner. He is experienced in weight control, exercise physiology, stress management, early detection of heart disease, has counseled in all areas of nutrition and has lectured extensively on supplementation and anti-aging for 30 years. He has also established multi-phasic screening prevention programs for numerous safety departments, city governments and executive health programs for over 40 major corporations.

Dr. Bader has authored 23 books including "The Encyclopedia of Kitchen & Cooking Secrets." "Cookbook's Companion," "1,001 All-Natural Secrets to a Pest-Free Property" "20,001 Food Secrets, Chefs Secrets & Household Hints," "The Wellness Desk Reference," "1,001 Secret Household Formulas & Money Saving Tips," "10,001 Food Facts, " "To Supplement or Not to Supplement," "Grandmother's Kitchen Wisdom" and many more. Dr. Bader's books have formally been marketed by; Barnes & Noble, Amazon, Reader's Digest, Book of the Month Club and Doubleday.

TABLE OF CONTENTS

INTRODUCTION

TOXIC CHEMICALS ARE HARMFUL TO THE ENVIRONMENT

The use of toxic chemicals is really taking the "easy way out!" Our grandparents and great grandparents managed to grow flower gardens and vegetables long before the invention of pesticides. They knew how to control and eliminate the bugs and insects without poisoning the environment, your surroundings or the ground water.

There is presently about 3.4 billion pounds of synthetic pesticides manufactured in the United States annually, which is 25% of the world's total. The EPA has recognized the problem and has stated that the pesticides are a major threat to groundwater in all areas of the Unite States.

The sad fact is that 67% of all pesticides are thought to cause cancer in humans and pets. When trying to get rid your garden of pests using poisons, we need to learn to eliminate them naturally instead of putting ourselves and the planet at risk. Remember, the poison you are using on the garden pest can kill you and your pets as well!

INTELLIGENT INSECTS

Bugs and insects have been around for millions of years before we ever appeared. They have learned how to adapt to almost every situation and are the most successful creatures on earth. They are part of an army of possibly over 10 million species of which we have only identified about 1 million.

They are capable of changing their colors, shapes and have the ability to live in the harshest environments on earth, from the highest mountains to the depths of the seas. They are capable of out-lifting us, out-jumping us, out-work us, poisoning us, paralyzing us and fly and burrow into the earth living underground.

Insects are our biggest competitors for the earth since they eat our food, ruin our clothing, destroy our homes and give us diseases that can kill us.

However, the good news is that only 1% of all insects are really pests, and without the beneficial insects as well as the pests, birds, fish, reptiles and even certain mammals would have nothing to eat. In fact, many people in all areas of the world rely on insects for one of their sources of sustenance.

PUBLIC AWARENESS

The public needs to become more aware of the dangers involved from using toxic chemicals and start using a more natural approach to getting rid of insect and bugs that are pests. While many of the methods mentioned in this book provides ways of ridding your property of the pest without killing them, a number of the methods, even though they are all-natural may harm certain insects and small critters that burrow underground.

There are natural methods of dealing with almost any type of insect and critter but the information has been difficult to obtain until now and not easily found on the Internet or literature. The information in this book is accurate and has proven very effective. Hundreds of the facts and solutions have been handed down for hundreds of years and long before pest control services and toxic products became popular and caused harmful chemical effects.

In 2011 more than 3.8 million people suffered medically related side effects from the use of pesticides. Some of the immediate effects included dizziness, nausea, headaches and loss of energy.

This book has been designed to make it easy to find the information you need and the answers to your questions are very precise. The substances that are recommended are easy to locate and easy to assemble into a usable controlled substance. Always try the simplest method first before going to a stronger one. Some of the stronger methods may harm many of the beneficial insects and even some animals.

BORIC ACID (technical variety)

One of the more common ingredients used in this book is boric acid. Boric acid has been used for generations to kill insects and roaches and is very effective. However, it can be poisonous if ingested in large amounts and care needs to be taken when using and storing it. It is one of the least toxic substances we can use that is very effective.

Boric acid is produced from a naturally occurring mineral, borate, which is reacted with sulfuric acid to produce boric acid and can be found in a colorless crystal form or a white powder. The Greeks used it to preserve food as well as a house-cleaning product.

Originally, boric acid was used as a medicinal antiseptic. It has the ability to kill the insect in two ways; first, it is a stomach poison and can be picked up on the insect feet and transferred to its mouth, second, the powder is capable of penetrating the insect's outer covering.

It can be sprinkled in corners and secluded areas and will not get into the air. Most hardware stores sell boric acid in a colored powder and add an anti-caking agent to prevent lumping. The color helps, so that it will not be confused with other food substances, such as flour or sugar. However, a good substitute for boric acid is diatomaceous earth (food grade), pyrethrum or silica gel.

DIATOMACEOUS EARTH (DE) (Food Grade)

It consists of silicate shells of microscopic sea creatures called diatoms. The shell fragments contain millions of razor sharp edges, which enter the exoskeleton and disturb the waxy coating that retains moisture. Diatomaceous earth can lead to dehydration in 12 to 24 hours and is more successful when it is hot but less humid.

DANGER: One teaspoon of boric acid can kill a child and give an adult a very bad stomachache. However, it is excellent for use inside bathroom cabinets and under the sink!

IDENTIFYING YOUR PROBLEM

Before trying to remove the pests and critters from your home, garden or yard, you must first identify the problem pest. This may not be easy since there are many pests that will do similar damage to your plants making it hard to find out which pest is guilty.

It is first necessary to study the damage and solve the mystery. If the plants leaves are full of holes, the type of hole and its shape may give you a clue. The plant may be cut off at the base and pulled underground. The leaves may be chewed around the edges or there may be a small hole in the stem. Was the damage done during the day or during the night?

A careful study of the surroundings and the underneath side of the leaf is important to see if the culprit has left behind a clue to its identity. Many insects lay their eggs on the underneath sides of leaves and the color of the eggs can be another clue.

Droppings from insects and critters are an excellent clue to follow up; however, you must narrow the possibilities down so that you can attack the pest with the most efficient natural means available.

If the ground is moist you may be able to find tracks, which are an excellent method of identification. If you do find out that it is a night intruder than you will need to check the garden after dark with a flashlight. Many insects can be caught in the act after dark, which makes identifying them much easier.

The damage, however, may not be done by insects and may be caused by animals in which case you will have to approach the problem from a totally different angle. There are many methods of eliminating the problem such as trapping, spraying, use of pathogens, placing barriers, glue strips, baiting or parasites may be used. Initially trapping is one of the best methods of identifying the pest or pests.

This book provides many methods of solving insect and bug problems and you can pick the best method for your yard that will cause the least amount of damage to your healthy plants.

Identification may include bringing a sample of the problem to your local garden or agricultural supply store. In some cases you may have to bring the sample to a local college or university entomologist.

BEETLES

Almost 40% of all insects are beetles! They can be found everywhere except in the oceans. They are easily recognized wing covers, which meet in a straight line down the middle of their backs. Most beetles are unable to, or rarely fly. If they do fly, they may tend to bump into things since they have very poor eyesight.

The larvae of beetles, is called a "grub." Grubs develop below ground and are usually pale white and have well, developed front legs used for digging. They have very strong jaws and have the ability to chew and cause extensive damage. The larval form has three pairs of legs on the thorax and can be found on the surface or on the plants. The bodies of bark beetle larvae look like a piece of puffed rice and have a dark colored head.

CATERPILLARS/BUTTERFLIES/MOTHS

The immature or larval stages are called caterpillars and have three pairs of claw-like legs on their thorax. They also have fleshy legs known as prolegs on a number of their segments. To identify this caterpillar from others each have 2-5 pairs of prolegs that are tipped with a crochet tip. The cycle goes from the egg stage to 5 stages of caterpillar then to a butterfly or moth. The eggs are always laid on a leaf.

LACEWINGS/ANTLIONS

This is a group of predators that have curved, lance-like jaws that project prominently from their head. The larvae have legs on the thorax but do not have prolegs on the abdomen. Lacewings have a tendency toward cannibalism, which forces the female to lay each egg on the end of a hair-like strand, which separates them at birth, thus protecting them. Lacewings may be considered a beneficial insect and loves to consume aphids.

ANTS/BEES/WASPS/SAWFLIES

The larval stage is difficult to identify and are not easily found since they develop in specialized nests that are somewhat unique to each species. However, bees, wasps and sawflies; can be identified by their two pairs of transparent wings. Flies have only one pair of wings. Ants: can be easily recognized by their enlarged abdomen.

FLIES/GNATS/MOSQUITOES

The larvae of true flies do not have any legs and thus making it difficult to identify a head. The head is usually tapered to a point and surrounded by tiny hooks that can be retracted. The larval form is called a "maggot" and is produced by flies. The larval form of mosquitoes also lacks legs; however, they have a visible head that is darker than the rest of the body.

THRIPS

The main difference between the adult thrip and the larval stage is the absence of wings. The larval stage and the adult are often found together on plants. Thrips are so small that they are almost invisible and about the width of a fine sewing needle. They damage the plant by sucking the sap out by scrapping the tissue. The plant damage; is sometimes mistaken for damage by mites, except there are no webs.

APHIDS/SCALES

Aphids are soft-bodied, pear-shaped and less than 1/10th inch long. They can be winged or wingless and have a pair of tiny tubes at the end of their abdomen. The immature stages of these insects are very similar to the adult; however, they lack wings. They can be found in almost any color and will suck the sap from the plant. Scales are usually reddish-brown, round-shaped orange circles with a small knob in the center of a cap-like covering. They are only 1/12th inch long.

GRASSHOPPERS/CRICKETS/KATYDIDS/MANTIDS

The immature stages and the adult are very similar with the exception of fully developed wings in the adult.

TERMITES

The only noticeable difference between the immature stage and the adult will be the size. The reproductive forms of termites have large functional wings and distinct wing buds in their early development stages.

TICKS/SPIDER MITES

After their eggs hatch, ticks have six legs in their larval stage. After they molt they have 8 legs and look like an adult until they complete their development. To check a plant for mites you will need a magnifying glass. Mites can reproduce every 3-7 days and are not insects. To control them spray the plant every few days since they won't multiply if the area is kept damp.

WHITEFLY

This small white fly is difficult to control since they will leave the plant as soon as you spray the plant. It is best to identify the immature stage, which is scale-like and can't move. The scale can be eliminated with dipping in a soapy solution.

GARDENER-CAUSED PLANT DISEASE

Care must be taken when handling or touching plants in the garden, especially wet plants. Disease: can be spread by just touching an area that is diseased and then touching another plant.

If you see a diseased area, just remove it, destroy it and wash your hands before continuing with your gardening. Some diseases live in the soil and are easily transmitted to your plants. The problem may not be from insects. Good soil enrichment by compost will be the key to reducing many plant diseases.

The following are a few more rules to follow

➢ **Keep the area around your plants clean and clear of any rotting debris**
➢ **Plow the garden area in the fall to plow the old plants under and remove locations for pests to winter**
➢ **Plowing will also allow some of the insects and their eggs to become more visible for the birds to see and eat**
➢ **Cover the rows with cheesecloth netting to deter Japanese beetles and similar bugs**

GENERAL GUIDELINES FOR HOUSE PLANTS

❖ Be sure and use clean pots & planters when you re-pot a plant.
❖ Use only sterile potting soil since garden soils may contain insect larvae or other harmful components.
❖ Be sure and isolate any newly purchased plant for around 30 days while checking them frequently for signs of disease or insects.
❖ If you are going to bring any plants that have been outside for the summer in the house, be sure to check them over carefully.
❖ Be sure and use a magnifying glass to look for insects.
❖ Wash the leaves occasionally with a soft cloth and warm, soapy water.
❖ Be sure the air is circulating freely around the plants.
❖ Nutrient sticks work very well to feed a plant and keep it healthy so that it can fight off disease and insects.

NATURAL METHODS OF CONTROL

❖ Removing the pest by hand picking
❖ Introducing parasites to eat the pests from the inside
❖ The use of a natural predator to eat the pest
❖ Microbes that will make a pest sick
❖ Removing debris, eliminating their living quarters
❖ Planting protective plants to repel them
❖ Trapping the pest using "pheromone"
❖ Crop rotation

INSECT-CAUSED PLANT DISEASE

There are many plant diseases caused by insects. Houseplants are especially susceptible to white flies and aphids that will suck the juices from the plants by piercing the plants leaves and stem. They are capable of transmitting viruses and bacteria into the plant from their saliva. The damaged areas may also decay, making these areas more susceptible to other airborne diseases. Certain soap sprays can alleviate this problem and prevent damage.

FREEZE THEM OR HEAT 'EM UP

Before we had hundreds of poisons and pesticides, we had other methods of dealing with pests and insects.

Using very high heat or very low temperatures will kill most insects and pests. Subzero or high heat, such as 140^0F or above will usually do the trick. When grandma wanted to protect her woolens and furs, she placed them in cold storage for the summer.

In Europe exterminators blow hot air at a temperature of 150^0F or higher into homes and apartments to get rid of the pests. Using your furnace or freezer, you too can duplicate some of the methods that worked in the past. However, it is not really safe to try and get your furnace up over 150^0F without doing damage to some fabrics and even flooring.

BUGS LOVE TO EAT CLOTHING

Prevention can save a fortune in clothing! Best to rotate your clothes and wear them as often as possible, especially woolens. This may eliminate moths and silverfish from eating them. If you are not going to wear clothes for an extended period of time, it is best to have them dry cleaned and place them in a protective bag. If you have a woolen garment in your closet over 2 years, it would be best to examine it carefully, then send it to the cleaners and protect it.

CHAPTER 1

ANTS & THEIR RELATIVES

ANTS & THEIR RELATIVES

There are literally thousands of methods of controlling and killing ants. However, there are only a handful of methods that are really effective. Ants can be viewed as a well-organized military unit that is trained to find food and water at all costs. They are tenacious and if there is any food or water to be located they will find it. There are over 12,000 species of ants in the world with California having over 200 species.

The average life expectancy of an ant is only 45-60 days. An ant brain has about 250,000 brain cells. The human brain has about 10,000 million brain cells; however, a colony of 40,000 ants has the same brain capacity as a human.

There are fewer ants running around when there is a lot of rain. When there is a dry weather period they multiply very quickly. Ants can be both a help to and a real pest. When they are just in the soil, they will aerate the soil and will even kill other pests like termites and other insects.

Ants are found everywhere in the world and number more than any other land creature. Their societies are well organized and revolve around a queen and males with neuter workers and females doing the day-to-day chores. They know who is a member of a particular colony and will not allow an outsider to enter their nest. They protect the colony by squirting formic acid at predators and can spray up to 1-foot away.

A colony is capable of having as many as 250,000 ants with the queen being imprisoned for life in a special chamber. In large number, they are capable of killing a baby chick or small bird. Ants that win a battle with another colony may even bring back workers as slaves to work for their colony.

Ants are not all bad and if they are not pestering us in our homes should probably be left alone to assist us in reducing the number of other pests that are on our property such as cockroaches, larvae of the filth fly, scale insects, mealybugs and some beetles.

IDENTIFYING CHARACTERISTICS:

Ants are very close relatives of wasps and bees and are easily recognizable. Their wingless adult form is known as "workers." The winged variety is often confused with winged termites, especially when they leave their nest to mate and for a new colony.

There are 3 characteristics that will help to determine the difference between ants and termites:

> ➤ The hind wings of ants are smaller than its front wings; the termite's front and hind wings are approximately the same size. Both termites and ants will lose their wings after a short flight.
> ➤ The ant has a thin waist and the termite does not, it is about the same thickness.
> ➤ The female and worker ants have a bent or elbowed antennae; the termite's antennae are not relatively straight and not elbowed.

Ants undergo a complete change, called a metamorphosis, which includes passing through stages such as egg, larval, pupae and adult. The larval are relatively immobile and resemble a worm and look nothing like the adult. Ants are also very social insects and they have their own duties, which are divided among the various types of adults.

The queen is responsible for all the reproductive functions of her colony and she is much larger than the other adult ants. They lay eggs and will sometimes take part in the feeding and grooming of the larvae. The female workers are all sterile and are involved in the gathering of food, taking care of the larvae, build tunnels and defend the colony. The females take up the bulk of the colony since males do not take part in colony activities only mate with the queen. The males are fed and cared for by the female workers.

One of the best methods of keeping ants out of the house is to regularly spray an all-natural deterrent solution around the outside of the home. If you have any bushes or trees that touch the house, remove the problem.

The following are identifying features of common household ants:

There are specific characteristics when identifying ants and you will need a magnifying glass to determine the number of nodes at the back of their abdomen. By counting the number of nodes you can determine the identity of the ant.

One-node ants are the Argentine ant, carpenter ant, common house ant and the velvety tree ant.

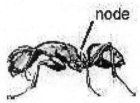

Two-node ants are the pavement ant, pharaoh ant, red imported fire ant, southern fire ant and thief ant.

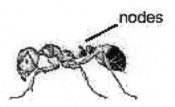

Ants also hate termites and will kill and eliminate their nest when they can find one.

PREVENTION INSTEAD OF POISONS
➢ Be sure and keep all tree branches and bushes away from the house, which makes it easier for them to reach the windows and cracks.
➢ If you find cracks, best to patch them.
➢ Never leave any traces of foodstuffs around, they will find even the smallest trace. Not even on dishes.
➢ Standing water near the house will also invite ants.
➢ Foods left in containers or packages that have been opened and left in the cupboard need to be sealed **VERY TIGHTLY**.
➢ Rinse off and wipe dry and medicine bottles, syrups and jelly jars.
➢ Be sure and clean your kitchen floor every day.

GENERAL ANT REMEDIES

OLD TIME REPELLANTS

There are many herbs that will repel ants naturally and these will be recommended as ant repellants. One of the best natural ones is fresh mint. If you have an ant invasion, just place some fresh mint (if you have a plant) anywhere they are congregating and they will all pack their bags and leave, very fast!

GET OUT THE MAGNIFYING GLASS

If you have an ant problem, one way to eliminate the problem is to follow them back to where they made their entrance into your home and seal it up tight. Killing them before you find out where they are coming from will not eliminate the problem, just make them mad.

WATER TORTURE MAY NOT WORK

If you are lucky enough to locate the nest, this will be the best way to eliminate the entire colony. Pouring cold water into the colony nest will not work since ant can survive a long time under cold water. You must use either boiling water or hot paraffin to do the trick.

GIVING THE QUEEN HEARTBURN

This concoction is a treat for the queen and when left for the workers they will bring the treat home to their queen as a present. The queen gets excited and quickly gobbles up the goody and within a few hours dies of heartburn. Make sure this treat is out of reach of children and animals that you wish to have around for a while. If they do ingest it the boric acid may make them very sick. However, it doesn't take very much to do the job and eliminate the queen so don't make it too toxic. A little boric acid goes a long way.

Mix the following ingredients together in a small bowl:

   3 ½   Ounces of Strawberry jam (any sweet jam will do)
   1 ½   Tablespoons of wet, canned cat food (cheap brand)
   1   Teaspoon of boric acid

Make very small balls from the mixture and leave them where you have seen the workers foraging for food. **Keep mixture away from pets and kids.**

ANT DUST
The following ingredients will be needed:

   ¼   Pound of dried peppermint (from health food store)
   ¼   Pound rock dust (from nursery)
   ¼   Pound seaweed powder (from garden supply)
   ¼   Pound alfalfa meal (organic, from health food store)
   ¼   Pound cayenne pepper

Place all ingredients in a well-sealed jar or plastic container and shake well to mix. **Avoid getting any of the powder on your hands and possibly into your eyes.** Use a small amount of the powder where the ants frequent. This will keep them away but not kill them. **Keep away from children and pets.**

WINDOW BOX PROTECTOR
If you have window boxes and have an insect problem in them, just clean them out and whitewash them. This will stop the insects and reduce the risk of dry rot.

FEED THEM MELON
If you have a bad ant problem and can't get rid of them, just leave a slice of watermelon or cantaloupe in your yard far from the house. They would prefer melon to anything you have in the house (most of the time, unless you spilled honey on the floor).

BEAN THEM!
Soyabean® (glycine max) is an excellent ant repellant and has been used for many years in Africa. Just prepare the spray by soaking the plant stems in water for 24 hours then using the water as a spray. This also works for aphids and codling moths.

REPEL THEM WITH TANSY
If you sprinkle some fresh tansy leaves in the corners of your kitchen counter and in the windowsills it will repel ants 100%.

GET OUT THE MAGNIFYING GLASS
If you think you know where the ants are entering the house and need to be sure, just place some strips of masking tape glue-side up and put some sugar or honey on it. Check it in the morning and see how many ants you trapped.

SLIPPERY SUGGESTION
To keep ants from getting on your plants, just place some lard, Vaseline®, Crisco®, butter, etc. around the base of the plant.

TREAT THEM TO A GREAT BREAKFAST CEREAL
Ingredients:
1½ cup Cream of Wheat

Kaboom!
Just place a dish of Cream of Wheat where the ants can easily access it. After they eat it, the cereal will expand and the ants will explode.

KILL THEM WITH KINDNESS

If you want to trap ants and make them really happy, all you have to do is open a bottle of cheap maple syrup (not the real expensive stuff); the ants will find the bottle very quickly, enter it and drown.

DON'T CHEW IT FIRST!

The only chewing gum that works to repel ants is a mint-flavored or spearmint gum. Just place an opened piece in all the drawers of the kitchen or wherever you are having a problem. Also, works great at the base of a houseplant.

THE ANT TRAPPER

The following ingredients will be needed:

6	**Tablespoons of granulated sugar**
6	**Tablespoons of active dry yeast (fresh)**
½	**Cup standard grade molasses or honey**
10	**Small plastic lids or bottle caps**

Place all the ingredients in a small bowl and mix thoroughly until it is smooth. Place a small amount of the mixture into the lids or caps and place them near an ant trail or near their mound. The mixture can also be spread on a piece of cardboard or small stick and placed in their pathway or in a crevice.

ANTS BY THE POUND

It takes 500,000 sugar ants to equal 1 pound. If you weigh all the ants on earth, they will weigh more than all humans on earth.

BIG NEWS! ANT KILLS ELEPHANT

In Africa a hungry ant can enter an elephant's ear and eat them from the inside out. A number of elephants every year fall prey to ants.

GETTING RID OF ANT HILLS

The following ingredients will be needed:

¼	**Cup of liquid hand soap**
1	**Gallon of cool tap water**

Place the ingredients into a bucket and mix well, then pour 1-2 cups on the anthill and repeat after 1 hour to be sure that the mixture penetrates deep into the chambers.

FOLLOW THAT ANT

All ants leave a scent trail, which you need to follow by observing the ant's behavior. If you can find the nest, you can eliminate the entire nest thus solving the problem.

ANT SPRAY FOR THE GARDEN

The following ingredients will be needed:

2	**Tablespoons of flaked Ivory soap**
1	**Tablespoon of Tabasco Sauce™**
5	**Drops of sesame seed oil (from health food store)**
5	**Drops of Jungle Rain™ (from garden supply)**
1	**Gallon spray bottle**

Place all ingredients in the gallon bottle and shake to mix well. This can be sprayed directly on the ants or on their pathways. **Keep away from children and pets.**

POWDER THEIR NOSES

Place diatomaceous earth (DE food grade), powdered charcoal, powdered pyrethrum-silica dust or bone meal around the base of the plants in an area; in which the ants are bothering the plants. **Do not breathe in the dust, best to wear a mask when mixing the ingredients.**

ARGENTINE ANTS

This ant has become very popular in the southern part of the United States as well as California. It is very active and protects honeydew-producing insects such as aphids, whiteflies and soft scales.

They are one of the more common house ants that come in when it rains or gets too hot outside. They are a little bigger than the sugar ant and are usually brown to black in color. You need to locate the colony and their point of entrance to stop them. The remedies are the same for the general ant solutions.

These are hard colonies to get rid of since they usually have more than one queen. It is best to give them a bait to take back to the queen instead of trying to spray killer on them. They like to establish their colony near the base of an aphid-infested plant.

SLIPPERY SUGGESTION

To keep ants from getting on your plants, just place some lard, Vaseline®, Crisco®, butter, etc. around the base of the plant.

CARPENTER ANTS

Identification:

Carpenter ants come in five sizes from about ¼ inch to ¾ inches and are about ½ inch longer than most other ants. It has a pinched wasp waist and elbowed antennae and will be black or bi-colored red and black or black and brown depending on the area of the country they reside in.

The colony consists of a queen (larger ant), male (smaller ant), minor workers, intermediate workers and the major workers. One nest may contain ants of all five sizes and they are easily confused with termites, but will usually not have wings. The termites also tend to remain at home while the carpenter ants travel about. When disturbed, the carpenter ant will emit a strong odor.

General Information:

These are normally beneficial insects that chew up mountains of dead wood and turn it into sawdust. However, when they get into a wood structure the damage can be horrendous. Their initial nest is established in decayed wood, however, after they get established they tend to head for healthy wood and end up doing extensive damage.

If the ant colony becomes too large they tend to form satellite colonies in a nearby structure. There is usually only one queen and she remains in the parent colony. The ants will go back and forth from satellites to parent colonies. There may be as many as 20 colonies related to the parent colony. Peak traffic hours on their trails are usually at night starting at sunset. They are attracted by sweets but can survive on insects and other animal remains.

Queens can live up to 15 years and lay over 70,000 eggs. It is best to eliminate the queen if you have a problem with carpenter ants. A pest control service is best if you have a large infestation. Carpenter ants are often confused with termites and may be winged.

LOVE CERTAIN TREES BEST

Carpenter ants prefer evergreen, cedar and Douglas fir trees best and will look for the for satellite locations as the original nest fills up and gets over-crowded.

LONG LIVE THE QUEEN

Carpenter ants are very resourceful and if you kill the queen the workers can produce special eggs that will produce a new queen.

Most of the ants remain in the nest and only about 2% are out foraging for food. If the food supply is low the queen will eat her own eggs and the smaller larvae.

THE GOURMET ANT FEAST
Carpenter ants as well as all other ants love to eat aphid's honeydew or tree sap. They also feast on grasshoppers, crickets, craneflies, aphids, spiders, moth larvae, earthworms, bees and flies.

They really like our food as well when they can get it and prefer soda pop, candy, syrup, honey, raisins and pet food. They are smart enough to take more solid foods over to water and allow the food to soak and get soft before they eat it. They are very good at eating insect parts and extracting nutrients and liquid from them.

These are normally beneficial insects that chew up mountains of dead wood and turn it into sawdust. However, when they get into a wood structure the damage can be horrendous. Their initial nest is established in decayed wood, however, after they get established they tend to head for healthy wood and end up doing extensive damage.

TYPE OF HOUSE TO BE ATTACKED
Wood frame
Crawl spaces
Houses with cedar or plywood siding
Slightly slopping roof

Houses more than 7 years old
Houses with vegetation next to the house
Houses near a forest

PUT A TAIL ON THEM

If you spot a carpenter ant, it is best to follow them to their nest. They come out late at night and you will need to place some honey out for them on a piece of cardboard or any other object that you can easily clean up. They will take the honey back to the nest.

When you find their entrance, drill small holes and blow boric acid in to fill their living spaces. Boric acid will kill them! They may not be in the house and you may have to follow them outside to find the nest. It is critical to find the parent nest if you plan on getting rid of the colony.

ELIMINATE THE PROBLEM

❖ Correct any water leaks on your property.
❖ Eliminate any wood to ground contact points, especially where soil has been pushed up to the side of the house.
❖ Make sure that there are no tree limbs or bushes touching the house.
❖ Firewood should be a good distance from the house and elevated off the ground since this is their favorite location for a nest.
❖ Old wood stumps are their favorite

A good quality poison-free killer is **VICTOR POISON-FREE® ANT & ROACH KILLER. Comes in mint or cedar scents and is safe around kids and pets.**

MAKE THEM SNEEZE

Mix together 1 teaspoon of table salt and ½ teaspoon of fine white pepper in 1-quart of water and mix well, then strain and spray the ants. This will work great to repel them and will kill the workers but not the queen.

OUTSIDE NESTING LOCATIONS

Forest, if within 100 yards of house.............25%
Live trees..18%
Dead stumps, buried wood.......................16%
Landscape wood...................................... 7%
Stacked lumber/woodpile........................... 3%

INSIDE NESTING LOCATIONS

The outside walls.......................35%
Attic.......................................21%
Ceilings & crawl spaces...............20%
Stacked lumber, firewood, etc.

YOU MUST FIND ALL NESTS

Since carpenter ants have satellites as well as a home nest, it is necessary to locate all satellites as well as the home nest if you ever plan on eradicating them. You can find the nest in your home and destroy it but the workers will find a new nest in the home in very short order. Once you find the nest in your home you can spray the entire perimeter to stop a new housing development.

FIELD ANTS

General Information:

Field ants are a very large group of ant species that make their nests in the ground in lawns, gardens and fields. Depending on the species, the workers range in size from 1/8" to ¼". The color of field ants may be red, black or a combination of red and black. The ants usually nest near trees, sidewalks, fences or around the base of buildings. A number of species make a mound with the soil that they excavate under the ground.

Sometimes these mounds are mistaken for fire ant activity; however, field ants do not sting and only bite when they are disturbed. A number of field ants can spray formic acid while they bite, so their bites are painful.

Field ants love to eat honeydew, which is a sweet substance that they get from insects like mealybugs and aphids.

They locate the aphids on trees and shrubs, but some species of field ants, like the silky ants, keep herds of aphids so there is always a supply of honeydew. Field ants will also eat other insects and they are attracted to meats. Most species of field ants are scavengers.

Field ants do not usually invade homes but workers will often hunt for food on decks, porches, and patios. Sometimes people see black field ants on the wood deck and assume they are carpenter ants.

To prevent field ant problems, begin with a careful inspection and look for things that the ants might use as nesting sites such as firewood. It would be best to move mulch far away from the foundation to discourage ants from nesting. Make sure exterior doors close tightly and replace weather-stripping where it is missing.

RED FIRE ANTS

General Information:

Fire ants are known for their aggressive behavior and will swarm over anyone or anything that disturbs their nest, often even attacking wild animals, small pet or people and in rare instances, even killing them.

Their very painful sting affects about 42% of people in infested areas each year. About twenty million people are stung by fire ants in the United States every year!

Identifying Fire Ants
Fire ants have been known to enter home in search of food and water when outside conditions become intolerable for them. They may look like ordinary house or garden ants, but have some very distinguishing characteristics:

- They vary in size within one nest, from 1/16 to 1/5 inch long.
- They are dark reddish brown in color on the head and body, with a darker abdomen.
- Their mounds can be more than 15 inches high, 15 inches in diameter and up to 5 feet deep.
- When they are disturbed they are aggressive, especially near the nest.
- They cause painful stings that raise a small welt.
- If you are not sure if what you saw is fire ants, find a long branch and disturb the dirt in the mound then stick the branch into the top of it. Stay as far away as possible and the fire ants will climb right up what they perceive as an invader (the stick). Other ants will run around in a fit trying to protect the queen.

Anatomy of a fire ant

Fire ants have tiny waists, called petioles, so that they can wiggle their rear parts freely allowing them to twist and turn their bodies in the nest. It also makes it easier for them to enter tiny cracks in your house.

They are also very fastidious little critters since they clean dirt off their antennae by dragging them through the strigil (a comb) in the notch of their front legs. They also have scent glands on their abdomen, which release chemical odors that they use to mark trails when foraging food.

North American fire ants are unique in that they form colonies with multiple queens. The queen can live up to 2 to 7 years and in that time will bear 1,500 to 1,600 eggs per day. Some colonies may have 100,000 to 500,000 fire ants.

Life cycle of fire ants

There are four stages to a fire ant's metamorphosis:

1. Egg – They are laid by the queen and are small and white. They can be deposited throughout the year, but mostly deposited during the summer months. The eggs are divided into two types: Unfertilized – become winged males who mate with the queens and fertilized, which become female workers which and are either: winged virgin queens or worker fire ants, divided into different duties in the nest.

2. Larva – These are light in color and immobile, they depend completely on the worker fire ants for transportation, protection, and food.
3. Pupa – These are mature larvae that transform into pupae and pupate for several weeks. Worker fire ants continue to protect them until the adults emerge.
4. Adult – They are social insects, like bees and wasps, and duties are divided among different types (castes) of adults. Total time from the egg stage to adult fire ants averages 30 days. Worker fire ants can live up to 180 days.

What fire ants eat

Fire ants will eat almost anything since they are omnivores and will eat any plant or animal material, including other insects, ground-nesting animals, mice, turtles, snakes, young saplings, seedlings, plant bulbs, fruit and grass.

When they forage for food, the oldest and most expendable 20% or so of the colony's workers explore within 50-100 feet of the nest in a looping pattern.

Worker fire ants can chew and cut with their mandibles, but can only swallow liquids. When they find liquid food in the field, they swallow it to one of their two stomachs. One stomach saves food to share with the colony and the other one digests food for themselves. They cut solid food into carrying size and bring it back to the colony for "processing."

Fire ants prefer protein foods (insects and meats) but will feed on almost anything and everything. By regurgitating their food from the one stomach, fire ant workers are able to share it with the colony.

Other ants lick or suck up the liquid and the nest is fed equally. This food sharing is why slow-acting poison baits can be very effective in eradicating the colonies.

When they invade an area, they do it with a vengeance and their sheer number can dramatically reduce populations of native ants, other insects, and even ground-nesting wildlife. They also invade homes, schools, sand boxes, athletic fields, golf courses and playgrounds. They will cause damage to crops and electrical equipment, costing millions of dollars each year in repairs and eradication.

Fire Ant Facts:
➤ Fire ants are capable of digging up over 16 billion tons of dirt every year, which would fill at least 3 billion dump trucks.
➤ Ant fossils date back to the time of the dinosaurs
➤ They are the strongest of any animal on earth and able to lift 5 times their weight
➤ Fire ants are social insects
➤ They cannot survive very long without the colony

How fire ants communicate
They communicate through signals and pheromones (which are chemical substances excreted by insects). They play an important role in the complex organization of fire ant societies.

Fire ants tend to spend most of their time in direct contact with the ground and when a worker comes across food she will leave a trail along the ground, which in short time other fire ants will follow. When they return home they reinforce the trail, bringing other fire ants, until the food supply is depleted. Once the food supply is gone, the trail is not reinforced and slowly disappears.

When the violent death of a fire ant occurs, it will emit an alarm pheromone that in high concentration sends other fire ants into the vicinity and into attack frenzy, but in lower amounts, just attracts them. A few fire ants use what is referred to as propaganda pheromones to confuse their enemies.

Fire ants, like other insects, use their antennae to smell as well as provide information about direction. With the use of pheromones, fire ants are able to exchange information about one another's health and nutrition. Fire ants can also detect what task group each other belongs to.

The queen is also able to communicate with the workers to determine which one will begin raising new queens.

The importance of fire ant senses

Touch:
If a fire ant is hungry, they will stroke each other or tap one another with their antennae asking for food.

Taste:
Fire ants will trade food with each other by mouth to mouth exchange. This is their method of sharing nutrition and chemicals and saying that they are related.

Smell:
Fire ants will use their antennae to smell the pheromones that come from other fire ants, which warn of danger or just say "hello" and inspire other fire ants to work harder.

Sound:
If a fire ant gets trapped in a cave-in, they will rub the joint between its waist and abdomen and produce a squeaky sound, which alerts the other ants saying "help me." The other ants will hear the noise through their legs and come to help.

Sight:
Fire ants have two compound eyes, which have multiple lenses and they see things broken up like a kaleidoscope therefore seeing movement better than shape. Since they are underground they do not rely on sight for communication.

THE SOUTHERN FIRE ANT

The southern fire ant was accidently introduced into the Unites States in 1929, when a cargo ship used soil as ballast arrived at the port of Mobile, Alabama from South America. The problem became worse in North America since we do not have as many natural enemies as the ant has in South America.

They are commonly found in Alabama and Florida but can also be found in 12 other states as well as Puerto Rico. Some have even been found in California and Kansas.

Somehow they have even found some in the state of Hawaii. However, they cannot survive in freezing temperatures for more than 2-3 weeks.

NATURAL HERBAL REMEDY

These ants can easily be driven away by scattering the herb "sweet fern "*Comptonia asplenifolia"* around where they are frequenting. This is not really a true fern but a small shrub. Check with your local garden store for more information.

SULFUR WORKS GREAT

If your place small bags of sulfur in areas that the red ants frequent; you will never see them again. *Be careful around animals and children.*

HARVESTER ANT

General Information:

These ants live mostly in western North America and they will build very large mounds. They live mainly in grasslands and are rarely found near buildings or gardens. Harvester ants love seeds as their preferred food and if annoyed will sting if their colony is disturbed.

PHARAOH ANT (sugar ant)

Identification:

Very small (approximately 1/16th inch long or 2.0 millimeters) light yellow to reddish brown ant with the hind portion somewhat darker color and sometimes banded. The petiole, which is the narrow waist between the thorax and abdomen, has two nodes and the thorax has no visible spines.

The antenna, terminate in a distinct club shape and have 3 longer segments. They have a stinger and poor vision.

General Information:

A pharaoh ant colony may contain many queens (as many as 200). The colony usually has1-2000 workers and there are usually many colonies in one area. However, there is no hostility between neighboring colonies. The colonies will produce sexually reproductive ants about twice a year and will produce more under laboratory conditions.

Colonies will add new colonies by "budding" when the queens, workers and larvae leave the main colony and start a new nest. This continual budding or starting new nests is a major factor in the invasiveness of these ants. A single colony can be responsible for populating a city block in less than six months while keeping all other ants out.

When you bait a colony, the other colonies will withdraw and consolidate into smaller colonies for protection then re-populate when it is safe to do so. Hospitals have a problem with pharaoh ants since their small size allows them to enter and access wounds, driplines and medical instruments causing the spread of infections and electrical interference in the equipment.

They are capable of carrying pathogens such as salmonella, staphylococcus, and even streptococcus. They like to build their nest near sources of food and water.

They are not fussy eaters and will feed on a variety of foods, mostly sweets, peanut butter, baked goods, soft drinks, grease, other insects, shoe polish and will gnaw holes in silk, rayon and rubber.

Spraying and killing visible ants will not eliminate the problem, however, spraying pesticides in possible locations where their nest may do the job. Foraging ants have been found in almost everything including sealed packages of sterile dressings, IV bottles, water pitchers, car engines, etc.

Life cycle & habits
The female sugar ant is capable of lying over 350 eggs during her lifetime and can lay about 12 eggs per day. The eggs can hatch in as little as 6-7 days. They only live for about 45 days depending on the climatic conditions. A colony can consist of up to 300,000 ants.

They breed all year long, especially in heated buildings and mating will occur in the nests. Nests have been found between sheets of paper, in clothing, under stones and especially warm, dark locations such as near a water heater.

THEY LOVE LIVER
Just grind up some liver, it doesn't matter if it beef or chicken, they like it all. Mix the liver with a small amount of boric acid and make small balls then leave the balls where they forage for food or near their nest.

DON'T SPRAY THEM!
Never use a spray of any kind to kill pharaoh ants, since they will just scatter and unless you get them all it will do you no good.

SUDS 'EM UP
Place 1 tablespoon of Ivory Liquid Soap® into 1 quart of water and mix well. Place the mixture into a spray bottle and squirt the little devils. Ants don't like to wash and this will get rid of them and wash away their scent pathway.

SERVE THEM A SALAD
However, only serve them cucumber peelings. Most ants have a natural aversion to cucumber peelings and will avoid them like the plague. The best location to place them is on the  windowsills. Dry the peeling then grind them up for the best results.

SCRUB-A-DUB-DUB
Clean your counters once a week with a solution of ½-white vinegar and ½-water. A mild solution of Clorox™ can be used but white vinegar and water is safer.

HERBS TO THE RESCUE
There are a number of herbs that will repel ants:
> **Bay Leaves**
> Place these in all the drawers in the kitchen or cupboards where a problem exists. They can be placed in a cookie jar, flour container or sugar jar. Be sure and only use fresh whole leaves.
> **Cloves**
> Place them anywhere a problem exists.
> **Mint Leaves**
> Crushed mint leaves have been used for thousands of years to repel ants.
> **Cinnamon**
> Place some powdered cinnamon to block their path back to their home colony.
> **Garlic**
> If you place a few small pieces of garlic in cracks where you have a problem, it will deter the ants.

I DARE YOU TO CROSS THE LINE

Ants will not cross a line of certain food items such as cayenne pepper, baby powder, bone meal, powdered charcoal, citrus oil soaked into a piece of string or coffee grounds.

KILLING OFF THE COLONY

Mix up a batch of sweet stuff consisting of honey and boric acid, about ½ teaspoon of each should do. Place the mixture into very small bottle with the lids off. The ants will carry the mixture back to the colony and **ZAPPO**, no colony. **This is a danger to pets and children so use with caution.**

20 MULE TEAM TO THE RESCUE

A good organic recipe to get rid of ants is to mix ¼ cup of granulated sugar and 1 teaspoon of borax into 1 cup of water. Place some of the mixture into small caps and place in areas where the problem exists.

Make sure you change the sugar source every month since the ants are smarter than you think. **Do not use around pets or children.**

FEED THEM PEANUT BRITTLE

Leave a large piece of peanut brittle out for the ants and it will be covered with trapped ants. The peanut brittle can be washed off and re-used over and over again.

THEY MAY USE SUNGLASSES

Ants like to work at night as well as the daytime. However, if you leave a small light on at night in areas that they frequent, it will discourage their foraging for food and water. Ants do not like changes in light patterns.

POWDER THEM UP

An excellent ant deterrent is talcum powder or any medicated body powder. These work excellent and will repel many insects, especially ants. Talcum powder would be the safest choice since the powder dries the ant out and kills it.

CERTAIN PLANTS WILL SCARE THEM AWAY
Growing spearmint, southern-wood and Tansy plants around the border of your home will deter ants and the aphids they carry.

A SOUR SOLUTION
If you can find a hole where ants are entering the house, squeeze the juice of a lemon in the hole or crack. Then slice up the lemon and put the peeling all around the entrance.

THE DOCTORS PERSONAL SOAP
To make your own spray for ants, just purchase a bar of Dr. Bronner's Peppermint Soap™ at a health food store. Mix 1 tablespoon in 1 quart of cool tap water and place the mixture into a sprayer.

Spray all the baseboards and wherever you are having a problem. If you add a small amount of the soap to your mop water it will act as a deterrent on the floors. The spray works well on the outside as well as inside the house.

ANTS LOVE AFFAIR WITH APHIDS
Aphids are one of the ant's favorites. They will find an aphid and stroke the aphid with their antennae until the aphid releases a drop of honeydew, which they bring back to their nursery to feed their young.

CLEANER THAT DETERS ANTS
You can purchase a natural cleaner called Citra Solve™. It is a natural citrus based cleaner that is not soap but is very effective in repelling ants. It does have a pleasant citrus aroma, so smell it before you purchase it to be sure that the smell will not be offensive to you or anyone in your family. This product will actually dissolve most insect bodies and is safe around the house. Use ½ tablespoon per 1 quart of water.

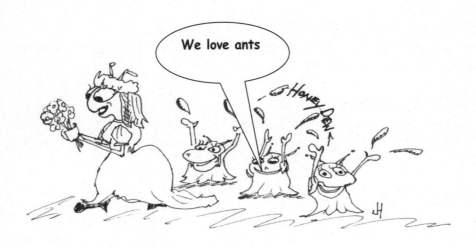

PROTEIN IN PLACE OF SWEETS
You can replace sweets in all recipes with a protein source such as peanut butter or any type of moist pet food for excellent results mixing it with either boric acid or borax. Keep away from pets and children. If you place the mixture in a shallow dish, be sure and leave a small glob of honey in front of the dish to attract them.

INSTANT KILLS
The use of instant grains has been popular to kill most ants in recent years. The grains tend to expand in the stomachs and cause the stomachs to burst killing the ant. The best grains to use are instant rice and instant grits.

Trail Locations inside Homes
Next to wiring or plumbing that has been cut through studs
Trails through insulation in wall spaces
Edges of cabinets and close to furniture
Tree branches or bushes that touch the house
Old stump root channels that may go underneath the house

PUT OUT THE STOP SIGNS
Ant activity in the home tends to increase 5-10 minutes before sundown and is at its busiest between 10PM and 2AM; however, some species prefer to be active from 8PM to 4AM in some parts of the country. The temperature and rainfall does not affect the ant's activity.

FOLLOW THE FAT ANT

If you can get a good look at the ant, check out their abdomen. If the abdomen is distended it means that they have had a great dinner and are heading back to the nest to watch some TV. This is the ant you want to follow, not the skinny one looking for a meal. Most of the full ants will usually be carrying a doggie bag back to their friends.

OUTSIDE KILLER

Pyrethrum is a natural substance that can be purchased in any garden shop. The powder does not blend well with water, but if you add a few drops of liquid soap to 1 cup of water and add 1 tablespoon of pyrethrum it will make a great paste that can be used outside and can be used in a sprayer if strained well.

IT'S TEA TIME FOR ANTS

If you prepare a tea using molasses and Jungle Rain™, which is a natural, organic soap based product it will act as a great ant deterrent when used in a sprayer.

GERMANS PROTECT ANTS

Since ants have a vital role in the health of a forest, the German government protects ants from being eliminated by natural or artificial means. However, since they are not welcome in homes, you will find lavender blossoms near the doors and windows in German households to repel the ants.

SKIP THE EXPENSIVE SPRAYS
Window cleaner will kill all ants, so keep that in mind the next time you are going to purchase the expensive bug spray.

CAUSING STATIC
The essential oil called Tea Tree Oil interferes with the ant's antennae signals and they are unable to transmit or receive information. This oil is safe to be used inside or outside the home. Ants will never frequent an area where they cannot communicate with the other ants.

CITRUS PEEL WORKS GREAT
Place orange and lemon peels in very hot water and allow it to remain overnight. Strain and pour the liquid around any plants that the ants are bothering.

"T" IS FOR TURMARIC
If you can locate the tunnel entrance to an anthill, just place a small powdering of turmeric powder around the opening. Ants hate the herb turmeric and will never come back to that location.

TUMARIC

IT WILL TAKE <u>SENSE</u> TO FIND THE <u>SCENTS</u>

Trail Locations Outside of the House
❖ Edges of the foundation or sidewalk
❖ Edge of the driveway
❖ Fence stringers
❖ Edge of the lawn or border of flowerbeds
❖ Separation grooves in the sidewalk
❖ Next to cement blocks or wood steps

PROTECT YOUR GARBAGE
Planting tansy and peppermint around your garbage can area will eliminate ants and flies from taking up residence there.

SAVE YOUR OLD COFFEE GROUNDS
If you spread coffee grounds around your windows and doors the ants will not come near them. Coffee grounds are a natural ant repellent.

NOT JUST FOR A TOOTHACHE

If you place some oil of clove or camphor on a cloth and wipe down any areas that are a real problem it will stop the ants from using that entrance. Be sure and wipe the door and windowsills.

WHITE-FOOTED ANTS

General Information:

 These are harmless to humans and don't bite or sting. They seem to love the weather in Florida and are only found in that state at present. The colonies can have over 2 million members and their favorite meal is sweets. They will protect aphids, mealy bugs and scales since they produce honeydew. The workers tend to eliminate pesticides from the food before the queen gets any, which makes it hard to eradicate the ants.

Finding the nest and eliminating it with boiling water is the best method of eradication. Any other ant remedy should work to repel them.

BAIT THEM OR LIVE WITH THEM

The only method found to date that will eliminate the colony is to bait them into a trap. The AntPro™ is one of the only recommended traps; that seems to work.

VITAMIN C BAIT

Mix together 1 part of baking soda with 1 part of powdered sugar and 1 teaspoon of powdered vitamin C.
Place the mixture into a mixture of ½ teaspoon of DE and honey, mix well and make into small balls. This should eliminate the queen and get rid of the colony. **Keep away from pets and children.**

CHAPTER 2

TERMITES

TERMITES

General Information:

Termites change areas and homes by colonization flights from one colony to set up a new one. This usually takes place in the fall or early in the spring or summer and depends of the species of termite. Even if your home has been protected you may still be at risk of the colony setting up housekeeping. When the termite lands both the male and female break off their wings, run around in circles and then hides under a rock for protection and seal themselves in and mate for life.

Colonies have to grow very slow at first so that they can develop their workers. Colonies can have hundreds to thousands of termites with colonies reaching 500,000 individuals in some areas. The winged termites are the reproductive ones and after mating, the queen will lose her wings. Termites cannot digest wood with the support of microscopic, one-celled protozoa, which are responsible for breaking down the cellulose in the wood so that they can digest and utilize it. The termite develops the protozoa by consuming each other's fecal material.

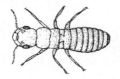

Termites must have moisture and have contact with the soil so if you find a nest and open it they will probably die off.

Formosan subterranean termite

One of the worst varieties: causing considerable damage. Their nests are located in building walls, under roofs and in trees. They are more common in the Gulf States, Hawaii, areas of Georgia and southern California. Their colonies can number millions of termites and they have soldiers that can secrets a gluey type of defense fluid from their heads. They are strong enough to displace other types of termites if they enter an area. To identify their soldiers, look for the oval-shaped heads instead of the typical square head.

WORKER

The king & queen

After the female has flown, mated and has produced eggs she is called a "queen." A male that has flown, mated and is in the area of a queen is termed a "king." Only one male (king) produces mates within the colony. When mature, a primary queen has a great capacity to lay eggs and it has been reported that they can produce more than 2,000 eggs a day.

The distended abdomen with eggs increases the queen's body length to several times more than before mating and reduces her ability to move freely. Attendant workers provide assistance. The queen is also widely believed to be a primary source of <u>pheromones</u> useful in colony integration, which are thought to be spread through shared feeding.

The king grows only slightly larger after mating and continues to mate with the queen for life, which may be as long as 45 years. This is very different from ant colonies, in which a queen mates once with the male(s) and stores the gametes for life since the male ants die shortly after mating.

Worker termites

Worker termites are the labors are responsible for foraging, food storage, brood and nest maintenance and some defense duties in certain species. Workers are the main caste in the colony for the digestion of cellulose in food and are most likely to be found in wood. This is achieved in one of two ways. Entomologists that study termites found that termites can produce their own cellulose enzyme and can digest wood in the absence of their symbiotic microbes, however, there is now evidence suggesting that these gut microbes makes use of termite-produced cellulose enzymes.

The workers also feed the other members of the colony with substances derived from the digestion of plant material. This process of feeding of one colony member by another is one of the keys to the success of the group. It frees up the parents from feeding except but the first generation of offspring, allowing for the colony to grow much larger and ensuring that the necessary gut relationships are transferred from one generation to another.

Soldier termites

The soldier caste has anatomical and specific behavioral specializations, providing strength and armor, which are primarily used against ant attacks.

The number of soldiers within a colony varies among species. A number of soldiers have jaws so large that they cannot feed themselves and are fed by workers. Some soldiers have the ability to exude noxious liquids through either a horn-like nozzle or holes in their forehead.

Many species are easily identified using the characteristics of the soldiers' heads. Termite soldiers are usually blind, but in some families, particularly among the damp wood termites, soldiers may have at least partly functional eyes.

The soldier caste is primarily a defense against predatory ants. A tunnel-blocking soldier can rebuff attacks from many ants. Usually more soldiers stand by behind the initial soldier in case the first one falls another soldier will take the place.

Termite nests & mounds

The workers are responsible for building and maintain nests which house the colony. These elaborate structures are made using a combination of soil, mud, chewed wood/cellulose, saliva, and feces. The nest has numerous functions such as providing a protected living space and water conservation. It has nursery chambers deep within  the nest where eggs and larvae are tended. Some species will actually maintain fungal gardens that are fed on collected plant matter,  providing a nutritious substance, which the colony can feed on. Nests have a maze of tunnel-like rooms that provide air conditioning and control the CO_2/O_2 balance, as well as allow the termites to move through the nest.

Nests are usually built underground, within fallen trees or even atop living trees. Some species build nests above ground, which can develop in giant mounds. Mounds can be as high as 30 feet.

Termites as food source

There are many cultures where termites, especially the winged ones are used for food. The winged ones are nutritious, having a good store of fat and protein and are palatable in most species with a nutty flavor when cooked.

They are easy to gather at the beginning of the rainy season in, especially in areas of Africa when they swarm, since they are attracted to lights and can be gathered up when they land on nets that are placed around a lamp.

The wings can be removed by a technique similar to winnowing then they are gently roasted on a hot plate or lightly fried until just crisp. Since their bodies are naturally high in oil, no oil is needed to fry them.

Formosan subterranean termite

One of the worst varieties: causing considerable damage. Their nests are located in building walls, under roofs and in trees.

They are more common in the Gulf States, Hawaii, areas of Georgia and southern California. Their colonies can number millions of termites and they have soldiers that can secrets a gluey type of defense fluid from their heads. They are strong enough to displace other types of termites if they enter an area. To identify their soldiers, look for the oval-shaped heads instead of the typical square head.

NATURAL METHODS OF ELIMINATION

DOWN WITH THE QUEEN

Termites; are really not a bad insect. They are the best wood recycler around and will turn a dead log into food for many other insects. Unfortunately, they are not fussy where they find wood and your home is a handy source of food. The queen is the key to the termite "swarm."

There are over 300 varieties of termites in the world; however, only four varieties can be found in the United States. The problem termite is the "subterranean termite," which is responsible for 95% of all damage.

Termites cannot be attracted to bait unless you place wooden stakes in the ground to see where they are. Once you can determine where they are foraging you can replace the wood with a bait to kill them. If you do identify a termite infestation the best thing to do is to call a professional.

GIMME A "D", GIMME AN "E"
Diatomaceous earth (DE) is one of the safest and most effective termite controlling natural substances. Best to paint it on the exposed wood surfaces by using 1 part DE to ¼ part boric acid. Add the mixture to just enough water to make a paint consistency and paint it on all wood surfaces.

SPRAY THE CRAWL SPACES
The attic and all crawl spaces should be sprayed with the same DE, boric acid mixture. Just make the mixture very watery so that it will be easy to spray.

CALL FOR SHERLOCK HOLMES
If you can locate their colony in the infected wood, just remove the wood and replace it with new wood that has been treated. Make sure all tube pathways are located and removed or sprayed to make them unusable.

CALL FOR TEAM BORAX

A good method of eliminating the termites is to use 20 Mule Team Borax™. Just dust their tunnels and it will eliminate the problem (providing you find all the tunnels). Try not to breathe in the dust particles (wear a mask). Borax can also be sprayed into their home and made into a paste and painted on the wood. Treating the wood with borax will provide you with a long-term solution.

BUILD A SAND MOAT
If you dig down 3 feet deep and 3 feet away from the house around your entire home, then place a layer of construction sand (90%) mixed with DE (10%) you will never have a termite problem. This is easier if you are building a new home since garden and trees tend to get in the way.

RING THE DINNER BELL
Nc nematodes (microscopic worms) have been used for hundreds of years to control and eliminate termites.

They can be ordered through a company called Arbico and are placed into the subterranean tubes to eat the termites.

TERMITE EATING PLANT
There is one plant in the world that is carnivorous and only eats termites. The pitcher plant **Nepenthes albomarginata** tends to entice the termites with white hairs that are all around the top of the plant. Termites find the hairs irresistible and fall prey to the plants sticky and slippery trap. Usually when the plant attracts one termite the rest of the nest follows. Unfortunately the plant only lives in the rain forest.

ESSENTIALLY YOURS
Two essential oils that can be purchased in a health food store are vetiver oil and clove bud oil. Vetiver oil has the ability to repel the termites and keep them away from your property, while the clove bud oil will kill the termites within two days of exposure. Both of these remedies are natural and safe.

HIRE SOME CARPENTER ANTS
Carpenter ants are sworn enemies of termites and will kill them every chance they get. Actually almost any ant will fight termites. As far as using carpenter ants it is a dilemma, which is worse, the termites or the carpenter ants. Almost any other ant, however, would be beneficial to have around the house to control the termites. To identify the termites, remember that they have very thick waists, while ants have very thin waists (they probably exercise more).

CLEAN OUT THE SANDBOX

A layer of sand that has uniform particles will stop termite movement through the soil. This would be best if it were done pre-construction, especially for slab construction. Sand is a physical barrier through which termites avoid and cannot build tunnels in, since the tunnels would collapse easily.

PASS THE FUNGUS AMONGST US

A recently developed fungal strain (Metarhizium anisopliae) has been produced by the EcoScience Corporation and is an effective termiticide. It is odorless, has no vapors and will not stain. The termites can pass the fungus to other termites, which in turn spread it throughout the colony eliminating it.

CALL IN THE SPECIALISTS

There is one Nc nematode **(termask)** that is very effective of getting rid of termites. You need to purchase them through an agricultural supply house and use injection equipment to apply them. Depending on how well the colony has sealed certain compartments will determine the effectiveness of this method.

TERMITE PROOF A NEW HOME

Check with pest control companies regarding the type of foundation that will deter termites from entering the house. Brick and concrete foundations are among the best but there are no guarantees.

THE TERMITE DOG

Some termite companies now employ specially trained dogs to locate the termite colonies in and around your home. These dogs are called "Tadd" dogs and for additional information call (800) 354-TADD.

ALOE THE TERMITES

Crush all the plant parts of an aloe plant in water and use 1 part aloe to 5 parts of water to be used as a spray. Allow it to stand for 1 hour before use and strain before placing into the sprayer. This spray works very well on termites

POPPY OIL DOES THE TRICK

The oil of the Mexican poppy is very effective in repelling termites from your property. It can be mixed with water as a spray or you can use the powder.

BIOLOGICAL CONTROL

If you place a piece of wood where the workers will find it and place the chemical "methoprene" on it, it will prevent the termite nymphs from maturing into adults, which are capable of reproducing. The workers will take the infected wood back to the colony for food.

YUMMM
Filet of hut!

GIVE THEM A HOTFOOT

A relatively new method employs heat to kill the colony. A portable propane heater blows hot air into a tented home. The temperature reaches 150^0F, which is needed to acquire the minimum kill temperature of 120^0F. The termites can only survive for about 20 minutes at this temperature.

However, this does kill a number of the beneficial insects that might be living in the home as well as the bad insects. Computers, chocolates, some plastics and certain pharmaceutical medications must be removed from the house. This is usually completed in one day.

ZAP, ZAP, ZAP

You can also use Electro-Gun™ to electrocute them and hot air treatments for the entire house. This is manufactured by the Etex Company and can be leased to zap the termites. It is used against drywood termites and can also be used to kill powderpost beetles.

It literally zaps them with and electrical charge but can only be used in parts of the home that you can get to. The arc of electrical current is shot directly into the burrow and then travels along the moist tunnels killing the termites. This pulsed high frequency current does not damage the wood in any way.

TERMITE-PROOFING YOUR HOME

- ➢ Never allow the paint on the outside of the home to deteriorate and expose the wood.
- ➢ Never allow any wood to come into contact with the soil or a bush.
- ➢ Never leave any tools or other objects leaning against the house for any length of time. This includes planter boxes.
- ➢ Never have any wooden trellises attached to the house and touching the ground.
- ➢ Be sure that all firewood is stacked on a cement base with adequate room around it. If you do find termites burn the wood as soon as possible or pour soapy water on it to kill them.

- ➢ Check stumps that are near the house regularly.

- ➤ If you have a crawl space under your home, be sure that it is kept as dry as possible.
- ➤ Shrubbery next to a home is one of the most common entry points for termites.
- ➤ Repair all cracks in concrete or masonry.
- ➤ Check any separation in wood joints; they should be inspected on a regular basis.
- ➤ Trees that overhang your roof are a great entry point for termites.

PUT OUT THE STOP SIGNS

Ant activity in the home tends to increase 5-10 minutes before sundown and is at its busiest between 10PM and 2AM; however, some species prefer to be active from 8PM to 4AM in some parts of the country. The temperature and rainfall does not affect the ant's activity.

GIVE THEM A DOSE OF CASTOR OIL

Use the castor oil plant and soak the green seeds, leaves and the roots in 2 quarts of water for 24 hours, then strain and use in a sprayer or use as a drench if you know where their nest is. The seeds and leaves can be dried and used as a powder.

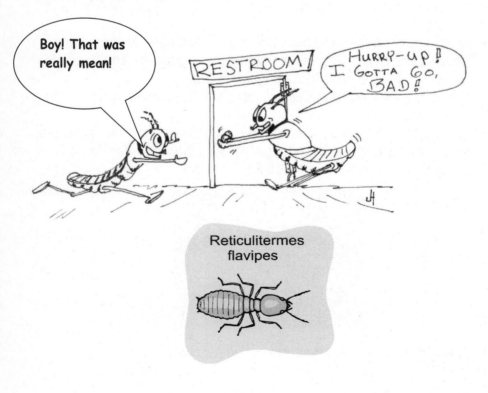

Reticulitermes
flavipes

CHAPTER 3

COCKROACHES

COCKROACHES

A ROACH BY ANY OTHER NAME, IS STILL A ROACH

Roaches do not mind living outside, but if you give them a chance, they will move in with their whole family. Roaches are known by a number of different names, such as water bugs, palmetto bugs and cockroaches.

They are bugs of the night and will go looking for any drop of water or food that may be within their grasp, since they are not fussy eaters. Outside they will take up residence almost anywhere, such as a tree, woodpile, planter, under rocks, etc. In many instances roaches will find a warm, damp location, which is where they prefer to breed.

Cleanliness will reduce or eliminate most roach problems, but frequent professional spraying if a problem exists by an expert or placing out bait also works well. Roaches will not come back to an area where they are frequently poisoned.

Cockroaches can be found all over the world and are going strong. They can be controlled or eradicated but it will take some effort. The best method of controlling cockroaches is to have a clean kitchen. Any small piece of food or readily accessible water source will be located.

Americans spend about 1.5 billion dollars annually trying to get rid of cockroaches, but to no avail. The roaches are now becoming resistant to most pesticides and chemicals.

There are over 3800 species of cockroaches worldwide and they have been around for 360 million years. People who are allergic to house dust will be allergic to cockroaches, since parts of their bodies when they die become mixed with house dust. Asthma can be induced from cockroach dust particles in susceptible individuals.

The roach can identify poisons with their fine sensory hairs and will avoid areas that have been baited with poisons. In the late 1800's people would place a mirror in front of a cockroach and felt that its reflection would scare it away.

Threats are real!
Cockroaches in general have been reported to spread approximately 33 kinds of bacteria, at least six kinds of parasitic worms and seven other kinds of human pathogens. They pick up the germs on the spines of their legs and bodies as they crawl through decaying matter, garbage or sewage and then carry these into food or onto food surfaces.

Germs that cockroaches consume from decaying matter, garbage or sewage are protected while in their bodies and can remain infective for several weeks longer than if they had been exposed to cleaning agents, rinse water, or just sunlight and air. Recent medical studies have shown that cockroach allergens cause allergic reactions in children. They were also shown to cause asthma in children. These allergens will build up in deposits of droppings, secretions, cast skins and dead bodies of roaches.

The most common roach's in the United States

American Cockroach
General Information:

The American cockroach is the largest of the common cockroaches measuring on average about 2 inches in length. It is commonly found in buildings throughout Florida especially in commercial buildings. In the northern United States it is mainly found in warm areas or large institutional buildings. The American cockroach is second only to the German cockroach in abundance. Has also been called a water bug or Palmetto bug.

Distribution:
The American cockroach was brought to the United States from Africa as early as 1625. It has spread throughout the world by commerce and is often found indoors as well as outdoors.

It is normally found in basements, sewers, steam tunnels and drainage systems and is readily found in commercial and large buildings such as restaurants, grocery stores, bakeries and anywhere food is prepared and stored.

The American cockroach is rarely found in residential homes, however after heavy rain the cockroach can occur in homes. They can develop to large numbers, usually greater than 5,000 in sewer systems. Outdoors they prefer moist shady areas in yards, hollow trees, wood piles, and mulch.

Description:
Egg: The female American cockroach laid their eggs in a hardened, purse-shaped egg case about one week after mating. The females on average produce an egg case about once every month for ten months lying about 16 eggs per egg case. The female deposits the egg case close to a source of food by either simply dropping it or gluing it to a surface with a secretion from her mouth.

Larva or Nymph: The nymph stage starts when the egg hatches and concludes with the emergence of the adult. The nymphs are white then become a uniformly reddish-brown with the rear margins of the thoracic and abdominal segments being a darker color.
Wings are never present in the nymph stage. Complete development from egg to adult is about 600 days.

Adult:
The adult American cockroach is reddish brown in appearance with a pale-brown or yellow band around the edge. The males are longer than the females because their wings extend 4 to 8 mm beyond the tip of the abdomen.

Smoky Brown Cockroach
General Information:

 The smoky brown cockroach is a large species of cockroach, winged, and growing to a length of 1¼–1½ in. It is brown in color and is closely related to the American cockroach, however, is easily distinguishable from it. It has a uniformly dark brown color and its body is dark and shiny, unlike the light rimmed pattern of the American cockroach.

It likes warm climates and is not cold tolerant, however, it may be able to survive indoors in colder climates if it finds a warm location. It does well in moist conditions and it seems to be found in moist concealed areas. It often lives around the outside of buildings, and it is common species outdoors in the southern United States.

Oriental Cockroach
Description:

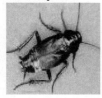

Oriental cockroaches are often called water bugs, black beetle or palmetto bugs because of their preference for dark, damp, and cool areas such as those under sinks and washing machines and damp basements. It is about 1¼-inches long and has wings but is unable to fly. Usually found around garbage cans and does not need a water source. It is a glossy dark brown to black in color. Prefers decaying organic matter and is the filthiest of all cockroaches. They will invade a building when the weather turns cold, and is more commonly found in the eastern states.

Both male and female adults are very dark brown or almost black; their bodies usually have a somewhat shiny sheen. The females have small, functionless, wing pads and broader, heavier bodies, while the males have wings that cover about three-quarters of their abdomen.

Both nymphs and adults are very sluggish and usually located at or below ground level indoors. They are rarely found on walls, in high cupboards, or in the upper floors of buildings; however, at times large numbers occur in one great mass around leaks in the basement or crawl space areas of homes. Oriental cockroaches are generally found outdoors during warm weather.

German Cockroach

German cockroaches are 1/2 to 5/8 inch long and tan to light brown. They have fully developed wings, but do not fly. The nymphs are similar in appearance to adults except that they are smaller and lack wings. The German cockroach is best identified by its small size and two dark parallel lines running from the back of the head to the wings.

It is usually found in kitchens, close to dishwashers, stoves and sinks as well as bathrooms. They prefer a moist environment with a relatively high degree of warmth, they love water heaters.

The insects are mostly scavengers and will feed on a wide variety of foods and especially starches, sweets, grease and meat products. Garbage is one of their principal food sources.

German cockroaches are mostly active at night, which is when they forage for food, water and mates. During the day they hide out in cracks and crevices and any other dark site that provides a warm and humid environment. Their relatively wide, flat bodies enable them to move in and out of cracks and narrow openings with ease and they may be seen during the day, especially if a heavy population is present or if there is some other stress, such as a lack of food or water or an application of pesticides.

The German cockroach is the most successful cockroach producing a larger number of eggs per capsule and undergoes the shortest time from hatching until maturity, resulting in a very rapid population growth. A greater number of nymphs hatch successfully since the female carries the egg capsule during the entire time.

BrownBanded Cockroaches

These are a light brown and are usually found in warmer climates especially in the Southern States. They are only about ½ inches long and have two light, irregular bands along their wings. They are often confused with the German roach, which has two dark bands behind their head. They prefer starches, but will eat anything.

The males have full wings, which reach beyond the tip of their rather abdomens, but females have underdeveloped wings, which are much shorter than their broad, rounded abdomens.

Male brownbanded cockroaches have been observed to fly indoors and among cockroach species, they have the most distinctions between sexes with females having larger abdomen and shorter wings than males. Brownbanded cockroaches often hide their egg cases in or under furniture.

Wood Roach

Very similar to the American roach and is light brown in color. They are attracted to light, which is their major difference and can usually be found under a log or in a woodpile.

NATURAL METHODS OF ELIMINATION

THE ROACH EXTERMINATOR

The following ingredients will be needed:

½	**Pound of borax**
30	**Ounces of powdered sugar**
½	**Ounce cocoa powder**
1	**Ounce of sodium chloride (salt)**

Place all the ingredients into a medium plastic container and mix thoroughly. This bug poison should be sprinkled around wherever the problem exists. ***This is harmful to pets and children and should be used with caution.***

HERB TO THE RESCUE

There are a number of herbs that will repel cockroaches. They are bay leaves, cucumber and cayenne. Cucumber peelings work very effectively to deter them. Place them wherever a problem exists and the cockroaches will not frequent that area.

THE CATS MEOW

A natural repellant to cockroaches is catnip. The chemical in catnip is called nepetactone, which is harmless to humans and pets.

If you leave small sachets of catnip in locations that the cockroaches frequent, you will never see a cockroach. If you make a tea from catnip, allow it to cool and then place it in a spray bottle it will eliminate you're ever seeing a cockroach again.

A CLEAN ROACH IS NOT A HEALTHY ROACH

A method of killing cockroaches is to place 1 tablespoon of Ivory Liquid Soap™ into 1 quart of water then place the mixture into a spray bottle and spray the cockroach. This is an instant kill since they hate to be clean.

ONE OF THE MANY USES FOR BAKING SODA

If you place a small shallow bowl where you are having a roach problem with equal parts of baking soda and powdered sugar it will kill the roaches. *Make sure this is kept away from pets and small children.*

BOTTOMS UP, LITERALLY!

Take a 1 pound coffee can and place 2 slices of bread in it that have been soaked with beer. Place the can anywhere a roach problem exists. Save the lid and dispose of the canned roaches.

A LITTLE HERE, A LITTLE THERE

Sprinkle boric acid down any cracks or crevices in non-food areas. *This is toxic so keep it away from children or pets.* This is usually the treatment of choice in hard to reach areas only. This is also one of the items that roaches have not developed a resistance to. Boric acid is a poison.

THE SWEET ROACH EXTERMINATOR

The following ingredients will be needed:

½	**Pound of borax**
2	**Pounds of powdered sugar (10X)**
½	**Ounce of cocoa powder**
1	**Ounce of sodium fluoride (from pharmacy)**

Place all the ingredients in a small bucket and mix thoroughly. Sprinkle in areas where the roaches frequent. *Keep out of reach of children and pets.*

DOING THE BACKSTROKE

The reason you see roaches lying on their back when they die is that they are killed by an inhibition of cholinesterase, which is an enzyme that transmits nerve impulses to the muscles. When they die there is a loss of muscular control resulting in violent twitching that forces them to end up on their back. The violent twitching causes their center of gravity to become higher than their center of balance.

THIS APPLE WAS PROBABLY USED BY THE WICKED WITCH

Hedgeapples have been used for hundreds of years to repel cockroaches. They are the fruit of the Osage orange tree and contain a natural chemical that repels roaches. It only takes one small apple in a room to eliminate the roaches. Hedgeapples will last about 2 months before needing replacement. Hedgeapples can be obtained through the Internet at www.hedgeapple.com.

WALKING THE PLANK

Place Vaseline® around the inside rim of a medium size jar, then place half a banana in the jar and put a piece of wood or tongue depressor on the outside of the jar to be used as a ramp so that they can easily walk into the jar to get the banana. The Vaseline® will make it too slippery for them to get out and they die.

HERE YE, HERE YE DOCTOR DOES IT AGAIN

One of the best all-natural methods of pest control, especially cockroaches is to place 1 capful of Dr. Bronner's Peppermint Soap™ in 1 quart of warm water and spray the areas where you have a problem.

THE LARD ROACH EXTERMINATOR
The following ingredients will be needed:

½	**Cup of all-purpose flour**
1/8	**Cup of granulated sugar (any sugar will do)**
¼	**Cup of lard**
8	**Ounces of boric acid**
	Cool tap water

Place all the ingredients into a small bowl and blend thoroughly making the solution into small balls of dough. Place 1-3 dough balls into an open small plastic bag and place in areas where the roach problem exists. ***This is toxic and needs to be kept out of reach of children and animals.***

SPICE 'EM UP
For a really hot roach, just place 2 tablespoons of Tabasco Sauce™ or other very hot sauce in 1 quart of water then mix well and spray the areas where a problem exists. You will never see another roach!

BAITING THE GERMAN ROACH
If you are going to use bait on a German cockroach there are certain foods they prefer over others. They are very fond of flour, brown sugar and light Karo® syrup. They prefer carbohydrates to proteins as well. Being German they love their beer but it has to be stale since they don't like the carbon dioxide. If you lace any of these foods with 5% food-grade DE or borax it will do the trick. ***Be careful of pets and children around the baits.***

THE KILLER VACUUM
If you are sure that you have roaches, wait until at least 1 hour after dark and go into the room you suspect with a red light (don't turn on the room lights) and a vacuum, then vacuum up all the roaches. If you are going to use a dry vacuum, place 1 teaspoon of cornstarch in the vacuum bag to kill the roaches.

THE ROACH MOTEL

Use a 2-liter plastic soda bottle and cut off the top about 3-4 inches down. Place some Vaseline® around the inside of the top and the bottom that is left, then place the top you cut off inverted (like a funnel) back into the bottle. Then duct tape the top back on and place masking tape around the bottle to make it easy for them to climb up. Then place a few pieces of bread soaked in beer inside. They will enter and not be able to leave because of the Vaseline® is too slippery.

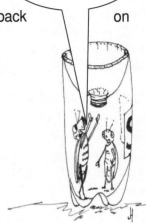

There must be a way out

THE ROACH TRAP

There are a number of roach traps on the market, which have a one-way door. The bait is placed inside and they can't get out.
These are very effective if placed in the right areas where they frequent.

BAKING 101 FOR ROACHES

To prepare roach dough, just combine ¼ cup of Crisco® with ½ cup of 10X powdered sugar, ¼ red onion, ½ cup of all-purpose flour and 8 ounces of baking soda (very fresh). Add water as needed to prepare a dough-like consistency. Make the dough into small balls and leave out for the roaches to find.

ROACH & ANT REPELLER

The following ingredients will be needed:

1	**Cup of borax**
¼	**Cup of crushed fresh black pepper**
¼	**Cup of crushed bay leaves**

Place the ingredients in jar with a well-sealed lid and shake well. Sprinkle a small amount of the mixture in the corners of the cupboards and drawers. You should never see another cockroach or ant again.

ROACH SPRAY

To 1 quart of tap water add 1 crushed clove of garlic, 1 tablespoon of cayenne pepper and 1 small crushed white onion. Place the mixture on the range and allow it to come to a simmer. Remove from the heat and allow the mixture steep for 1 hour before placing it in a sprayer and spraying the locations that the roaches frequent.

DUST THEM OFF

As a last resort insecticidal powder will need to be forced into all cracks and crevices. Check with a pest control company and ask them to use a safe powder that can be used around pets and children. **Remove all pets such as birds, cats, fish and dogs from the premises when dusting is being done.**

WORKS ON VAMIPRES BUT NOT COCKROACHES

Some species of cockroach are actually attracted to garlic, so best not to try and use garlic to get rid of roaches.

CHEMICAL KILLER

Silica gel (aluminum silicate) can be used to dust areas where the roaches frequent. It has the ability to scratch their protective coating away and kill them. Caution should be used, when dusting and a mask and gloves should be worn even though the dust is considered non-toxic.

The names of commercial silica gel product are Dri-Die™ and Drione™ and can be purchased in your local garden or agricultural supply stores.

WHY DID THE CHICKEN CROSS THE ROAD?

Probably to get to a cockroach! Chickens love to chase and eat cockroaches and in some countries the chickens are allowed to go in and out of the house freely to control the cockroach population.

PREVENTION IS STILL THE ANSWER

Best to prevent the problem by following a few rules:

> ➤ Clean out the back of the refrigerator and any food that has been pushed underneath by children.
> ➤ Vacuum regularly.
> ➤ Make sure the kitchen floor is always clean.
> ➤ Wipe off counters daily.
> ➤ Clean out pet food dishes and don't leave them out at night.
> ➤ Your garbage can should have a tight lid.
> ➤ Seal all cracks and crevices.
> ➤ Fix any leaky pipes since they love a cool drink.
> ➤ Repair loose wallpaper since they will eat paste.
> ➤ Eliminate any stacks of lumber near the house.
> ➤ Remove any foliage that is too close to the house.
> ➤ Eliminate stacks of magazines or newspaper. These make great places for them to reside.

HIRE A GECKO

Gecko's love cockroaches and will chase and consume them when they can find them. They hunt them at night and they are one of their favorite meals. If you let just one gecko loose in an apartment building it will eliminate all the roaches and their relatives in about 7-10 days. However, remember that they don't like cats and the cat will eat the gecko for dinner.

CHAPTER 4

SPIDERS

SPIDERS

There are 40,000 species of spiders worldwide and they are all carnivorous. Spiders are beneficial insects and are welcome in most homes. There are only four spiders that are poisonous in the United States, the black widow, the hobo, the yellow sac and the brown recluse. Spiders will consume about 100 bugs every year and you are never more than 12 feet away from a spider at any time. An orb web spider will eat their web daily and spin a new one. Spiders can regenerate their lost limbs. The only thing a spider does is hunt for food and makes new spiders.

Spiders kill more bugs than birds do and the total weight of bugs that spiders consume in one day will be more than the weight of all the humans on earth. In China spiders are so revered that farmers even build them small teepee-like homes to hibernate in during the winter months. Spider's silk is stronger than tensile steel of the same diameter and is so fine it has been used as cross hairs in gun sites.

Spiders only live for about one year. Their hairy legs contain their organs for hearing, touch and smell. All spiders inject a chemical that liquefies their host and then they suck up the goodies.

99% OF ALL SPIDERS ARE HARMLESS

A FEW OF THE MORE COMMON SPIDERS

ARIZONA BROWN SPIDER

Arizona brown spiders; are about ½ inches in size and is closely related to the Brown Recluse Spider. Its venom contains powerful cytotoxins that cause large ulcerous soars that are difficult to heal. The Arizona brown spiders are hunters and move from place to place in search of small insects to feed on.

They prefer to hide in daytime hours and when inside a building, clutter is very attractive to this spider for hiding. They have also been commonly found hiding in shoes, clothing, and boxes.

Most bites occur when the spider is accidentally trapped against the skin and are normally not very aggressive. It is best to wear gloves and use a soapy spray directly on the spiders to kill them.

Recluse bite

This spider is excellent at hiding and the most effective form of inspection and detection is done with the use of glue board traps..

Fun Fact:
This spider is also known as the Fiddle-back Spider or violin spider because of the violin-shaped marking on its back.

BLACK HOUSE SPIDER

 The black house spider is also known as the window spider and appears dark and strong. The body of the black house spider is shiny black, while its legs and sides range from black to dark brown. Their abdomens are dark gray in color and their backs exhibit a series of white V-shapes. The females are commonly twice as large as males.

Black house spiders are known to weave lace webs and are frequently mistaken for funnel webs. They also make complex tunnels with more than one portal with the tunnels leading to a hollow, silken retreat for the black house spider. The web of the black house spider will appear gray and tangled as a result of constant repair.

They spin their webs in dry, dark locations and can be found in cracks in walls, rusting iron and the angles of windows, as well as many other sheltered crevices within a house.

Black house spiders may also inhabit the bark of unhealthy trees and use the sap from these injured trees to attract prey. They prey upon a variety of flies, butterflies, beetles and bees.

Even though their bite is not lethal, humans may experience negative side effects from their bite. Vomiting, muscular pain, weakness, nausea, sweating and shortness of breath may occur if the bite is severe. The bite itself is painful and usually swells. However, black house spiders hardly ever attack humans and if they do, only bite only when threatened.

BLACK WIDOW (poisonous)

Spray with a strong soapy solution. Spray all cracks and areas where they are located. It is best to spray the areas once a month. Black widows will only bite you if you provoke them. They prefer to run away rather than confront you in any way. Their bite is very painful and medical treatment may need to be initiated immediately.

Their outer covering is very shiny black with a red hourglass on the underneath side of their abdomen making them easy to identify. After mating, the female kills the male and eats him for dinner.

BROWN HOUSE SPIDER

The brown house spider; is also known as cupboard spiders and reside in numerous locations throughout the world. They may be found in dark, moist areas within a house and prefer basements, crawl spaces and garages. They may also be found outside, beneath rocks and piles of wood.

Brown house spiders are less aggressive than other spider species and their bites are not as dangerous as those of their close relatives. The worst you may experience is some swelling around the bite area with symptoms dissipating within hours.

The male brown house spiders reach up to about ¼ inch, while females may grow to exceed almost ½ inch.

The males are more slender and females more corpulent. Brown house spiders are also known to have long legs and small bodies and may be found in many shades of brown or black.

Some specimens are even tinged red or purple while others exhibit sporadic, white markings all over their bodies. Brown house spider webs are woven with fine silk strands that are entangled with no specific pattern and designed to trap prey. They most commonly prey on insects and sometimes consume other spiders, as well.

BROWN RECLUSE (poisonous)

Usually found in wooded area, attics or woodpiles. They are a yellowish/tan to dark brown spider and have a light-colored, violin-shaped mark on its head and body. It is a small spider with long slender legs and has six eyes. It may be found in old piles of paper, woodpiles, back of closets and even clothing that has not been worn for a long time. It is best to wear gloves when working in these areas. A soapy spray will get rid of them. Their bite requires immediate medical attention since its poison causes destruction of tissue and the area is very slow to heal.

COMMON HOUSE SPIDER

The common house spider is widely distributed throughout most of the world. It is very common in barns and houses and constructs webs in the corners of walls, floor joists, and windows. The common house spider may also be found outside under rocks and boards, as well as beneath bridges and similar structures. In homes, it is most often encountered in damp areas such as basements and around water heaters.

This spider frequently abandons its web to build a new one nearby and can produce numerous webs in a short period of time. This web-building behavior causes homeowners to do a lot of cleanup.

The common house spider female is about ¼ inches in length with a yellowish-brown upper body and a dirty white to brown abdomen with gray chevrons.

The legs of this spider are yellow, with darker rings at the end of each segment. Some members of this species have a triangular, black spot on the top of the abdomen. The male is a little smaller than the female in length and has orange legs. Males and females can be found anytime of the year and they can live for a year or more after maturing. The male and female will coexist in the web and mate repeatedly.

CRAB SPIDER

The crab spiders has a short, wide, flattened body with the first two or three pairs of legs longer than the rest and are normally held out from the sides of the body as a crab would hold its claws. Crab spiders can usually walk forward, backward, or sideways similar to fiddler crabs. There are about 2000 known species of crab spiders worldwide, 200 of which occur in North America.

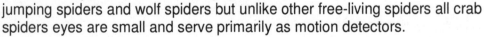

The majority of crab spiders are less than 1 cm (0.4 in) in length; however, the giant crab spider may reach 2.5 cm (1.0 in). They never spin webs to trap prey, but hunt on the open ground or on vegetation or flowers. They resemble free-living spiders such as jumping spiders and wolf spiders but unlike other free-living spiders all crab spiders eyes are small and serve primarily as motion detectors.

Crab spiders are predators that lie in wait to ambush their prey and even though their jaws are rather small and slender, many crab spiders have potent venoms that quickly immobilize their prey.
Many crab spiders are well camouflaged, blending in with their backgrounds and some even resemble tree bark, leaves, or fruits; others appear to mimic bird droppings.

GIANT HOUSE SPIDER

This spider is also known as the greater European house spider. With very long legs, the giant house spider is known to reach up to ¾ inches in size. The species are most commonly brown in color, with a pale mark at the middle of the breastplate. On each side of its breastplate it has four small circles arranged longitudinally.

It is also believed to be the world's fastest spider. On a flat surface, giant house spiders are known to move at a speed of 1.73 feet per second. Giant house spiders are originally native to Europe but were introduced to North America through Vancouver Island in the 1920's. Coastal areas and beaches are most susceptible to giant house spider infestations.

Giant house spiders usually live in flowerbeds, woodpiles and other sheltered, outdoor areas. However, inside, they can be found in dark crevices and basements.

JUMPING SPIDER

There are about 4,000 species for the jumping spider alone making it one of the largest of all other spider species, with more than 300 of those species found in the United States and about 75 found in Europe. The jumping spider averages almost 1-inch in length; the female spider is usually larger than the male. These spiders are also well known for their appearance and because of it they are easily spotted. They are typically brightly colored, have very outstanding patterns, and are also hairy and sometimes stocky.

Jumping spiders have four pair of eyes, two of which give it extremely sharp vision; so sharp that it actually allows it to see better than almost any animal of the same size. The jumping spider's eyes allow it to have a 360-degree eyesight and also has the ability to turn its breast around 45 degrees. The jumping spider is typically found in tropic regions, from the rain forest to the Himalayas. The spider can be found on the ground, on rocks, in the grass, or on trees.

Because their great eyesight, their prey can be noticed anywhere from 12 to 18 inches away. At this point, the jumping spider scans their prey with eyesight similar to that of a zoom lens on a camera. When the prey is regarded as eatable, the jumping spider will move closer and attack with a line of silk and jump or pounce on it.
The jumping spider is not poisonous to humans and like a wolf spider, the jumping spider typically does not attack humans unless they feel threatened or in danger.

LYNX SPIDER

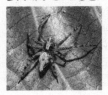
They are more common in the southern United States. They use their green camouflage to sneak up on their victims in the daylight. The lynx spider can be found on grass and low herbage. It is a long legged hunting spider capable of running fast and jumping on their prey. They do not make a web but hunt their prey but do not have the greatest eyesight.

They can only see prey for a distance of about 4-inches. Lynx spiders have two large front eyes and a smaller pair, two on the side of their head and two large ones looking above and backward giving them an almost 360 degree view. They can be found in a variety of colors. These spiders are active during the day, preferable in the sunshine, running and jumping over leaves and grasses.

PSEUDOSCORPIONS

In North America there are over 200 species of pseudoscorpions and although very common, they are only occasionally found indoors and then only a few at any given time. Pseudoscorpions can be found in any room in a house; however, they are usually more common in damp areas, such as laundry rooms, basements and bathrooms. They look scary in appearance, but are harmless to people.

Pseudoscorpion, means "fake scorpions." They are small (most are about 1/5 inch long) and reddish or brown. They have oval, flat body with two pincer-like appendages. When they walk, they often look crab-like and are able to move as quickly backward as they move forward. They are actually a type of arachnid and are related to spiders, ticks and scorpions. In fact, without their pincers, they look very much like ticks.

Pseudoscorpions are also similar to scorpions but do not have the long tail and stinger that is common to scorpions. They live in many different types of habitats, including forests, grasslands; sand dunes and even around beaches. They prefer to live in crevices and similar spaces and can be found in leaf litter, moss and even under tree bark and stones as well as in bird and mammal nests.

Many pseudoscorpions favor sites that have with high humidity, although some species can tolerate a degree of dry conditions. Even though they are not commonly seen, pseudoscorpions can be quite abundant. If the conditions are favorable, hundreds can be found within just one square yard.

These "false scorpions" will feed on many types of small insects and other arthropods, including springtails, bark and book lice, beetles, flies, ants, and mites. They may even stalk their prey while others prefer to ambush insects. They have poor vision, usually possessing two eyes, four eyes and some have no eyes. They use sensory hairs to sense when prey is nearby and when a small insect brushes against these sensory hairs, it triggers a reaction and they seize the insect.

The majority of pseudoscorpions have poison glands in their pincer-like claws which they use to paralyze prey, while they inject saliva into the victim then feeds on the liquid contents. Pseudoscorpions produce silk from glands on their mouthparts and use the silk to spin cocoons in which they overwinter and deposit molted exoskeletons. They also use silk to make sacs that protect their eggs.

When they mate, they usually first engage in a complex courtship dance and after the female is fertilized, she carries her eggs in a sac attached to her abdomen. Once the young is hatched, they remain on their mother obtaining nourishment for a short time before moving away on their own.

RED HOUSE SPIDER

The red house spider is a tropical arachnid, also known as the red-legged house spider and is often mistaken for the dangerous redback spider. However, the bite of the red house spider is not dangerous and symptoms typically are no more severe than localized pain.

The red house spiders are rusty red and are about the size of a dime. Their bodies are spotted, with females bearing a red, vertical band as well as an hourglass-like shape along the underside of the abdomen.

They are often found in dark, undisturbed, indoor spaces and may be found spinning their tangled webs under eaves, in doorframes and along the corners of baseboards.

HAIR DRYER TO THE RESCUE

Pseudoscorpions prefer damp areas and that is where you most likely will find them. Drying out these areas with a hair dryer or dehumidifier should do the trick.

RED SPIDER

Usually found on plants that have poor air circulation and suffer from malnutrition or lack adequate water. Spray the plant with a mild soapy water solution to get rid of the spiders, then feed and water the plant well.

RED SPIDER MITE

General Information:

These adult and nymph spiders will suck the juices from your plants and turn the leaves yellow, silver or even speckled.

They lay their eggs on the plants and are closely related to the horseshoe crab than to insects. They are so small that you should check your plants with a magnifying glass to locate them. They make tiny tents that look like cobwebs on the underneath sides of leaves. They like it dry and too much moisture will drive them away.

If you water your plants and fertilize them regularly, it will limit damage from spider mites.

SALT THEM

Red spider mites can be eliminated from an area by spraying with a solution of 1 ounce of table salt mixed into 1 gallon of water. Seawater will work great but be sure that the plant will tolerate being salted.

DUST THEM WITH POISON

Spider mites: can easily be eliminated by using tobacco! If you dry and powder the tobacco leaves and then dust the plants it will eliminate the mites in short order. Never use nicotine on roses or they will turn black. **Nicotine is a poison to humans, fish and animals.** High concentrations will also kill plants.

BUTTER THEM UP

To prepare a plant dip for houseplants that have become infested with spider mites, just place 2 cups of buttermilk in 1 gallon of water. Dip the plant in the solution and allow it to remain overnight before rinsing it off.

PREDATORS WORK GREAT

There are two predators that really work great in eliminating the red spider mite. They are the lacewing and the ladybug beetles.

LIME THEM

You can spray them with an insecticidal soap or a combination of soap and lime. Dusting them with a lime dust will also eliminate the problem.

GET THEM DRUNK!

Red spiders; can be eliminated by mixing 1 cup of rubbing alcohol with 1 quart of cool tap water. Place the mixture into a spray bottle and be sure and test a leaf first before spraying to be sure you won't damage the plant. If the mixture is too strong reduce the alcohol to ½ cup. Best to wait one day after the leaf test to be sure no damage will occur. Never use this spray in the hot part of the day for the best results.

GREAT SPRAY FOR SPIDER MITES

1	Cup of all-purpose flour
4	Tablespoons of buttermilk
1	Gallon of cool tap water

Prepare a paste from the flour and water before adding the balance of the liquid. If the mite infestation is mild, then just paint the mixture on the leaves instead of using a sprayer. It is best to do the underneath, sides of the leaves as well.

SPEARMINT SPRAY

1	Cup of chives
1	Cup of crushed spearmint leaves
½	Cup of hot peppers or ¼ cup Tabasco Sauce™
1	Small horseradish plant (ground)
1	Quart tap water
¼	Cup Ivory liquid soap

Grind all the ingredients in a blender or food processor and add just enough water to liquefy. Add the quart of water and the liquid soap and refrigerate. To use mix ½ cup of the base to 1 quart of water then strain into a spray bottle. It works great for mites, cabbage loopers and most caterpillars.

GREAT KILLER

The United States Department of Agriculture (USDA) reports that coriander oil will repel the red spider mite. Prepare an emulsion of 2% coriander oil and spray the areas where the spider mite condition exists.

TARANTULAS

These cute hairy spiders will usually not harm a human and just want to be left alone. They live in burrows and go out hunting after dark.

WOLF SPIDER

These can either be a hairy gray or brown color with eight eyes. These are excellent hunters and will chase down their prey. However, wasps kill 99% of all wolf spiders.

They have very stout bodies and thick legs.

NATURAL METHODS OF ELIMINATION

AN APPLE A DAY KEEPS THE SPIDERS AWAY

If you want to repel all types of spiders without killing them, just place a hedgeapple or two in the room where the problem exists. These are the fruit of the Osage orange tree and have been used for hundreds of years as a crawling insect repellant. For more information see www.hedgeapple.com.

GOOD USE FOR OLD PANTYHOSE

If you place cedar chips in the toe of some old pantyhose and hang it where you have a problem, the spiders will avoid the area. However, so will your friends and neighbors when they see the pantyhose hanging all over your home.

AN HERBAL SOLUTION

If you sprinkle the herb pennyroyal in areas that spiders frequent they will never come back. Pennyroyal can be purchased in any health food store.

CHESTNUTS ROASTING ON AN OPEN FIRE

Fresh chestnuts have been used for centuries as a spider deterrent. You can't use packaged shelled or roasted, only fresh, shelled chestnuts. If they are placed across any entry point it will stop them dead in their tracks.

WHAT IS A COBWEB?

Cobwebs are actually *"draglines"* laid down by spiders wherever they go. This is their lifeline that can be used to drop from one place to another or to help them get out of danger. When they get coated with dust they are called cobwebs.

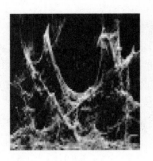

SOLVING CORNER PROBLEMS

To prevent cobwebs from returning to the corners, just spray the area with a solution of 5% white vinegar with a teaspoon of coconut oil added. The spiders will leave the area alone.

SPIDER SPECIFICS

It is best to purchase an all-natural soap that contains pyrethrum and no other chemical substance to use on spiders. Jungle Rain™ is excellent as well as Dr. Bronner's Peppermint Soap™.

SALT KILLS

To eliminate spiders just mix 1 ounce of table salt in 1 gallon of warm tap water. This will kill them within a short period of time. Best for use outside and keep away from plants.

SMOKE 'EM IF YOU GOT 'EM

Place a whole package of chewing tobacco in 1 gallon of boiling water, remove it from the heat and allow it to cool. Strain the solution into a container, then place 1 cup of the solution and ½ cup of lemon-scented liquid soap into a hose-end sprayer and spray your yard and around the outside of the house. This will eliminate all spiders even the good guys for some time to come. Never use nicotine on roses or they will turn black. **It is poison to humans, animals and fish.** Cigarette smoke will also kill spiders, but we do not recommend taking up smoking to kill them.

KILLER OILS

Only one drop of the following oils in 1 quart of water will kill spiders. Use citronella oil, lavender oil, cinnamon oil, peppermint oil, citrus oil and tea tree oil. It will also kill a number of other insects as well.

When mixing citrus oil in a quart of water add 5 tablespoons of Dr. Bronner's Peppermint Soap™ to give it some extra kick.

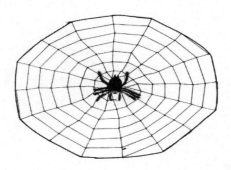

CHAPTER 5

MISCELLANEOUS

GARDEN & PLANT BUGS

MISCELLANEOUS GARDEN & PLANT BUGS

General Information:

There are many natural and chemical remedies to eliminate insect pests. Some remedies work better than others; however, I am providing the ones that tend to work the best. Most of these concoctions can be made with readily available products that will easily be found around the home or purchased from a supermarket or garden supply store. It is always best to only spray the plants that are infested, since many sprays will damage healthy plants that are not infested.

APHIDS

Identification:

These pear-shaped 1/10th to ½ inch long insects are also called plant lice and are not fussy as to which plants they infest. They can be green, yellow or black. They are usually found on the underneath side of leaves with over 4,000 species identified at present. If you see an aphid that looks swollen and somewhat metallic or is a dull brown or black, it is called a "mummy" and has been invaded by a parasitic wasp. It is best to leave it alone so that the larvae can fully develop.

General Information:

You can find aphids on shrubs, potted plants, all garden plants and even trees. They will cause plant stunting, wilting, yellowing and will eventually kill the plant. They prefer the tender tips, buds and stems of most plants. They insert their piercing mouth into the plant stem or leaves, and proceed to suck out the sap from the plant and deposit honeydew, which attracts other insects. Their nutrition is mainly nitrogen and if you use a high nitrogen fertilizer, it will attract them. Aphids usually appear in the fall.

They tend to transmit a number of diseases and are a serious threat in most gardens. If you see ants traveling up and down a plant, they are probably harvesting the honeydew from the aphids. Predators that eat aphids include ladybugs, lacewings, daddy longlegs, and parasitic wasps (Aphidius wasp).

Beneficial insects that will kill aphids can be used in a greenhouse and raised by placing some aphid-infested leaves in a plastic bag, making sure that the aphids are still on the leaves. In a few days the beneficial larvae will emerge and can be harvested with the tip of a small paintbrush while they are crawling about inside the bag. They can then be released inside the greenhouse to eliminate the aphid problem.

If you use a poison pesticide to kill off the aphids, you will also kill off all the beneficial insects that may control them.

OIL THEM UP
Mix 1 tablespoon of canola oil and add 3-4 drops of Ivory soap, then add to 1 quart of water and mix well. Place the contents into a spray bottle and spray the plants from the top down and then from the bottom up making sure the underneath sides of the leaves are saturated.

ICKY STICKY MESSY
Flypaper is very effective in your garden to trap aphids. If you want to make your own, just use a heavy paper stock and spread Tanglefoot™ on it. Tanglefoot™ can be purchased at most garden supply houses.

THEY SMELL NICE AND DIE
Mix together:

¼	**Teaspoon of eucalyptus oil**
½	**Teaspoon of Ivory Liquid Soap™**
½	**Teaspoon of canola oil**
½	**Gallons of water**

Place all the ingredients into a bucket and mix well. Place the mixture into a spray and spray the affected areas.

SIC THE ANTLION ON THEM

There are a number of natural predators that will eliminate aphids. One of the most effective is the aphid lion, which are also known as Dobson fly, green lacewings or antlions.

They can be purchased in most garden stores or nursery's, especially on the east coast of the United States or can be purchased by mail order through an agricultural supply house. They also feast on

 mealybugs, scales and love to munch on thrips for dessert. Most garden supply stores will sell 1,000 eggs for about $10.00.

A GOOD USE FOR TOBACCO

Aphids love roses and will do a lot of damage if not discouraged from  getting to them. A good natural method of deterring aphids is to bury a mixture of 1 cup of tobacco (cigarettes are a good source, organic tobacco would be better) mixed with ½ cup of powdered garlic and 1 cup of compost mixed into the soil around the base of the bushes.

THE KILLER LEMON

Bring 1 pint of tap water to a boil, remove from the  range and add the grated rind of 1 lemon. This mixture needs to steep overnight to release all the citrus oil. Strain the mixture and either, spray it on the aphids or use it on a soft bristle brush and paint the plant with the solution. Any citrus rind can be used, but lemon and lime seem to be more somewhat more effective. The two active ingredients are limonene and linalool.

PEPPER SPRAY WORKS GREAT

1	Tablespoon of Tabasco Sauce™
6	Cloves of garlic
1	Quart of warm tap water

Chop the garlic up very fine, and then add the Tabasco Sauce™ and the water. Allow it to stand for 1 hour before you strain and place in a sprayer. One teaspoon of cayenne pepper may be substituted for the Tabasco Sauce™.

NO LADY WHEN APHIDS ARE AROUND
Ladybug beetles love to eat aphids and will assist you in controlling them very effectively.

SMOTHER THEM WITH OIL
A relatively new agricultural product that was developed for aphid infestations is called "Sunspray™." This is horticultural oil that will smother aphids and their eggs.

ARE APHIDS DOING THE BACKSTROKE?

Water garden plants, can be attacked by aphids and get their juices sucked out just like any other plant. One of the easiest methods of removing them is to hold the plant under water until they release and get drowned. If you have fish they will really love you for the treat, which they rarely get. If you plant fennel or butterfly weed in your water garden it will attract aphid eaters.

DIPPER
Dipping houseplants upside down in a bucket of water is a popular method of getting rid of most bugs. A soapy water bath cleans the leaves as well as getting rid of the pests. Do not use this method on African violets, cactus or plants that have hairy leaves and stems. This method works especially well to eliminate aphids and spider mites. Make sure that the soil is very secure before you do the dipping. Make sure the container is big enough so that it will not break off the stems.

DE-BUGGING A DELICATE PLANT
African violets and other types of delicate plants that will not tolerate a severe water spray to dislodge the bugs need to be placed into a plastic bag that has been sprayed with hair spray.

The plant needs to be quickly inserted into the bag after the spray, then tied with a tie and left to stand overnight. This will kill all bugs on the houseplant.

A SPOT OF TEA WITH A DASH OF AMMONIA
If you want to keep bugs off your indoor plants, try spraying them with a solution of 10-parts weak tea mixed with 1 part household ammonia. **Keep the ammonia away from pets and children.**

HOUSE PLANT PROTECTOR
When you clean your plants leaves, try adding a few drops of liquid detergent to the water and it will keep the bugs off the leaves.

WASH 'EM DOWN THE DRAIN
If you get pests on your houseplants one of the easiest methods of removing them without chemicals is to just place the plant under running water in the sink. The force of the running water will wash off aphids, mites, whiteflies, etc.

INDOOR PLANT PROTECTOR
Sprinkle diatomaceous earth (DE) in the saucer under houseplants to eliminate all insects from setting up housekeeping.

ODOR DETERRENT
If you place one peeled garlic clove, narrow end up, just under the soil of a houseplant it will keep most bugs away from the plant.

BORROW YOUR CHILDS SQUIRT GUN
If you think that you have a pest problem on a houseplant, take the plant outside and give it a few squirts with a strong stream of water. However, be careful not to damage a delicate plant.

POISON GAS???????????

If you have a plant that is already infested, place the plant into a plastic bag and blow a good quantity of cigarette smoke into the bag then seal it up with a tie. This will kill any bug that is in the plant. Allow it to remain overnight and hopefully the plant will survive the smoke.

DON'T BECOME A BUG MAGNET

A variety of different bugs are attracted to different colored clothing. If you wear blue the thrips will follow you around and whiteflies love yellow. Best to wear basic brown or green since these colors don't seem to attract bugs.

SPRAY THEM WITH COOKING OIL

Aphids will suffocate if sprayed with cooking oil. You can make a cooking oil spray by adding 1 teaspoon of insecticidal soap and ½ teaspoon of cooking oil to 1 quart of water. You can also use a commercial spray, such as Pam™.

GETTING TO THE ROOT OF THE PROBLEM

Cassava root is a very effective root when it comes to controlling aphids. You will need to crush the root to obtain the juice then dilute it with equal parts of juice to equal parts of water.

Spray the area, affected by the aphids immediately and wait 15-20 days before planting.

PLOW UP YOUR GARDEN

If you plow up your garden in the fall it should eliminate the aphid eggs. Then if you plant some mint plants that will end their cycle.

LIME DOES MAGIC

Use ¼ cup of lime **(use with caution)** in 1 gallon of warm tap water, add 4 drops of liquid soap and place the mixture in a sprayer. A soap that works really well is ***Ringer Aphid-Mite Attack Insecticidal Soap™***.

MARIGOLD SOLUTION

To get rid of aphids, just soak 15 mature diced-up marigold plants in 5 pints of boiled water and allow the mixture to cool before adding 3 drops of liquid soap. Strain and spray on the affected areas and be sure to spray the underneath sides of the leaves.

SWEET POTATO WATER

Next time you boil sweet potatoes be sure and save all the water to use in a spray to get rid of aphids. This works really well on small insects such as aphids and ants. The leaves of the sweet potato plant can also be soaked in water and the water used as a very effective spray.

WOOLLY MAMMOTH - NO RELATION TO WOOLLY APHID

Tea (cammelia sinensis) can be very effectively used to combat woolly aphids. The leaves are high in caffeine and can be used to prepare a spray.

Make a tea from the leaves and allow it to cool then place the tea in a sprayer and spray the aphids. The crushed tea, leaves can also be placed around plants as a deterrent.

TOMATO JUICE SPRAY

| 2 | Cups tomato leaves and stems |
| 1 | Quart of tap water |

Grind-up the tomato parts them process them in a food processor with 2 cups of water. Allow the mixture to stand overnight, then strain it and add 2 more cups of water. Use as a spray to get rid of aphids.

DON'T BE SCARED OF THIS MUMMY

If you are aphid hunting and spot an aphid that is swollen and looks metallic, brown or blackened, you have found a "mummy." This is an aphid that has been parasitized by a wasp. Don't kill it or you will kill the wasp larva.

A PLANT REPELLENT
If you plant nasturtiums around plants that are susceptible to aphid attacks it will keep the aphids away. Garlic and onion plants are almost as good but nasturtiums seem to be more effective.

FOILED AGAIN
Placing aluminum foil around plants that aphids like seems to work very well; in fact, it tends to keep a number of insects away due to the reflection from the aluminum foil, which confuses the insect. This also aids in reducing weeds and helps the soil retain moisture.

THE CLAY KILLER
A dilute solution of soft wet clay will kill the soft-bodied aphids.

RUB-A-DUB-DUB
Be gently and rub the affected leaves between your fingers to remove the aphids. This method has been the preferred method for hundreds of years.

SQUASH THAT BUG & CHASE HIS FRIENDS AWAY
If you find a plant that is infested with aphids, just crush up a few and leave them on the plant. When they are crushed they will release a chemical signal and all the other aphids will leave the plant.

BORERS

General Information:
There are two main types of borers; they are the caterpillars that eat plants and the grubs of beetles that attack trees.

They are called borers because they can bore into the plant or tree and proceed to feast on the insides, usually in an upward direction. They are difficult to find before they do a great deal of damage.

Tree diseases in many trees can usually be traced to borers, especially if you have plants or trees that are weak and undernourished. These weak trees or plants are prime targets for borers.

Woodpeckers love to go after borers and find them a tempting meal. If the trees are wrapped, however, it usually stops most borers from getting up the tree and getting a foothold. If you can spot the gum and sawdust mixture that they leave behind when they are boring into the tree, it is best to locate and go after them right away.

ASH/LILAC BORER

Identification:

The ash borer belongs to the group of insects called the clear-winged moths. However, these moths fly during the day, not at night. They have slender bodies that are yellow to brownish-black. The wingspan is about 1-inches and the females are larger than the males. Their larvae, does the damage.

General Information:
These bugs tunnel into the trunk of ash trees usually at ground level or below ground. The tunnels can be 12-inches long and up to 1/3 inches wide. They can cause extensive damage to the tree and even kill the tree.

To reduce the infestation it is sometimes necessary to remove the section or limb of the tree where the infestation is taking place. All methods of control for any borer will be viable for these ash borers. If left alone they can kill a tree!

CLEAR THE WAY

If you keep the ground around the trees clear of any grass or weeds the birds will be able to spot the bugs and handle the problem very efficiently. However, pheromone traps are one of the preferred methods of control.

EUROPEAN CORN BORER

Identification:

They are about 1 inch long, gray-pink in color with brown spots. They bore holes in corn and a variety of grasses. Check the underneath side of leaves for their egg masses.

> I'll have mine scrambled

GETTING CONTROL

The eggs can be attacked by ladybugs, lacewings and trichogramma. If there is a bad infestation and the holes are in the corn, it would be best to spray the corn with Nc nematodes or they will enter the stalk and kill the entire corn stalk. As a preventive measure if you feel that the problem is going to occur, spray the corn with Bt. You can also cut a hole and physically remove the borer.

LESSER CORN STALK BORERS

Identification:

These are green, brown or blue-banded caterpillars that will tunnel into corn stems. The caterpillar will exit the stalk through a silken web that resembles a tunnel and pupates in the soil. The adult moth has a wingspan of about 1-inch.

The male's front wings are a yellowish-brown with gray margins. The female's front wings are almost all black.

General Information:
The caterpillars tend to prefer the southern United States cornfields. Georgia, Alabama and South Carolina are the favorite states for the lesser corn borers; however, they can be found from Maine to Georgia. Mexico and Central America has also had a problem. Even though they prefer corn, they will feed on many other plants if the corn is not available.

GET OUT THE SYRINGE
Many farmers prefer to inject Nc nematodes into the boreholes. However, a number of farmers will make a small cut near the borehole and physically remove the pest screaming and kicking. Keep a bucket of soapy water with you if you decide to remove them.

BEFORE THEY SET UP HOUSEKEEPING
Prevention is always the best method of control. Spraying the field with a solution of Bt or NVP will solve the problem.

POKE 'EM
If you find their holes, just poke a stiff wire into the hole to kill them.

POUND THEM ROOTS
Crush up 2 pounds of French marigold roots and place them in 2 quarts of water. Allow to soak for 1 hour, strain and place in sprayer and spray on infested soil.

LIMA BEAN POD BORER

Identification:
This is green or reddish caterpillar with a light yellow head that prefers the southern United States. It grows to about one inch long and will wriggle violently when bothered.

General Information:

This bug will pierce through the Lima bean pod and eat the seeds. It has the tendency to pass from one bean to another and has the tendency to destroy beans even if it is not hungry. When it does finish eating it will enter the ground to pupate.

PICK'EM UP

The best method to eradicate these pests is to handpick them from the plants before they do too much damage. If the crop is planted late they will do more damage than they will to an early, planted crop. If you do plant early you may avoid the pest all together.

PACIFIC FLATHEAD BORER   Adult

General Information:

Attacks fruit and nut trees above the ground and usually attack trees that already have some form of damage, usually a sunburned area, making it easier for them to bore into. Their tunnels cause sap to be released from their holes. The beetle has a dark mottled appearance with a bronze colored shell.

PAINT WITH LATEX

Paint the tree trunk with an indoor white latex paint or use whitewash. You will need to paint the area of the trunk at least 2 feet from the soil line and about 1 inch under the soil to be effective.

RASPBERRY CANE BORER

Identification:

 This is a thin beetle that has black wings and a yellow body and about ½ inches long. They have long black antennae and take 2 years to complete their life cycle.

General Information:
The female lays her eggs on a young shoot and the grub that hatches eats the pith inside the cane. The top of the cane will then turn black, wilt and die. The best control is to cut off the wilted shoot well below the point of injury and be sure to burn them.

SQUASH VINE BORER

Identification:

 This is a red and black moth that has clear wings and is about 1½-inches long. Larvae are wrinkled, white with brown heads. The adult moth flies in the daytime and looks like a small wasp. The front wings are reddish-brown and the front wings are clear. The body is orange and it has black bands on its abdomen. The larvae, is a caterpillar that is wrinkled and is white with a brown head capsule.

General Information:
These are wasp-like moths that lay a single egg usually near the base of the plant stalk. When the caterpillar hatches it bores into the stalk or a leaf stem and then tunnels along the inner tissue, pushing brown garbage out of their tunnel entrance. They usually attack squash, pumpkins and cucumbers. If you see a sudden wilting of a leaf check for borers and remove the leaf or plant part and destroy the borer. The Baby Blue and Butternut varieties of squash are fairly resistant to these bugs.

TRICH THEM

Releasing trichogramma will attack the borer eggs and kill them. Use Nc nematode infested mulch around the base of the vegetables for excellent control. If you find a borehole, just inject Nc nematodes into the borehole with a medicine dropper.

SAVE THOSE RUNNERS

Use a weekly spray of Bt as soon as you start to see the vine runners to keep the borers away.

PASTE 'EM UP

Prepare a thick paste made from water and wood ash and paint it on the trunk of the tree to stop the borers from climbing up.

PUT DOWN A CARPET

Fabric row covers (from garden supply stores) are a great way to stop moths from laying their eggs since they are looking for moist soil.

ALUMINUM WRAP

Try wrapping the base of the plant with a layer of aluminum foil to stop the moths from laying their eggs on the stem of the plant.

SMELLY ONES WORK GREAT

These borers hate the smell of garlic and onions. If you intersperse these plants among your vine plants it will keep the borers at bay. Planting radishes is said to work well to keep the borers away.

IT'S RAINING SOAP SUDS
There are two good methods to deter these bugs. You can hang bars of soap on the tree and when it rains the soap will run down the tree or you can squirt liquid hand soap on the limbs and the soap will run down the tree when you water the tree.

STRAWBERRY CROWN BORER

General Information:

The grub does the major damage by boring into the main root of the plant and weakening or killing it. The adult is a brownish beetle with red patches on its wings and feeds on stems and leaves. Strawberry plants can usually defend against the beetle if they are good strong plants.

Adult Beetle

KEEP NEW BEDS AWAY
Since the beetles cannot fly, planting a new bed 300 yards away from an old bed where a problem exists usually eliminates the problem.

BOX ELDER BUGS

LEMON TREE VERY PRETTY

If you have a problem with box elder bugs on your plants, just spray the plants with a solution of diluted Lemon Joy® or any dishwasher detergent (use 1 ounce per 1 quart of tap water). Spray a few leaves first to be sure you will not damage the plant before spraying. To make the Lemon Joy® even more effective add 1 drop of essential peppermint oil to the mixture.

MILLIPEDE

General Information:

 These creepers can grow up to 200 pairs of legs and usually help to eliminate decaying material.

However, they are also pests and may attack roots and stems of healthy plants, especially if they need water during a dry spell. When they get a taste of sweet sap they will keep feeding. They have been known to do a lot of damage to seedlings.

They prefer damp and dark locations, such as a basement. When bothered they will curl up in a "C" shape similar to a pillbug. When they curl up they will remain still when touched and play dead.

FUNGUS/MOLDS

THERE'S A FUNGUS AMONG US
Mix 2 tablespoons of baking soda in 1 quart of water and mix well. Place the mixture into a spray bottle and spray directly on fungus every 2-3 days as needed.

PASS THE SALAD DRESSING
Over 85% of all molds can be killed with white vinegar. Make sure that the vinegar is at least 5% to be effective.

MOLD KILLERS
Borax, sodium borate, table salt and lime are all commonly use mold killers. Baking soda and food-grade diatomaceous earth (DE) can also be used very effectively.

MILD LOVES HUMIDITY
Dehumidifiers, fans and air conditioners will reduce the amount of mold by reducing the level of humidity in the home.

BLEACH 'EM OUT
To control mold place 1 cup of household bleach into 1 gallon of water and mix well and sponge or spray on to control the mold spores.

SURGICAL REMOVAL
If you are having a problem with black spot fungus, you will need to remove and destroy the affected limb. It is best to find all the areas where it is hiding and remove it before winter sets in. The fungus is able to survive the winter on fallen leaves and even the stems of roses.

AMARANTH FIGHTS FUNGI

Use about 2 pounds of amaranth leaves or fresh grain and extract the juices. Mix the juice with 2 quarts of water and use as a spray. Strain if necessary and allow the mixture to sit for 1 hour before using. This will combat the following fungi: Alternaria, cercospora, colletotrichum, curvularia, helminthosporium and pestalotia. Bring a leaf with fungus on it to your local gardening supply house for identification.

FUNGI AND GINGER
A number of fungi can be killed using ginger. These include leaf mold, early blight, frogeye and leaf spot. The rhizome needs to be crushed and the juice used in a spray. Test and area first to avoid any plant damage and allow it to remain overnight.

GRASSHOPPERS

Grasshoppers; are a real pest in the family garden because of their big appetites. They prefer grasses, clover and weeds, but when these are not available will go for the veggies. Their powerful hind legs allow them to jump up to 30 inches and they can fly long distances. Their powerful jaws can make short work of plants.

If you dig up the soil in the fall you can kill most of their eggs, however, you will need to go down about six inches to reach all of them. Heavy mulch also makes it difficult for them to get out of the ground.

 Grasshoppers are more of a serious threat to crops in areas that receive between 10-30 inches of rainfall. The areas of more concern are the Midwestern United States and Canada and sometimes in the Mountain States. They spend 6-8 months in the egg stage and if fields are plowed in late fall it will help to reduce the possible infestation in the spring or early summer.

TILLER AWAY!
One of the best methods of killing grasshopper egg pods is to till the garden area.

BEGONE LITTLE HOPPERS
You can purchase products made from naturally occurring protozoans called Semaspore™ or Nosema Locustae™ in many garden or agricultural supply houses. Grasshoppers eat the protozoan, become infected and die as well as spreading the disease to newly hatched grasshoppers.

ALTERNATIVE METHODS
All praying mantis' love to feast on grasshoppers! Spray them with Nc nematode and soap spray in the late evening or at night.

PLANT TOMATOES OR SQUASH
To keep grasshoppers away from your plants, just plant tomato plants around the garden instead of just one area. Tomato plants are a natural insect repellent and really work great. Grasshoppers do not like squash plants and will avoid them.

HUNT THEM DOWN
Grasshoppers sleep at night on plant leaves and can easily be found if you hunt for them with as flashlight.

They can easily be picked off and drowned in a bucket of soapy water with a little cayenne pepper added. They are not early risers and if you get up early you can still pick them off the plants.

HOT PEPPER SPRAY WORKS

Prepare a spray using onions, garlic and hot peppers or Tabasco Sauce™. Blend the onions, peppers and the garlic in a food processor with 2 cups of water and allow it to stand for 1hour.

Strain and use ½ cup in 1 quart of water to stop grasshoppers from attacking your plants. It is best to test a few leaves first to be sure that the spray is not too potent if it is add more water to dilute it.

ELIMINATE ROADSIDE WEEDS

Roadside weed areas are the home for many grasshoppers. If you clear these areas and plant a perennial grass such as crested wheatgrass it will reduce the problem.

MULCH THEM

If you place a good layer of mulch or compost down it will stop the grasshoppers from surfacing in the spring.

HIRE A GUINEA HEN

Guinea hens are one of the best grasshopper catchers around. They will patrol your garden and eliminate the hopper problem. When they have cleared the area, cage them!

IMPORTED CABBAGEWORM

Identification:

One of the more common cabbageworms is the Imported Cabbageworm. The adult is a small white butterfly that has black-tipped forewings, which has a span of about 1½- inches. The males having 1 black spot on top of their wings and the females have 2 black spots. The hind wings are all white with a black spot.

Their eggs are laid on the underneath side of leaves and are a yellowish color. It is best to crush the eggs when found to reduce the number of larvae.

Their larvae are a velvety green with faint yellow stripes. The larvae are about 1 inch long, green with a yellow stripe down their back and love to eat leaves. Those common white butterflies come from this caterpillar.

STANDARD CATERPILLAR CONTROL

Very effective control can be achieved if you release trichogramma and lacewings, or spray or dust with Bt or NPV. You can also handpick the larvae off plants and then use a butterfly net to catch the butterflies. If you plant rosemary, thyme or sage in your garden they will stay away. A Bt spray is also very effective.

LEAFROLLERS

Identification:

The forewings are usually walnut brown to a light tan in color. These moths are active at night. Their eggs are usually very hard to spot since they are the same color as a leaf.

General Information:

The caterpillars may spin their web in leaves and then roll them up making them easier to spot. They will infest large numbers of leaves and can do a lot of damage. They are not too fussy and will use plant leaves if a tree is not handy.

BEST TO SPRAY

One of the best methods for these caterpillars is to spray them with Bt, then use a mixture of NVP or soap and lime spray. An alternative method would be to release lacewings and trichogramma to destroy the eggs.

MITES

Identification:
They are grayish black to red and their mouthparts are all grouped in the front of their body, which looks like their head. The adults have four pairs of legs and are very slow moving. They may look like a little moving spot (about the size of a grain of salt). They only measure 1/100th of an inch. They have eight pairs of legs and have no wings or antennae. They can be found in water, on land and in the air.

General Information:
There are over 40,000 species worldwide and 50% of them live as parasites on animals. The most common ones we encounter is the house dust mite who usually inhabits the folds in mattresses waiting for a meal of dead skin to munch on. They cause numerous allergies and may even cause asthmatic attacks. Mites are distant relatives of spiders.

Spider Mites
One of the more common mites is the spider mite especially in the urban landscape and can inflict serious damage to trees, shrubs and flowers. Both evergreen and deciduous plants may be attacked. Spider mites are not insects but they are more closely related to ticks and spiders and their name is derived from their ability to produce silk, which most species spin on host plants. Mites are tiny, about the size of the period at the end of this sentence. They are very prolific, which is why infestations usually go unnoticed until plants exhibit significant damage.

Spider mites have a simple, oval-shaped body and no wings or antennae. All species pass through an egg stage, six-legged larval stage and two eight-legged nymph stages before transforming into an eight-legged adult. The immature stages resemble the adults except in size and an adult female may live for several weeks and lay many dozens of eggs during her lifetime.

Under optimum conditions, spider mites can complete their development from egg to adult in less than one week, so there may be many overlapping generations in a single season. Therefore, populations increase rapidly and can cause extensive plant damage in short period of time.

Spider mites possess needle-like mouthparts and feed by piercing the leaves of host plants and sucking out the fluids from individual plant cells. This causes the leaves to have a stippled or flecked appearance, with pale dots where the cellular contents have been removed. Most of the mites feed from the undersides of leaves, although the damage is most evident from the upper surface.

 Most spider mites have a habit of covering leaves, shoots, and flowers with very fine silken webbing, produced from a pair of glands near the mouth. The silk strands aid in dispersal by allowing the mites to spin down from infested to non-infested leaves, and to be blown by wind currents. When abundant, the silk also may shield the mites from pesticide sprays.

Spider mites are one of the more difficult landscape pests to control; however, infestations are easier to control when detected early, before the populations have reached very high levels. Spider mite infestations can often be traced to the purchase of infested plant material. When purchasing new plants; always inspect the lower leaf surfaces for evidence of mites.

An efficient way to sample vegetation for spider mites is to hold a sheet of white paper under a branch and tap the foliage sharply. If spider mites are present, they will be dislodged and look like slow- moving, dark specks on the paper.

VACUUM, VACUUM, VACUUM
The best method of reducing the mite population or eliminating the problem it is to vacuum regularly.

NOT TOO MITEY AFTER THIS
Mix 2 tablespoons of cayenne pepper or a very hot, spicy sauce with 3-4 drop of Ivory Liquid Soap™ in 1 quart of tap water. Mix well, then place into a spray bottle and spray plants making sure that you spray the underneath sides of the leaves well. Make sure that the mixture stays in solution by shaking the bottle frequently.

HIT THEM WITH A SYRINGA
Soak 2 ounces of fresh "syringa leaves" in 4 cups of cold water for about 24 hours then strain and use in a sprayer. Test a few leaves and leave overnight. If the mixture is too strong it can burn your plants. **The fruit is very poisonous, so use with caution.**

USE SULFUR POWDER
One of the best insecticides for mites is to use sulfur powder from your drug store. There are a number of different preparations that contain sulfur. *Use with caution.*

MITES LIKE MARIGOLDS
Unlike most bugs, spider mites love marigolds and are not repelled by the plants.

SQUIRT THE BOXWOODS
The boxwood plant; can be damaged by boxwood mites. The leaves will become withered, bronzed and may drop to the ground making the plant look scraggly. The best method of eliminating the problem is to squirt the plant with water several times during the spring and summer months.

BULB MITES MAY RIDE A MOUSE OR FLY

These mites love bulbs and can do significant damage. They are whitish and have a few brown spots and grow up on onions and potatoes and then go on to the bulbs. While the mites will not do a lot of damage they allow decay organisms to enter and damage the plant. When the mite enters a stage where it develops a hard shell it will stop eating and look for a free ride aboard a mouse or fly looking for its next location. If you have a problem, just dip the bulbs in hot water for 20 minutes and make sure that you clean up any rotting or old bulb material.

ONE OF THE GREATEST SOLUTIONS

A glue spray really does the job, just mix 2 quarts of tap water in 4 ounces of Elmer's Glue and allow it to stand for about 12 hours. Spray the solution of the infected plants.

This will glue the mites, killing them and will not harm the plants. As the glue dries, it will just flake off. This should only be done in the evening and not in the hot sunlight. Be sure and clean out your sprayer immediately afterwards.

CHEESE MITE

General Information:

 The cheese mite will cause dermatitis (skin irritation) and is larger than the grain or mold mite. It needs an ideal temperature of 73^0 and humidity of 83% to thrive.

CONTROLLING CHEESE MITES

- Make sure you inspect cheeses that are not wrapped.
- Inspect pet food that is purchased in bulk.
- Store foods in a clean, dry area.
- Never place new grains on top of old grains in storage bins.
- Store foods in well-sealed containers.
- Vacuum up spills and never leave them around.

FREEZE THEM

If you think that you have mite-infested foods, just place the foods in the freezer at 0^0F for seven days or in a shallow pan at 140^0F for 30 minutes in the oven. If you wish to use a microwave place the foods in there for 5 minutes on high.

THEY MAY WEAR SUNGLASSES

Dust mites will be killed by direct sunlight. If you place upholstered furniture in the sun for a few hours it will kill any mites that may reside there. Bedding should be washed and changed weekly and washed in water that is at least 120^0F.

THERE GOES THE TEDDY BEAR

Plush animals are usually loaded with dust mites and need to be placed in a plastic bag in the freezer for 24 hours once per week. If they are washable they should be washed once per week.

NOW I LAY ME DOWN

Pillows are one of the most common items that contain dust mites. Almost 25% of all pillows are contaminated and should at least be replaced every 4-6 months. If you ever had your bed evaluated for the dust mites you would probably never sleep in it again or buy a new one.

DUST MITES

Identification:

These microscopic insects can be found anywhere in your home and are related to other mites, and ticks, in the class Arachnida, which also includes spiders, scorpions, daddy-longlegs, and similar eight-legged creatures.

Mites can be distinguished from insects by a lack of wings and antennae, and by having eight legs (though larval mites may have only six legs). Mites can be distinguished from spiders by the fact that mites have only one body segment, as opposed to the two body segments spiders have.

One of the problems to the identification of house dust mites is their invisibility. Even the adult mites cannot be seen with the naked eye.

They measure a mere 1/100th of an inch, or 250-300 microns, one-fourth to one-third of a millimeter. The larvae and nymphs are even smaller and it takes a powerful microscope to see them.

What dust mites lack in size they make up for in sheer numbers and densities of dust mites in the typical used mattress after only 2-3 years can range from 100,000 to ten million individual mites. House dust mites feed and grow almost exclusively on the dead, shed skin cells that are shed by humans daily by the hundreds of thousands. While your bed is their favorite location the majority of house dust mites can also survive in pillows, stuffed animals, overstuffed furniture, even rugs and carpeting. The place where your pet sleeps is also a favorite location.

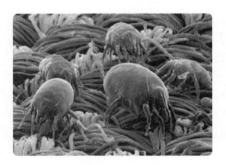

They thrive on dead skin cells and may be a hazard to people with allergies or asthma. It is best to reduce their numbers as best you can. There are 35 million people who have allergies to dust mites. **Every home collects about 40 pounds of dust per year, which contains 15 species of dust mite.** One ounce of dust can contain 42,000 dust mites. In England 33% of all cereals inspected was contaminated with dust mites.

General Information:

- Vacuuming works great on mattresses and pillows.
- Bedding should be washed in very hot water. Detergents and soaps will not kill the mites unless the water temperature is very hot.
- The bedroom should be kept clear of stuffed animals, clothes hampers and throw rugs.
- Stuffed animals should be periodically washed in very hot water.
- Problem areas should be dusted with tannic acid powder since this neutralizes the allergens. This is available at most health food stores.
- All mattresses and pillows should be covered with laminated covers so that the mites cannot penetrate them.
- Fabric-covered headboards are a perfect place for mites.
- Heating ducts should be covered with a special filter that can trap dust particles smaller than 10 microns.
- Mites love humidifiers and thrive on the warmth and moisture.

YOU'RE SLEEPING ON DUST MITES

The majority of dust mites in your home reside in your mattresses. Place 3-4 anti-static dryer sheets between the mattress pad and the box spring then place duct tape around the legs of the bed and around the base of the bed, sticky-side out. You also need to place an airtight plastic cover over the mattress and pillows.

EAR MITES

Identification:

 This is a very tiny infectious organism that looks like a tick and must be identified through microscopic examination. It usually results in a black discharge that resembles coffee grounds.

General Information:

Ear mites are a tiny spider like parasitic mite that infects the ears of dogs and cats. They usually live in the ear canals but may also live on other parts of the dog or cat's body. Ear mites are the most common cause of ear infections found more frequently in cats than dogs but are a considerable cause of ear infection in dogs as well.

Certain breeds of dogs are more prone to ear mite infections that others, especially dogs with long floppy ears. The ear mites live comfortably in the warm moist area where the air flow is restricted. They feed on dead skin debris & ear wax and burrow into the ear, causing inflammation which if you have a look inside the ear of an infected dog you will see dark reddish brown or black debris throughout the ear canal looking like coffee grounds.

Ear mites are actually visible to the naked eye and can be seen as white spots among the dark debris. You may even spot them moving around. Ear mite infections are serious if left untreated and can result in damage to the ear canals and eardrums and possible deafness.

Ear mites are uncomfortable for your cat or dog having thousands of little bugs running around in one of their most sensitive areas. The first symptom you notice will be your dog scratching his ears or shaking his head due to the extreme itchiness. Dogs may cause damage by scratching causing the ears to bleed and even shake their ears with such intensity that small blood vessels are broken.

OIL THEM

Place a few drops of olive oil on a cotton ball and place it in the ear for a minute or two, then be sure and remove all traces of the oil.

GRAIN MITES

Grain mites are not really insects, but are closely related to insects. They are microscopic, pale grayish white, wingless and soft bodied. Their populations can increase to such a large number that grain appears to be covered with a moving layer of dust. Adults have 8 legs, while larvae only have 6 legs and each leg has one claw on the end along with a sucker.

They will attack not only grain but cheese, flour, pet food, oilseeds, medicinal herbs, hay, abandoned beehives and just about any food used by man. Grain mites can even feed on fungi so food that is going bad is often infested. In grain, mites eat the germ and only eat the endosperm if it is moldy.

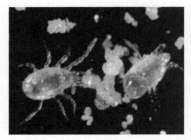

Populations of grain mites are sensitive to moisture conditions and if the grain moisture drops to below 13.4%, all individuals will die. Environmental conditions are perfect for extreme population growth at temperatures between 20 and 25°C (68 to 77°F). Development time for one generation ranges from 78 days at 4°C (39°F) to 9.2 days at 28°C (82°F). Their life span depends upon temperature, food, and reproductive activity. Females under ideal conditions live 42-63 days. Male survivorship is usually only a few days less.

Grain mite populations can explode when they feed on wheat germ, yeast, cheese, powdered milk, flour, or grain. In finely ground commodities such as flour and powdered milk, infestations are confined to the surface layer while whole or cracked grains and nuts may be totally infested.

THE GROCER'S ITCH
Since there are so many mites around, especially in foods, there are two, mite infestations that have been related to people that work with grains. The grocer's itch and the baker's itch are commonly found in markets and bakeries. It is best to keep humidity out of your grains.

HOT CHILI TO THE RESCUE
If you place a very hot chili pepper in the grain you will not have any insects residing there. The hotter the better but be sure that it is a whole pepper with no externally visible damage or you will ruin the taste of the grain.

MOLD MITE

LOVES HUMIDITY
The mold mites will invade almost any food, especially grains and breads if the humidity is relatively high. The drier the products are kept the better. If you have this problem in your area it would be wise to store grain and grain-related products in the refrigerator or freezer. They are harmless to people and pets.

Mold mites are part of a large group of similar species that are hard to tell apart. Similar members in this group of tiny mites include the cheese mite, flour mite, and grain mite. Mold mites are very common but usually go unnoticed except when they become abundant. They infest stored food and grain and can cause big losses although they are more usually an annoyance and nuisance and not injurious.

They are harmless to people and pets, furniture, house structures and clothing. Mold mites only develop where there is adequate moisture or high humidity. They feed on molds and are common only where mold and fungi can flourish.

Control of mold mites is difficult and is likely to require persistence. The first step should be to eliminate humidity or moisture that is producing favorable conditions for molds and mites.

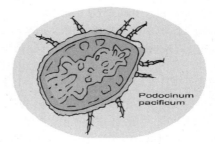

Podocinum
pacificum

STINKBUG

These are flat green, shield-shaped bug that will cause tomato plants to develop white spots as they suck out the juices. If they are not causing a problem these may be beneficial since they will act as a parasite and kill pest caterpillars and beetles. They will lay a cluster of brown or green eggs on the underneath side of leaves.

PARASITE TO KILL A PARASITE
The parasite that will eliminate the stinkbug is called **Trissolcus basilis.** You can also hand pick the stinkbugs and their eggs off your plants.

SPRAYS WORK WELL

A soap spray using 4 drops of liquid soap and ¼ cup of lime in 1 gallon of water will take care of the problem.

THRIPS

Identification:

 These are very small (almost invisible) yellow or black insects that attack plants and flowers and suck out their juices as well as spreading many plant diseases. Under a magnifying glass they will look like long, elongated bugs that have a double wing with fancy fringe. They can range in color from yellow to almost black.

General Information:

When you disturb thrips they will fly or hop for a very short distance and have the tendency to flip their abdomen over their head like a scorpion to try and scare you away. They will lay their eggs on leaves and plants and look like a walking spot that is only about 1/16th of an inch long. They may be yellow to black in color and there are over 600 species in North America.

They prefer to feed on beans, tomatoes, potatoes, carrots, cucumber and squash. They also like gladioli and roses. If you see a silvery spot or streak it may very well be thrips that have settled in.

CALL IN THE MITES

There are two predatory mites that can be purchased to control thrips. They are **Amblyseiulus mackenseii** and **Euseius tularensis**. Dragonflies also like to feast on thrips. Using Nc nematode mulch around the base of plants may also do some good.

SPECIAL SPRAY

Check with your garden supply store for a spray that contains sabadilla dust, which is usually combined with sugar. Soap sprays early in the morning are also very effective as well as yellow sticky traps.

YELLOW AND BLUE TRAPS

Thrips are attracted to the colors yellow and blue. If you use some construction paper and place a sticky substance on it they will go over for a look see and get all stuck up. If you place the sticky substance on the plant stems it will stop them from climbing up the plant. Tanglefoot™ is excellent to use as the sticky substance.

FOILED AGAIN

Foil collars work great for low-lying plants. Make sure that they extend at least 12 inches around the plant on all sides to be effective. If the plants are over 2 feet tall, you will need to place stakes around the plants and extend the foil from the stakes.

GENERAL METHODS OF INSECT CONTROL

CLOCHE ME

This resembles a miniature greenhouse and is used for seedbeds and very young plants as well as acting as a barrier against insects and pests. The cloche must be opened every day to allow watering, especially on hot days. However, this is a negative since when it is opened it may allow insects and pests to enter. It is, however, an excellent method of allowing plants to get a good start.

The healthier the plant the less likely insects stand a chance of damaging them. Check with your garden supple house about building plans or purchasing a ready-made cloche.

ALL-PURPOSE SPRAY PESTICIDES

The following formulations will be effective against most pest insects. Place the formula in a spray bottle and either spray on the insect or into its home.

Water to fill the bottle ¾ full, then add 4 drops of Ivory liquid soap, ¼ teaspoon of hot pepper sauce and ½ crushed garlic clove. This formula will need to be strained before you place it into the spray bottle.

Finely crush 2-3 habanero peppers, 2 large yellow onions and 1-large garlic clove. Place the mixture into 1 quart of very hot water and allow it to steep overnight before straining and using in a sprayer.

Mix together 1 tablespoon of Ivory liquid soap and 1 teaspoon of canola oil in 1 quart of tap water.

Finely crush 15 garlic cloves and allow them to soak in 16 ounces of mineral oil and 4 drops of Ivory liquid soap for 12 hours, then strain and add 3 pints of water. Best to test on a leaf or two before using this formulation on the whole plant.

Finely crush ½ cup of Serrano peppers in 2 cups of warm water, strain well and spray.

Place 2 cups of rubbing alcohol in 1 quart of water and spray the plants that are infected. Best to allow the mixture to remain on 1-2 leaves overnight and then check for damage.

Crush up some rhubarb or oleander leaves and place them into 1 quart of warm water. Allow it to stand overnight then strain before using. **This is very toxic so keep it away from pets and children.**

FLOATING ROW COVERS

This method uses lightweight opaque materials, which are draped over the entire garden bed. The material allows sunlight and water to pass through, but will keep insects and birds from damaging your plants. Since the material is so light, the plants will push it up as it grows. The edges are anchored with a heavy object such as a rock, to avoid being pushed up by the wind. The material will break down after a few years and is sold in rolls and is fairly inexpensive.

PHEREMONES

These are biological mating hormone scents given off to attract other insects of a particular species. Pheremones are sold by garden supply stores and can be placed on flypaper or in traps to attract insects. This method is a very effective method of ridding your garden of insects.

CHAPTER 6

CATERPILLARS

CATERPILLARS

ONE CATERPILLAR, TWO CATERPILLAR
One of the best methods of getting rid of caterpillars is to just pick them off and drive them at least 10 miles away from your garden and release them.

KILLS THE YOUNG ONES
This naturally occurring bacteria, is used to kill the young ones of the gypsy moth. Just spray them with **Bacillus thuringiensis (Bt),** a good natural biological caterpillar control weapon that you can purchase in a garden supply house.

HIT THEM WITH A BLACKJACK
Blackjack is an annual weed that has flowers with white and yellow centers. The seeds are small, black and thin with tiny claws on one end. They usually stick to people's clothes or pets fur. A spray can be made; by using the mature seeds if you just take a cupful in water and allow it to boil for about 8-10 minutes or allow them to soak for 24 hours. If you boil them allow them to cool then add 1 quart of water and 1 teaspoon of liquid soap and spray immediately. This will also eliminate aphids, beetles, cabbage root flies and whiteflies.

ELIMINATE THEM WITH PAWPAW

To prepare a spray using pawpaw (Carica papaya), use 2 pounds of shredded leaves and add them to 4 cups of water and mix well. Strain and add the juice to 2 pints of water then add 2 teaspoons of paraffin and 3 drop of liquid soap. Spray into the soil to get rid of caterpillars and cutworms.

SMELLY SOLUTION
Jimson weed (purple stink weed) can be used to combat aphids by just drying and then powdering the stems and leaves, then using the powder to dust the plants. This plant has also been called thorn apple.

This plant is poisonous to humans and animals so handle it with caution.

BAGWORM

This caterpillar lives in a silk cocoon that looks like a bag. It has small pieces of leaves attached to the outside as camouflage and carries the bag with it when it is feeding. The bag is about 2 inches long when it is fully matured. They lay their eggs in the fall and they hatch in May or early June.

HERE-A BAG, THERE A BAG

One of the best methods of getting rid of the bugs is to hand pick them from the trees or plants and burn them.

Adult Bagworm Moth

BURP 'EM
The Burpee Company, Inc. sells a pheromone trap that is prepared specifically for your bagworms.

HERBAL SPRAY

1   **Pound of quassia chips**
1   **Gallon of water**

Place the quassia chips in the water and allow it to stand overnight then strain and dilute with water in a ratio of 1:10. Add a small amount of liquid soap and spray. The quassia chips are available at most garden supply stores.

CABBAGE LOOPER

Identification:
These little white-striped green caterpillar critters just love broccoli, kale, kohlrabi, radishes, turnips, peas, cabbage and cauliflower plants.

Their body forms a loop as they travel along. You can easily identify the looper by its *"humpback"* appearance. The moth is brown with silver markings on the center of each wing.

General Information:
They tend to feed on the underneath sides of the leaves. They lay their greenish-white eggs singly on the upper surface of the leaves. To stop them from laying their eggs on your plants, just plant onion sets around the area totally surrounding your plants. The loopers will not come near a garden that has an onion fence around it. Space the onion sets about 4 inches apart for the best results.

BEGONE CABBAGE LOOPERS
For natural control of cabbage loopers it is best to release trichogramma and lacewings. If you want to get rid of them in a hurry then dust or spray with Bt or NPV from your garden supply or agricultural store. Best to begin spraying once a week after the moths or butterflies start appearing.

A SOUR SOLUTION
If your cabbage has been infested, just make some sour milk by adding 4 teaspoons of white vinegar per cup of milk to turn it sour. Spray or sprinkle the mixture over the heads of cabbage to get rid of the bugs.

HERE A LITTLE, THERE A LITTLE
This is an oldie but a goody! Prepare a mixture of ¼ cup of table salt with ½ cup of all-purpose flour then place the mixture into a large saltshaker and sprinkle the cabbage during the growing season. It is best to do this a few times and not depend on just once to do the trick.

ASHES WORK GREAT
Wood ashes can be sprinkled on the leaves to repel the cabbage loopers as well as the imported cabbageworms. This is an excellent method and won't hurt the plant.

TIDES IN

Ocean saltwater; is used very effectively by many farmers to kill the cabbage loopers and their eggs as well as stopping the caterpillars from eating the leaves. Cabbage plants can tolerate the salt from a spray of saltwater.

THIS REALLY ISN'T CORNY

If you sprinkle cornmeal or rye flour on cabbage plants the caterpillars will eat it and soon die. This is a very safe method of controlling these pests.

A CANOPY OF LEAVES

If you place geranium leaves over the cabbage plants it will deter a number of pests including the cabbage looper.

GIVE THEM A LAXATIVE

Try placing a small squirt of mineral oil into the tip of each ear of corn to smother the worm. This should be done after the silks are starting to wilt and turn brown. You can also add a small amount of cayenne pepper to the oil for an extra charge.

TIGHT HEADS KEEP THEM AWAY

There are a few varieties of cabbage that have very tight heads, which the bugs do not like. These are Mammoth Red Rock, Savoy Chieftain and Savoy Perfection Drumhead cabbage.

PLANTS THAT REPEL

If you plant any of these plants near your cabbage you will not have a problem with loopers. They are onion, garlic, celery, tansy, hyssop, mint, sage, rosemary, tomato or thyme.

CABBAGEWORM

PUT SALT ON THEIR TAIL

One of the best methods to stop cabbageworms is to spray them with a solution of 1 ounce of table salt in 2 gallons of water.

The salt may damage your plants, so be careful where you spray. Salt will also stop plant growth.

CABBAGE WORM CURE
The following ingredients will be needed:

½	**Cup of table salt**
1	**Cup of all-purpose flour**

Place the ingredients in a small dish and mix well. Sprinkle the powder on the plants early in the morning when the plants still have some dew on them.

CORN ARMYWORM

Identification:

These are around 2 inches long and light tan or dark brown in color. They also have; orange, yellow or dark brown contrasting stripes.

General Information:
The damage to the corn may appear in the form of chewed leaves and the damage usually appears on the edges of the leaves. They will eventually bore into the ear of corn and set up housekeeping until there is no more to eat before they move to a new ear.

SPRAY THOSE NEMATODES
Spraying Nc nematodes early in the season will help reduce the number of bugs. If you see a borehole it would be best to inject the nematodes directly into the hole. You can also hand pick them by making a slit next to the borehole.

KILL THEM WITH GRAPEFRUIT!

1	**Whole grapefruit**
2	**Cups of boiling water**
2	**Cups cool tap water**

Grind up the grapefruit in a food processor and add the mixture to the boiling water. Allow it to remain overnight then strain and add the cool water before you spray. When sprayed on the plants it will stop caterpillars and most beetle larvae from chomping on your plants.

CORN EARWORM

Identification:

This worm is about 2 inches long and may be found in shades of green, brown or yellow. Its sides will be darker than the bodies. The adults are light brown or gray moths with black spots and about a 1½-inch wingspan.

General Information:

These worms are also known as tomato fruitworms or cotton bollworms. Their garden food consists of corn, tomatoes, cotton, peppers, eggplant, okra, potatoes, squash, beans and peas. They will attack the tender shoots as soon as they break the surface. They love to chew on the corn silk and disrupt the germination process. They chew holes in green tomatoes and may move on and not even finish their meal. If you have flower buds that have become damaged it would be best to remove them.

CLOTHESPINS TO THE RESCUE
If you clip a clothespin to the tip of each ear of corn to keep the husk tight you will not have a worm problem. You will, however, have the funniest-looking cornfield in your vicinity.

PLANT RESISTANT VARIETIES

There are a number of varieties that can be planted that the worms will not bother with. These include ones with tight husks such as Try Country Gentleman or Silver Cross Bantam corn.

PLANT REPELLANTS

There a few plants will repel these worms very efficiently. These need to be planted within the rows and include smartweed or sunflowers.

BIOLOGICAL CONTROL

Bt sprayed on the plants works great. Tachinid flies and wasp parasites will also do the trick. The commercially available virus Elcar™ can also be used as well as NPV very effectively.

SCREEN THEM IN

If you have a number of valuable plants the best thing to do is to screen them in with a piece of cheesecloth or other porous material.

CUTWORM

Identification:

There are many species of cutworms and their color varies from green to white, brown and even black. They may also have stripes or be banded. They are plump, soft-bodied larvae covered with coarse hair.

General Information:

They seem to like vegetables the best and head for corn, beans and cabbage first if they are available. They will eat almost anything. One of their favorite foods, are tender seedlings. They don't eat a lot but can cause a lot of damage by cutting off the plants by the stems and killing them. Some cutworms will climb up the plant and eat the leaves. They will be on the soil surface at night, which leaves them vulnerable.

ATTACK THE EGGS FOR CONTROL
Use trichogramma and lacewings to attack and eat the eggs. They love cutworm egg omelets. Applying Nc nematodes around plants will also solve the problem.

FOILED AGAIN
You can wrap aluminum foil around the stems of plants that you may be worried about to stop cutworms from eating the stems. Rub a little garlic juice on the foil to make it more effective.

COLLARS FOR THE BUGS
If you are having a problem with cutworms, try placing small cardboard collars around the stem of the plant and place it just under the ground at least 1-2 inches. You can use old toilet paper or paper towel tubes. Just cut them; place them on and then staple them closed. You can also use tarpaper rolled up and aluminum foil will also do the trick wrapped around the stem.

LEAVES AS WRAPS
Hundreds of years ago cutworm infestations; were solved by placing hickory or walnut leaves around the stems of the plants. Cutworms shy away from these leaves.

SANDPAPER TO THE RESCUE
If you place a collar of sandpaper or roofing shingle around the base of the plant as a collar it will stop the cutworms from doing their thing.

AH CHOO
Cutworms can be eliminated with black pepper spray. Just crush up 1 tablespoon of the seeds into a powder, add water and spray any stored grains where you have a problem. The powder can also be used and spread around the affected area.

MUMMIFY THEM
Prepare a mixture composed of molasses, hardwood sawdust and wheat bran.

If the cutworm even crawls into this mixture it will dry them up and make sweet little wooden mummies out of them.

GRAIN KILLS CUTWORMS
Soak 2 handfuls of finger millet (grain with grass-like leaves) in 1 quart of water, strain and spray.

CRUSH THOSE SEEDS
The castor oil plant can be used to eliminate cutworms by placing 4 cups of the crushed, shelled seeds into 2 quarts of water and boiling for about 10 minutes, then adding 2 teaspoons of paraffin and ½ teaspoon of liquid soap to the mixture. Add 7 more quarts of water to dilute and spray into the soil in the affected areas. *Castor bean seeds are poisonous to some animals and humans.*

THEY HATE TO COMMUTE
You can go out at night and find this pest with a flashlight and look for them chomping on the plant leaves. In the daylight they tend to rest just next to the base of the plant so that they will not have far to go for their next meal.

PAWPAW SEEDS WORK
Crush 1 cup of pawpaw seeds and place them in 2 cups of water and allow it to stand for 24 hours. Strain and spray the areas. Test a leaf or two to be sure that there will be no plant damage. If there is damage add more water and dilute the spray.

LE PEW
Garlic spray for cutworms:

3	**Cups of warm tap water**
3	**Tablespoons of mineral oil**
3	**Whole garlic bulbs**
1	**Tablespoon of Ivory Liquid Soap™**

First separate the cloves of garlic and chop in a food processor. Place the cloves in a jar with the mineral oil and allow it to stand for 24 hours before adding the water and soap. It is best to store the mixture in the refrigerator with a tight cover. To use as a spray dilute ½ cup in 1 quart of water. Spray directly on the plants for an instant kill.

OUCH THAT HURTS MY FEET

If you sprinkle oak leaf mulch or use crushed eggshells around the plants it will stop the cutworms from attacking the plants. The sharp edges hurt their tender footsies. You can also sprinkle DE or wood ashes around to irritate them.

BLOATING UP A CATERPILLAR

If you want to kill them just sprinkle some cornmeal around the plants and they will eat it, bloat up and die.

EASTERN TENT CATERPILLAR

Identification:

The Eastern Tent Caterpillar has white stripes down their back as well as yellow and brown lines and blue spots on their sides. They spin tent-like waterproof webs, which is their distinct characteristic.

Tent caterpillar Web

General Information:

They will eat fruit and leaves but will not touch an evergreen tree. They lay their eggs in masses that will encircle twigs and they will hatch in the spring. There can be up to 300 caterpillars in a single web and they can remove all the leaves on a tree in a very short period of time. They are more active in the spring and make large tents or webs between tree branches.

SPRAY THE LEAVES

There are a number of ways to eliminate this pest. You can spray the leaves with Bt or a solution of lime and soap directly on the caterpillars. Lacewings, Bt and trichogramma wasps will also do the job.

SEAWEED TO THE RESCUE

Go down to the beach and collect seaweed and place the seaweed in all the crotches of the tree. This needs to be done in the spring to repel the caterpillars. As the seaweed disintegrates it also makes excellent mulch, full of trace minerals.

GET OUT THE MAGNIFYING GLASS AND YOUR OVERCOAT

Check the tree in the winter months for egg masses and remove them and place them into a bucket of soapy water.

TAKE DOWN THE TENT

Remove all the tents that you can locate and place them in a bucket of soapy water, which will kill them.

GET OUT THE LADDER

One of the easiest methods of controlling the caterpillar is to use a large stick or broom handle and when the caterpillars are in their nest (usually when it rains or at noon) poke the stick into the nest and roll it around. The fibers in the nest are sticky and will adhere to the stick. Squash them or place the nest in a bucket of soapy water.

GARDEN WEBWORM

This worm attacks beets, beans, corn, strawberries and peas primarily. They make webs from leaves and consume them. They may be found in a variety of colors but most have three dark spots on each side of each segment with one to three bristle-like hairs growing from each segment. All webbed leaves must be clipped off and destroyed.

GREEN FRUITWORM

These worms attack apple fruit trees and strawberries and feed on the leaves, tying them together with silk. They will do damage to fruit and begin their attack at petal fall. They are a large green caterpillar and are sometimes speckled. The mature ones have a cream-colored line down their backs. The best control is to use Bt.

Adult Fruitworm

GYPSY MOTH LARVAE

Identification:

These are 2 inch long gray caterpillars that little brown tufts of brown and yellow hairs extending from their sides. They also have 10 blue spots followed by 12 red spots on their back. If you find one there will be plenty more where they came from.

General Information:

They will totally defoliate a tree and kill it. After they kill the tree they will leave and look for another tree or work on your plants for dessert. They are usually only found from New England to West Virginia and are now being seen in other states. They leave large brown egg masses on trees.

PICK ME A CATERPILLAR

If you tie a rope around the tree and place a burlap bag on the rope the caterpillars will rest there for some time to chat about their daily activities. This will give you plenty of time to interrupt them and drive them 10 miles from your property and release them, or just snuff them out where they stand.

Female Gipsy-moth and Larva
(*Porthetria dispar*)

CHASE THEM DOWN WITH PARASITES

Control can be effective with a number of parasites such as the lacewing, **Glyptapanteles flavicoxis** and **Cotesia melanoscelus**. The eggs contain a scale that the trichogramma cannot seem to break. Spray Nc nematodes around the base of trees to kill migrating caterpillars.

The foliage should be sprayed with Bt or NPV at the first sign of an impending attack. You can also spray the Nc around the tree trunk.

MOUNTAIN ASH SAWFLY

General Information:

This tiny green caterpillar is only about ½ inches long and is covered with spines. They will strip the leaves and skeletonize them, leaving only the ribs and veins. They prefer the leaves at the top of the plant or tree. They will appear around the middle of May and are usually found only in the northeastern United States.

LOOKING UP

The bug lays eggs in clusters on the underneath sides of leaves. You can spot them by the white spots on top of the leaves.

NAVAL ORANGEWORM

General Information:

These caterpillars attack walnut, almond and pistachios and enter the nut after the hulls split, then feed on the nutmeats contaminating the nuts with their excrements. The caterpillar has a white to pinkish body with a reddish-brown head.

It has a crescent-shaped mark on the second segment behind the head, which makes it easy to identify from a codling moth. They will weave their home around a nut making it into a *"mummy nut."* These nuts should be removed and destroyed.

WATCH FOR NUT-SPLIT
You need to harvest the nuts as soon as nut-split occurs so that the worm will not have a chance to set up housekeeping.

PARASITES ARE AVAILABLE
There are two parasites that are commercially available that will combat the naval orangeworm problem. They are **Copidosommopsis plethorica** and **Goniozus legneri**.

ORANGE TORTRIX CATERPILLAR

General Information:

This is a brownish-colored caterpillar that has a larva that rolls up in a leaf with a web and will feed inside it. If you find that you have a number of oranges falling before their time it is probably due to this pest boring into the rinds.

It will lay their eggs on the surface of the leaves or underneath the leaf looking like cream-colored discs. The eggs will destroy the leaves. If you see one of these caterpillars with white eggs on its back it would be best to leave it alone. The eggs are from a parasitic wasp and will be beneficial to your garden.

TWO GOOD KILLERS
There are two good methods of getting rid of these pests; either use Bt or dust or spray with pyrethrum.

EXOCHUS TO THE RESCUE
The parasite wasp species **Exochus** attacks the larvae of the orange tortrix caterpillar and has been found to be very effective. Other parasites that are also effective in control are **Apanteles aristolilae** and a tachinid fly called **Nemorilla pyste**.

POTATO TUBERWORM

It attacks tomatoes, potatoes, eggplant and peppers at their terminal end and burrow in killing the fruit or vegetable. They are somewhat pinkish with dark heads.

Be sure and check potatoes before storing or they will kill most of the potatoes. If you have a problem with potatoes and this bug, be sure and do not plant tomatoes or eggplant near the field.

SALTMARSH CATERPILLAR

General Information:

These caterpillars attack beans, lettuce, tomatoes and love grapes. They will skeletonize leaves in short order and are not a very welcome visitor to your garden. They have very long hairs with orange, white and black tufts. They usually lay their eggs in a weedy area and then go to the garden for their meals. The best method of stopping them has been with a barrier of aluminum foil or Bt.

TOMATO HORNWORM

General Information:
These are 4-inch long caterpillars that are green with white bars and feed on tomatoes, potatoes, sweet peppers and eggplants. They have a horn but do not sting. A similar horned worm called the tobacco hornworm prefers tobacco plants. Handpicking is one of the best methods of eradicating these bugs.

BUGS VS WORMS
There are a few bugs that will keep these worms in line; they are the lacewing, trichogramma and the ladybug. Spraying Bt on the leaves will also help as well as planting strong-smelling herbs.

A PLANT BARRIER
Planting herbs or flowers that they do not wish to be around is an excellent method of controlling these pests.

If you plant basil, borage or marigolds around your garden you will never have a problem with the tomato hornworm.

SPARYING WORKS

Using a hot pepper or limonoid spray will keep this pest from eating you plants. Either crush citrus fruit peels in water overnight or mix Tabasco Sauce™ and water to make the sprays and be sure to strain before using. Always test a few leaves and allow it to stand overnight to be sure that you do not have too strong a formula for that particular plant.

PREDATORS TO THE RESCUE

Predators that will eliminate these bugs include ladybugs, trichograma wasps and lacewings. Also if you plant some dill they will head right for it making it easier to catch them.

TOMATO PINWORM

General Information:

These small caterpillars attack tomatoes and are usually found in coastal areas around Southern California and the San Joaquin Valley. They bore into the tomatoes at the stem end and make narrow blackened tunnels, which then expose the tomato to bacterial infestation and decay. The caterpillars are gray to a yellowish color with red or purple around each segment. If you are having a problem with this worm it is best not to grow tomatoes in the area for about 3 months and there should be no tomatoes grown within 4 miles of the area. Pheromone traps also work well.

WHITEMARKED TUSSOCK MOTH

General Information:

This is a weird-looking caterpillar that has a red head from which will sprout two hornlike tufts of long black hair with another tuft appearing from the tail. It has a black and yellow stripe down its back.

It will skeletonize leaves of a variety of plants including geranium, German ivy, rose and many fruit trees as well as a number of deciduous shade trees.

REMOVING THE PROBLEM
Look for the egg masses and remove them, then paint the areas with creosote. If you have birds around they will give you a hand and the scary looks of the caterpillar will not affect them at all.

LITTLE BEETLE SAVES THE DAY
The tiny dermastid beetle called *Trogoderma sternale* will feed on the eggs and are used as a natural control in Southern California.

PESTS FOR WHICH PHEROMONES ARE COMMERCIALLY AVAILABLE

CATERPILLAR PEST	CROP
Black Cutworm	Vegetable Gardens
Codling Moth	Apple, Pear & Walnut Trees
Leafroller	Orchard Crops, Grapes
Orange Tortrix	Citrus Trees, Grapes, Berries
Oriental Fruit Moth	Orchard Crops
Peach Twig Borer	Stone Fruits, Almond
Redbanded Leafroller	Orchard Crops
Tomato Pinworm	Tomatoes
Beet Armyworm	Vegetable Gardens
Cabbage Looper	Vegetable Gardens
Diamondback Moth	Cole Crops
Fruit Tree leafroller	Orchards
Tentiform Leafminer	Apple Trees
Apple Pandemis	Apple Trees
Variegated Cutworm	Vegetable Gardens
Artichoke Plume Moth	Artichokes
Sunflower Moth	Sunflowers
Carpenter Worm	Fruit Trees
Potato Tuberworm	Potatoes, Tomatoes
Peachtree Borer	Stone Fruit

CHAPTER 7

TREE PESTS

TREE PESTS

CRAWLEES ON FRUIT TREES
To get rid of most crawling insect pests on fruit trees, just mix 1 cup of canola oil and 2 tablespoons of Ivory Liquid Soap™ in a 1-gallon container of water. The oil and soap should be mixed first and then add the water.

STOPPING SNAILS AND SLUGS

To stop snails and slugs from climbing your fruit trees, just protect the tree by placing a 3-inch wide strip of thin copper sheeting completely around the trunk about 1-2 feet from the ground.

Slugs like a moist area to live and reproduce especially fruit rinds and damaged fruit that is left lying on the ground. The dryer the area is, the fewer slug problems you will have. Sprinkling any type of salty solution around the tress will deter slugs

GROUND APPLES ARE BAD
When apples fall on the ground they are perfect locations for a number of insects to start housekeeping in. Remove any apple or other fruit when it falls to the ground. This will reduce the bug population that may cause damage to your fruit trees.

KILLING THE WINTERING INSECTS
Many insects spend their winter in trees waiting for the warmer weather of spring. It would be wise to eliminate these insects before they become active again. Special winter or dormant oils should be used when the trees are dormant. These are heavy oils that are slow to evaporate and should be used before new growth starts to appear in the spring. The oils will not harm the tree but will kill the vacationing insects. Be sure that the tree is well watered before spraying any oil.

SCALE REMOVER

To remove scales on trees, just use mustard seed flour. The scales will suffocate if the flour is sprinkled or sprayed on them. To prepare a spray solution, just mix 1 pound of mustard seed flour with 1 gallon of water and use in a sprayer.

ALL AROUND OIL

The summer or superior oils are lightweight and can be used all year round. These oils have the ability to smother the pests and their eggs by clogging them up. Be sure that any tree that is to be oiled is well watered before spraying the oil. If the plant or tree is under, lack of moisture stress, it can damage the plant or tree.

SPECIAL OIL SPRAY

2	Quarts of tap water
1	Teaspoon of horticultural oil
2	Cups of isopropyl alcohol

The alcohol mixed with the oil will kill bugs on contact. The oil helps the mixture stick around long enough to really do some good.

MAKING TREE PASTE

This is only practical if you have a few trees that are bothered by aphids.

Make a paste of:

1/3	Sticky clay
1/3	Cow manure
1/3	Sand

Mix with water into a paste and paint it on the tree trunk and large branches.

NEVER USE ANY OILS IF THE OUTSIDE TEMPERATURE IS OVER 90°F

ALMOND TREES
ALMOND TREE PEST PROBLEM SOLVER

THE PROBLEM	CAUSED BY
Nut meat with worms, webbing with brownish fecal matter	Navel orangeworm
Young shoots die back to several inches from tip in spring	Peach twig borers, oriental fruit moth
Leaves tied together with webbing, young fruit eaten	Leafrollers

APRICOT TREES
APRICOT TREE PEST PROBLEM SOLVER

THE PROBLEM	CAUSED BY
Young shoots die back one to several inches from tip in spring,, small worms in shoots	Peach twig borer, oriental moth
Leaves and fruit webbed together and eaten in spring, sunken brown scars	Leafrollers, tussock moth, green fruitworm
Fruit may have whitish worm inside and fall off tree prematurely	Codling moth
Foliage infested with green bugs in spring, leaves and twigs have honeydew on them, Irregular holes in leaves with no webbing, holes	Mealy plum aphid, earwig
Tiny holes in ripening fruit, green beetle with black spots hanging around	Cucumber beetle
Fruit partially eaten	Birds and squirrels

APPLE TREES

APPLE MAGGOT

General Information:

 These are yellow-white legless larvae that will bore into an apple after they hatch from an egg. The eggs: are laid by the adults in small punctures in the apple. The punctures are so small that they are hardly noticeable. The problem may not become evident until you bite into the apple and find the worm. The telltale hole will appear in the apple when the worm leaves. After they become mature the maggots leave the apple and just fall to the ground, enter a pupate stage and remain for the winter. They are common everywhere apple trees are grown. These are also known as the apple tree fly or railroad worm.

GET THEM DRUNK
It is best to catch the pest when it is in the fly stage before you have a problem. Set a baited trap by mixing 1 part of molasses to 9 parts of tap water then add yeast so that it will ferment and pour the liquid into a wide-mouthed jar. After the fermentation relaxes, hang the jars in the trees.

YUK, PLASTIC FRUIT AGAIN!
This will really irritate and kill them at the same time. Hang plastic fruit from the trees and paint Tanglefoot™ or Stickem™ on the fruit. They will land and be stuck for the rest of their lives.

WORMS TO THE RESCUE
One of the best ways to eliminate maggots is to apply Nc nematodes to the topsoil around the apple trees in the late summer to early fall. This will kill all the maggots as soon as they fall to the ground.

PASS HE FAUX APPLE PLEASE
If you string some fake apples that are yellow and red in the apple trees and place Tanglefoot™ or any other sticky substance on them it will trap the females that are going to lay their eggs. This should be done in the spring or early summer for the best results. You can also purchase some traps that can hang in the trees.

APPLE RED BUG

General Information:

 These bugs are normally found in the north central and northeastern United States. The bark crevices hold the eggs until they hatch and they become mature about June. They feed on the fruit and leave small russet scars or slight dimples. If you do a delayed spraying of dormant oil it should eliminate the pests.

APPLE SEED CHALCID

General Information:

 This is a tiny wasp that is found in the northeastern United States and lays their eggs in apples and other fruit. The apple will have a dimpled appearance since the larvae feed on the seeds. Check the fruit for signs of dimpling and destroy the infested fruit to get rid of the problem.

BUFFALO TREEHOPPERS

General Information:

These bugs are triangular in shape and have a short snout and horns at each shoulder. They do their damage by puncturing the bark of the trees to lay their eggs. The young trees are more susceptible to damage than the older trees. The eggs are laid in September and October. If you have this problem, don't plant alfalfa, legumes or clover as a cover crop.

Their favorite plant is bindweed, which must be kept out of orchards. Spraying with a dormant oil spray should kill the majority of the wintering eggs.

CANKER WORM

General Information:

 These worms are yellow, green or brown and spin a silken thread from which they can descend from branches on apple trees. If you cultivate the soil under the apple tree during the first week of June, chances are you will eliminate most of these worms since this is when the larvae tend to descend and enter the ground.

The canker worm will go through 10 year cycles that, which may often peak for 2-3 years. Many of the canker worms; will be eaten by birds and other types of predators.

THE ELIMINATOR
Spraying with Bt is the recommended method of controlling these bugs. Spray in April or May for the best results.

BAND THE TREES
In the fall, try placing a plastic band that has been treated with a sticky substance such as Tanglefoot around the trunk. This will stop the wingless female moths from climbing the trunk to lay their eggs.

CODLING MOTH

General Information:

 This caterpillar will bore into the core of the apple and is one of the more significant apple bugs that do crop damage. There are a number of methods of controlling the bug naturally. When you hear someone referring to the "worm in the apple" it is usually this worm. The larvae, tunnels into the core of the apple and eats the apple from the inside out. The brown reside around the opening is their excrement and is called "frass."

APPLE PEST PROBLEM SOLVER

THE PROBLEM	CAUSED BY
Brown granular material around core that may leak out holes	Codling moth
Leaves and blossoms tied up and eaten, bronze-colored scars	Leafrollers
Leaves eaten in spring, small gouges	Western tussock moth
Irregular spots on upper side of leaves, looks like blisters	Tentiform leafminer
White cottony masses on woody areas of the tree, warty growths on limbs and roots, honeydew and black sooty mold	Woolly apple aphid
New leaves distorted and curled, honeydew	Rosy apple aphid
New growth stunted, honeydew present and black sooty mold on leaves and fruit	Green apple aphid
Pieces of apples missing	Birds and squirrels

WE NEED A GOOD BAND

One of the best controls is to band the tree. In the spring use strips of corrugated cardboard to tempt the larvae looking for a place spin their cocoon. Wrap the bands in several thicknesses then tie them on firmly. The exposed ridges should be facing toward the tree, if not; the larvae will not spin a cocoon. In warm weather you should remove the bands every 2 weeks and in cool weather about every 3 weeks, then remove and kill the larvae.

SANITATION WORKS GREAT!

In the fall if you clean up any fallen fruit and leaves, it will remove their winter home.

MAKE A TRAP

To prepare a trap, mix together 4½ cups of tap water, ½ cup of honey, ½ cup of molasses and 1 tablespoon of fresh yeast. Place the mixture into an empty plastic milk bottle and cut an entrance hole near the top. Run a piece of rope through the handle and hang it in a tree. It takes about two traps per mature tree. Be sure and empty them weekly and keep them up for about 2 months.

You can also use a special pheromone to trap them that can be purchased at your local garden supply.

NOT ONLY FOR VAMPIRES

Spraying garlic is very useful in controlling the codling moth. The natural sulfur tends to repel them.

WASP THEM

Parasitic wasps are employed regularly to eliminate the codling moth larvae and pupae.

EUROPEAN APPLE SAWFLY

General Information:

The sawfly spends its winter under the soil as mature larvae in a cocoon and comes out in the spring as a fly. This is a brown and yellow bug with many transverse lines. It is somewhat larger than a common housefly and is active in the northeastern United States. The larvae live just under the skin of the fruit until they are about one-third grown and then bore into the fruit and do extensive damage before entering the soil.

TRAP THOSE APPLE VARMENTS

Use white, sticky rectangular traps that can be purchased in most nurseries. This is the preferred method of elimination instead of poisons.

FLATHEAD APPLE BORER

General Information:

This is a pest with a big appetite and will infest the following trees: apricot, cherry, boxelder, elm, hickory, chestnut, linden, oak, peach, plum, sycamore and willow. Their feeding tunnels will actually show through the bark in sunken areas. The larvae, is whitish-yellow and legless with several front body segments, which are wide and flat. They spend the winter in the fruit tunnels that they made.

The tunnels will eventually fill with a dry powder known as "frass," which is composed of droppings and sawdust produced by their boring. The adults are dark bronze beetles that have a metallic sheen. The beetles come out in May and June and will relax on the sunny sides of the trees and lay their eggs in the crevices of the tree.

GET OUT THE BURLAP BAGS
Trees that have been transplanted and seedlings need to be protected with a wrapping of burlap or cardboard from the soil up to the lower branches.

PAINT THE TREES
You can apply a generous coating of white exterior latex paint to the tree trunk, protecting them from the bug.

ROUNDHEADED APPLE TREE BORER

General Information:

This borer likes to tunnel deep into the trunk of the apple tree near the ground. Infestations will weaken a tree and can kill young trees. They will also eat both the leaves and the fruit. If you find brown castings above or just below the ground you know that they are active. If you do see the holes, snake a wire into the hole to kill them.

SUDS-A-WAY
If you use a thick wash of soap applied to the lower trunk of the tree it will discourage the beetles from laying their eggs.

CATCH THE DROPPINGS
One of the best methods of reducing the problem with these bugs is to remove any fruit that has dropped on the ground. Most of the time when fruit drops prematurely it is due to an infestation.

HIRE A HOG
Many farmers allow a hog to run free in the orchard eating all the dropped fruit. This solves the problem of having to pick up all the fruit that has dropped.

CHERRY TREES

CHERRY FRUITWORM

General Information:
This worm hatches out toward the end of May in the northeastern United States. The green worm larvae; bores into the cherries and feeds for about  2 weeks. The adult fruitworm is actually a gray moth with black spots. It will lay its eggs on the fruit in mid-July and they hatch as small green caterpillars, which proceed to eat the cherries near the stem and build their web around a cluster of cherries.

Fruitworm Moth

PARASITES TO THE RESCUE
There are two parasites that are used to control these bugs. The first is a parasitic fungus called **Beauvaria bassiana**, which is also used against the cranberry fruitworm and the second is a parasitic wasp called **Trichogramma minutum**.

OPEN THE FLOODGATES
Large commercial orchards sometimes flood the orchard to get rid of these bugs and others. In smaller operations handpicking works well.

CUCULIO BUGS

General Information:

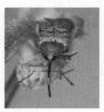
These tiny bugs feed on the tender foliage, buds and blossoms of different fruit trees as soon as they have finished blooming. They will drill circular hole in the newly set fruit. The females lay their eggs and the grub proceeds to eat the fruit for about 15 days, then bores out and enters the soil. It then proceeds to form a hard shell and turns into pupae.

SHAKE THEM UP

When these bugs are in the tree and the tree is shaken they tend to curl up in a ball and play dead. They will easily fall from the tree in a large tarp placed under the tree. When the tree is shaken they all fall out into the tarp for disposal.

CHERRY TREE PEST PROBLEM SOLVER

THE PROBLEM	CAUSED BY
Leaves curled in spring, cluster of black insects	Black cherry aphids
Leaves tied together with webbing and eaten in spring	Leafroller
Leaves have brownish patches, skeletonized leaves	Pear slug

GUARD HENS TO THE RESCUE

If you allow hens to roam around the fruit trees they will handle the problem by eating the grubs as they descend. This will end their life cycle very efficiently.

CITRUS TREES

CITRUS TREE PEST PROBLEM SOLVER

THE PROBLEM	CAUSED BY
Reddish-brown round scales on leaves and twigs, leaves may yellow and drop	California red scale
Fruit and leaves have honeydew and black sooty mold	Soft scales
Leaves curled and may have honeydew and mold	Aphids
Honeydew on fruit and leaves, flies fly away when disturbed	Whiteflies
Honeydew on fruit and leaves, cottony secretion on leaves and twigs	Cottony cushion scale
Fruit and leaves with honeydew and black mold	Mealybugs
Ring or partial ring of scarred tissue on stem and fruit skin, young leaves may be deformed	Citrus thrips
Fruit scarred but no ring around stem	Wind abrasion
Holes in blossoms, leaves or new fruit	Citrus cutworm
New leaves with holes, webbed together	Leaffrollers
Leaves and green fruit have yellow stippling	Citrus red mite

ELM TREES
MISCELANEOUS PESTS

EUROPEAN ELM SCALE

General Information:

These pests can easily be spotted on the bark of the trees during the early summer, which is when the scales reach their maturity.

The scales are oval, reddish-purple and have a white, waxy secretion. If you crush them with your fingers they will cause a red stain. They cause the leaves of the tree to become prematurely yellow, especially on the lower branches. If you have a bad infestation the leaves will turn a gray-green and wilt.

WHOOOOSH

One of the easiest ways to eliminate the scales is to use a forceful stream of water using a garden hose. If that doesn't work use a spray of dormant oil in the early spring.

EUROPEAN RED MITE

General Information:

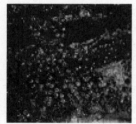

This mite attacks fruit trees. The adult is very small and the female is dark red with a few white spots. The most serious infestation usually occurs in the hottest part of the summer around July and August. They feed on chlorophyll and cause the foliage to become bronzed and the fruit may then drop prematurely as well as being small and low in sugar content. If the infestation is early in the season, the bud set for the following year may be reduced.

EGG KILLER

Apply a superior dormant-oil spray in early spring to kill the over-wintering eggs. This is one of the best methods of eliminating the problem. Most of the time natural predators will take care of the problem since the mites are at the bottom of the food chain.

154

FRUIT TREE LEAFROLLER

General Information:

The leafroller prefers citrus trees, apple trees and most stonefruit trees. The caterpillar likes to feed on the young leaves, buds and developing fruit. The majority of damage occurs in the spring and early summer months.

About mid-summer the pest will be inactive in the egg stage until the spring when it goes back into action. The caterpillar is green and has a shiny black head and it will feed inside of rolled up leaves or blossoms. When it is disturbed it will fall on a spun thread.

OIL THEM IN THE WINTER

One of the best methods of controlling these pests is to spray oil in January or February before any of the buds begin to open to kill the egg masses on the twigs.

ORIENTAL FRUIT MOTH

General Information:

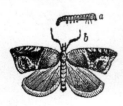

The larval stage tunnels into tender peach shoots and other fruit very early in the season and later enters the fruit. If you get a wormy peach it is usually this pest that is at fault. The mature larvae are pinkish and about ½ inches long. The first indication of a problem is the wilting of the terminal of growing shoots. It is not easy to identify the problem with the worms eating the peach around the pit. You may sometimes notice a gummy residue on the outside of the peach. If they enter through a tiny hole in the stem you may never notice them until it's too late. Dormant oil sprays do not work on these pests

PARASITE SAVES THE DAY

There is one parasite that is very useful and will save the crop. The wasp *Macrocentrus ancylivorus* has been used very effectively when this pest is identified.

STOP THE MATING

A relatively new pheromone product called Isomate-M™ will disrupt their mating and reproduction process. It is being used successfully in commercial orchards only.

PEACH TREE

PEACH & NECTARINE PEST PROBLEM SOLVER

THE PROBLEM	CAUSED BY
Young shoots die several inches from tip, worms living in shoots, ripening fruit infested fruit moth	Peach twig borer, oriental
Leaves become curled, tiny green insects visible	Green peach aphid
New leaves become yellow to reddish and curl	Leaf curl fungus
Leaves yellow, roots have galls	Root knot nematode

PEACH TREE BORERS

General Information:

Adult

These are a relative of the squash vine borers and are prevalent all over North America. They will do damage to peach trees around the bottom 10 inches of the trunk and 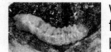 will get started at the soil line. The larvae, feeds below the surface of the soil or beneath the bark and may completely girdle the tree.

This is also a major pest of stone fruit trees.

They are capable of killing young trees and will cause the trees to be too weak to withstand adverse weather conditions as well as reduce productivity.

It is common to bring this borer home from a nursery and you should pay careful attention to any trees before you purchase them. If you find one better start looking for more. Most of the controls mentioned for squash vine borers will work for these borers as well.

POWDER THEM
Placing a layer of diatomaceous earth around the base of the tree in the early spring will stop the borers from getting to the tree. **Tobacco dust works great too but may harm pets and other animals.**

CRYSTALS WILL HELP
If you spread moth crystals (poison) around the base of the trees in late summer then cover them with 3-4 inches of soil, mounding it around the trunk of the trees it will eliminate the problem. Be sure and remove the mounded soil before winter rains come or you irrigate the trees. *Harmful to animals and humans!*

CALL FOR THE TIN MAN
To stop these borers, just force a piece of tin into the ground all around the tree trunk. Leave a space of about two inches between the tin shield and the tree bark. About mid-May fill the space with tobacco dust and when it rains it will become a potent barrier. This treatment should be done every May.

PEAR TREES

PEAR PSYLLA

Identification:

The nymphs are small yellow bugs that will feed on the tops of leaves and skeletonize them. The adults are dark orange with transparent wings and look like miniature cicadas.

Nymph

General Information:

They will hibernate under the edges of rough bark on tree trunk branches and come out during the first warm days of April. They will then deposit their eggs in old leaf scars, cracks and crevices. If the infestation is not caught in time by mid-summer, a badly infested tree will have blackening on the leaves, which will fall off prematurely.

Adult

PREVENTION IS BEST

Dusting with limestone will work; however, a good spraying with dormant oil in the spring is even better. Apply a 2% oil solution just as the buds begin to swell and the psylla are beginning to lay their yellow eggs on the twigs and buds. If they are already established then you will need to spray the tree with soapy water with as hard a spray as possible that will not cause damage to the buds.

NATURAL ENEMIES

There is a chalcid wasp that will eradicate these pests called **Trechnites insidiosus**. Just one of the parasitic wasps will parasitize up to 90% of the nymphs during July and August in unsprayed orchards.

SAN JOSE SCALE

General Information:

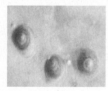
This little sapsucker will suck the sap from fruit trees such as pear or peach and just about any other they can get to. Serious infestations will damage the tree and kill off a number of branches. The mature female is yellow and the size of a pinhead. When the young are hatched they are so light that the wind will carry them to other trees. The Osage orange trees will support these pests even though the fruit from this tree (hedgeapples) will repel most other insects.

SQUIRT, SQUIRT

In order to control the scale you will need to spray the new buds in the early spring with an oil emulsion. This treatment should be repeated about one week later to assure good results.

PARASITE TO THE RESCUE

The parasite *Aphytis melinus* has been used very effectively against the scale. They are available commercially through you garden or agricultural supply stores.

SHOTHOLE BORER

 This small dark brown beetle lives and breeds under the bark of pear and peach trees. The holes that the beetles emerge from: look like small buckshot holes. They are usually found in the northern states and loves weak trees.

PEAR TREE PEST PROBLEM SOLVER

THE PROBLEM	CAUSED BY
Worms in fruit, brown granules in holes	Codling moth
Leaves and blossoms eaten and neatly tied together then webbed, young fruit gouged	Leafrollers
Leaves have brown or pink spots, skeletonization	Pearslug
Irregular spots on upper side of leaves, small blisters on underneath side of leaf	Tentiform leafminer
Fruit and foliage have honeydew and yellow insects on leaves, tree defoliated	Pear psylla
Fruit has clear honeydew and black sooty mold	Mealybugs
Leaves distorted, new foliage stunted, green insects on new shoots	Aphids
Fruit is brownish and rough, foliage has dry, rusty look	Pear rust mite

PLUMS & PRUNES

PLUMS & PRUNES PEST PROBLEM SOLVER

THE PROBLEM	CAUSED BY
Young shoots die back 1-7 inches from tip in spring, caterpillar inside the shoots	Peach twig borer
Leaves tied together with webbing in spring	Leafrollers, orange tortrix
Leaves attached to fruit with webbing in summer	Eyespotted bud moth
Brownish patches on leaves and skeletonization	Pearslug
New growth with green insects, leaves curled, fruit split, white mealy substance	Mealy plum aphid

WALNUTS TREES

WALNUT TREE PEST PROBLEM SOLVER

THE PROBLEM	CAUSED BY
Green nuts fall off or dry up on tree, webbing on nut, older nuts worm infested	Codling moth
Nuts are worm infested at harvest time, covered with webbing and brown material	Navel Orangeworm
Leaves tied with webbing and eaten in spring	Leafroller
Tiny black spots on husks turning into black areas that are soft, nut meat still OK	Walnut husk fly
Leaves covered with honeydew and black sooty mold, nuts become sunburned	Walnut aphid

CHAPTER 8

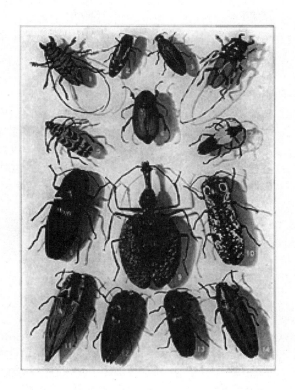

BEETLES

BEETLES

Many, many, many years ago farmers used to hang toads in the doorway of their grain storage facility to keep the bugs out. The toad had a string around its leg and would eat the bugs that tried to get in to get the grain. I am sure if we tried this now we would have animal rights people all over us, so best to forget this type of bug repellant.

GENERAL BEETLE REPELLANT
Use one handful of lantana (tickberry) and place the leaves in 2 quarts of water and allow it to remain for 3 hours before straining and adding 4 drops of liquid soap then using as a spray. The leaves can also be crushed and powdered and used as a dusting powder. If you just pound all parts of the plant and spread around the areas where grain are stored it will repel all beetles.

GARDEN BEETLES

ASIATIC GARDEN BEETLE (ASIAN BEETLE)

General Information:
This is a small brown beetle; that are capable of doing a lot of damage. They love crisp green leaves and are a night feeder. One of the best methods of getting rid of them is with an electronic trap purchased from a garden supply house. The grubs can also be killed using Derris.

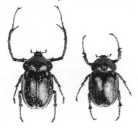

SPRINKLE THEM AWAY
One of the most effective methods of getting rid of the Asian beetle indoors is to food-grade diatomaceous earth (DE). Just sprinkle it around the baseboards to kill off the beetle. Try not to breathe the dust; however, DE is harmless to children and pets. Make strong DE spray for outdoors.

VAZOOM

If they get out of hand and are taking over the house, just vacuum them up and dispose of the bag or empty it in a bucket of soapy water.

ASPARAGUS BEETLE

Identification:

This is a small metallic blue-black beetle that has three yellow-orange squares along each wing cover.

General Information:

It loves to munch on the asparagus stalks and is capable of doing a lot of damage. It will damage both the garden varieties as well as the wild asparagus plants. They will hibernate in trash that is left around the garden and come out in the spring looking for tender young asparagus shoots to lay their eggs on.

REMOVE THEIR HOUSING PROJECT

If you remove all the trash and the beetle cannot find a comfortable home they will pack their bags and move on. Many beetles rely on people who do not clean up before winter sets in. Most gardeners tend to leave the clean up for the spring and this is usually too late.

GIVE THEM AN ALLERGY ATTACK

These beetles do not like to be around nasturtiums and calendula (pot marigolds). They will leave your yard and look for a box of tissues.

CHICKS AND DUCK AND GEESE BETTER SCURRY

If you have a bad infestation the best method of eradication is to release some fowl into the garden. They love beetles and will round them up in short order. Then you need to get rid of the fowl, possibly fried.

HOLD THAT CONTAINER

Asparagus beetles cannot be handpicked since they drop to the ground as soon as they spot you getting too close to them. If you place a jar or can under the insect and then get close it will fall right in the container. This will take a little practice but you will get the hang of it after a while.

DON'T FENCE ME IN

If you place a fence around the asparagus plants and allow some hens to run loose they will eliminate all the beetles for you.

If there is ample grass sod in the area the hens will leave the asparagus plants alone. Don't leave them there permanently just long enough to get rid of the beetles.

FEED TOMATOES TO ASPARAGUS BEETLES

To prepare a spray from tomato plants, just make the spray by using the freshest leaves you can find as well as the stems and even the tomatoes. Dice up the plant and parts and mix 2 handfuls with 8 cups of water then allow it to stand for 5 hours before straining and applying as soon as possible. This mixture loses potency rather quickly. You can add 4 drops of liquid soap to beef it up a little. This spray will also stop egg-laying by a number of insects. **Tomato leaves are poisonous to humans and animals.** You can also just plant tomato plants around asparagus plants and the beetles will stay away.

ASPARAGUS MINER

General Information:

maggot

This bug tends to tunnel close to the base of the plant; however, some will start their tunnel as high as one foot off the ground and tunnel in, going down, then under the soil in many instances. This pest is found in the Northeast and California and is only considered a "miner" pest. If you clean up all the old asparagus stalks and remnants you will eliminate a new problem in the spring.

Adult

BEAN LEAF BEETLE

Identification:

They are about ¼ inch long, reddish with black spots and a small black head. They will lay their eggs on leaves and their larvae will enter the soil to feed on plant roots. You will only find the adult beetle feeding on leaves.

USE FRIENDLY KILLERS

The best method of controlling these pests is to employ some ladybugs and lacewings to eat their eggs. You can also mix Nc nematodes into seed furrows and into the mulch you use around plants. Handpicking them also works well.

PLANTS THAT REPEL THEM

If you plant garlic, radishes, potatoes or cloves around your bean plants the beetles will leave them alone.

SPRAY THEM OFF

Using a jet of water sprayed directly on the plant will dislodge the beetles.

BLISTER BEETLE

Identification:

Blister beetles are black, flying beetles that may have yellow stripes and are about ½ inches long. They have long legs and a narrow neck. They will cause a blister on your skin if handled. They will also eat leaves, fruit and stems of plants.

General Information:
If these beetles get into your garden it may be the end of the garden. If a swarm gets in the best thing to do is to physically chase them out of the garden and as far away as you can. Chickens won't even help since they get sick when they eat these beetles.

IT'S A BIRD, IT'S A PLANE, NO IT'S A FLYING BEETLE
These beetles are solid, black flying beetles. They have long legs and a narrow neck and will cause you to get skin blisters if you handle them. They prefer to eat leaves and fruit and will prey on grasshopper eggs making them somewhat beneficial.

If you handpick them use gloves and wash the gloves afterwards. Nc nematodes work well since they lay their eggs in the soil.

THE SAME OLD SPRAY
Lime sprays work very well and also dusting damp plants with lime will make them leave the garden area and head for a neighbor's yard. As a last resort use a soap and lime spray or use pyrethrums.

CALOSOMA BEETLE

General Information:

This is a well-known beetle that looks like an Egyptian scarab. The wings are covered with a metallic blue color and are slightly ridged with a red border. They have long legs and are very speedy and release a foul smelly chemical when bothered. Their favorite meal is the tent caterpillar.

CARPET BEETLE

General Information:

Carpet beetles enjoy munching on wool, feathers and even fur. These beetles actually are the ones that leave small round holes not the jagged  hole that the clothes moth leaves in the clothing. Their larvae are hairy little worms that do most of the damage and they can live up to 3 years. If you give them the opportunity they will also dine on carpets, curtains and upholstered furniture. They will not feast on synthetic carpets or fabrics.

Adult carpet beetles are oval and approximately 1/8 inch long and uniformly dark brown-black and shiny. Carpet beetle larvae are elongate, reddish or light brown and covered with short hairs. Some species have distinct tufts of hairs extending from the posterior and their larvae repeatedly shed their skins and these old larval skins are often confused with the living insects. The full grown, the larvae are about 1/8 inch long.

The larvae feed on various materials of animal origin and commonly occur in bird nests, while adult beetles feed on the pollen of plants. Most household infestations originate from these wild populations. Carpet beetles also may be carried about by moving infested items. Inside the home, the female beetles lay eggs over a period of about three weeks. Common egg laying sites include areas anywhere dead insects occur, in accumulations of lint in dryer air ducts, along borders of carpeting and behind baseboards.

The eggs hatch in 10 to 20 days and the new larvae search for food. Depending on the quality of the food source and the temperature, the larvae become full grown in 2 to 11 months.

If you find the source of the problem, remove and destroy the infested material if possible. If you place small items in the freezer for 48 hours or heat-treat them at temperatures above 120^0F for several hours.

DANGER! BAD BUG LIVES HERE

Carpet beetles do a lot of damage to fabrics every year, even more than clothes moths.

They are difficult to get rid of once they get a foothold and love to munch on pet hair as well. One of the best methods of eradication is to vacuum frequently.

HERE LITTLE BEETLE, COME TO FISHY

Carpet beetles are attracted to fish oil and if you place some sardine oil on piece of flypaper or any sticky surface it will attract them into a trap. However, if you do this in your closet don't expect to have too many friends.

CIGARETTE BEETLES

General Information:

The cigarette beetle will feed on a variety of stored products such as paprika, chili, and dried dog or cat food. Both adults and larvae are capable of penetrating almost any type of packaging material. These small destructive pests can even feed on pyrethrum powder strong enough to kill cockroaches and most other insects. Adults are strong fliers and are attracted to light at night. In fact, flying around lights at night is often the first indication of their presence.

Cigarette beetles are native to Egypt and a beetle was found in King Tutankhamen's tomb! In the 3,500 years since then the beetle has hardly changed. The adult cigarette beetle is a tiny red-brown to yellowish-brown beetle and when viewed from above it appears oval and in profile humpbacked in shape.

It is 1/10 to 1/8 inch long and the antennae are serrate (the side edge of each antennal segment is pointed like a saw tooth). The wing coverings are smooth without longitudinal grooves. They can be found throughout the year, but seems to be more common in the fall and winter months.

The eggs are white, oval and too small to be seen with the naked eye. The cigarette beetle larvae are white and grub-like with long hairs covering the bodies giving them a fuzzy appearance. When full grown they are about 1/8-inch long. Larvae spin themselves into a cocoon prior to becoming pupae.

Adults lay their eggs on the food material so the larvae can eat. Adults live about two to four weeks. The females lay up to 100 eggs; the development time from egg to adult is six to eight weeks and there are three to six generations every year. The minimum development temperature is 65^0F.

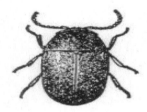

Cigarette beetles will infest a wide variety of food products such as: Aniseed, bamboo, beans, biscuits, cassava, chickpeas, cigars, cigarettes, cocoa beans, coffee beans, copra, coriander, cottonseed (before and after harvest), cottonseed meal, cumin, dates, dog food, dried banana, dried cabbage, dried carrot, dried fruits, drugs, flax tow, flour, ginger, grain and most herbs.

The cigarette beetle can be controlled without the use of dangerous pesticides. The first step in control of the cigarette beetle is to find the source of the infestation, which means inspecting all of the dried foods in the infested cabinets or drawers. Once the infestation is found, it should be destroyed and the cabinets and drawers cleaned with a vacuum cleaner (then throw the cleaner bag away).

Glass jars and plastic containers with air tight covers effectively keep food insect-free and are the best to use. Susceptible food items need to be tightly contained or stored in the refrigerator or freezer, or be consumed within two to three weeks of purchase.

COLORADO POTATO BEETLE

Identification:

This is a round ½ inch yellow beetle with black stripes down its back and a reddish head that loves to eat potato leaves. They lay yellow-orange eggs on the underneath side of the leaves. The eggs will hatch in 5-9 days. The larvae are fat and red with black spots and black heads. They chew on the leaves, skeletonizing them and several generations can emerge every year.

General Information:

The adults hibernate in the soil over the winter. In the last few years this beetle has become more prevalent. If you find black excrement on the leaves it may be this beetle.

This beetle consumes potatoes, tomatoes, eggplant, cabbage and peppers. You may also find them munching on your petunias. If you plant Sequoia potatoes they will not eat them.

BENNIES TO THE RESCUE

Beneficial insects are one of the best methods of eradication of these pests. Use **Edovum puttleri**, ladybugs or lacewings. The ladybugs love to feast on their eggs and are the best one to eliminate the beetles. They don't like green beans and if you plant them with the potatoes they will probably leave the area alone. Bt will also work very well against these insects.

KILLING THE LARVAE

Using a soap and lime spray will kill off the larvae by dehydration and a garlic and pepper juice spray will repel them and send them packing.

CRUSH THOSE EGGS
In early spring the beetles lay their eggs on the underneath side of the potato leaves. However, keep checking the underneath sides of the leaves regularly for eggs and remove them since this is one of the best methods of controlling the beetle.

NATURAL REPELLENTS
There are a number of plants that will repel these bugs if they are planted near the plants that they consume. These include marigolds, garlic, snap peas, onions, flax, catnip, coriander, nasturtiums, tansy, dead nettle and horseradish.

EXPLODING BEETLES
If you sprinkle wheat bran that has been well moistened around your plants the beetles will eat the bran before they eat your plants. They will then swell up and literally explode. The beetle's cuticle will actually give under the bloating pressure.

DANGER, EXPLODING BEETLES

GIVE THEM A CUP OF TEA OR A SHOT OF SALTS
You can prepare a tea made from basil or cedar chips and place it in a sprayer. This works very well in keeping the beetles at bay. You can also add 2 tablespoons of Epsom salts to a gallon of water and spray to protect your plants.

GET OUT THE SOAP BUCKET

If you know that the bugs are present, walk along next to the plants with a bucket of soapy water and lightly shake the plants allowing the bugs to fall off into the bucket. The slightest disturbance will cause the beetles to leave the plant. However, if you see eggs on the underneath side of the leaves they will have to be crushed.

CUCUMBER BEETLE

Identification:

These are green and yellow beetles with either three black stripes or 12 black spots on their back.

General Information:

The biggest problem usually occurs early in the season when their larvae chew through the stalks of a member of the squash family. They prefer cucumbers, acorn squash, melons of all types and summer squash. Usually two generations appear every year. They are also known as the southern corn rootworm. They will spend their winter in garden debris, weeds or under logs. There is a chemical in cucumbers called **"curcurbitacin"** that attract these insects. It is a bitter essence that they love.

They lay their orange-brown eggs at the base of the plants and eventually tiny whitish grubs will hatch. If you use quality mulch they will not lay their eggs there.

These beetles will cause the entire plant to wilt and fall over dead since the beetles carry the bacterial wilt disease in their digestive tracts. If you feel that the plant has been infected, just slice a vine in two and squeeze the ends until the plant juices are seen. If the plant juices are a milky white substance that can be drawn out in a thread, the plant; is being attacked by the bacteria and the rest of the plant is finished.

EASILY CONFUSED
Cucumber beetles are easily confused when they go in search of their favorite food cucumbers and summer squash. If you plant rattail radishes around the areas containing cucumber or cabbage plants it has the tendency to repel the beetles and they head for another yard. If you plant additional rattails between the plants it will provide additional protection.

CHECK THE DOWNSIDE
One of the best ways to control the beetles is to check the underneath sides of the leaves very early in the season. The leaves should be sprayed with a solution of insecticidal soap and water to eliminate the larvae and the eggs.

NEEM TO THE RESCUE
If you do end up with an infestation by mid-summer spray them first with Neem Oil™ to repel them from the vegetables and plants. Then you should follow-up with pyrethrums, which will kill them. These are both natural organic products, safe to use and fully biodegradable.

CALL FOR NEMA THE WORM
Nc nematodes will do the job nicely and eliminate the beetle. They don't like radishes and if you plant them with the other vegetables they will stay away from the garden. Lime and soap sprays irritate them and they won't come back.

PEPPER SPRAY

½   Cup of hot peppers or ¼ cup Tabasco Sauce™
2   Quarts of tap water
1   Tablespoons of Ivory Liquid Soap®

Place the hot peppers or Tabasco Sauce™ with 2 cups of water in a blender, blend thoroughly then allow it to stand overnight. Strain and add the balance of the water and the liquid soap and use as a spray.

VANILLA HELPS
These beetles will not go near your plants if you spray them with a solution composed of artificial vanilla flavoring and water.

WOOD ASH/LIME SPRAY

¼	Cup of wood ashes
¼	Cup of lime juice
1	Gallon of tap water

Mix all the ingredients together and allow it to stand for 1 hour before spraying on the plants. Be sure and spray the underneath sides of the leaves.

PLANT REPELLENTS

There are a number of plants that if planted between the plants that they eat it will repel them naturally. These are tansy, catnip, marigold and radishes.

DRUGSTORE BEETLES

General Information:

 The Drugstore beetle, also known as the bread beetle or biscuit beetle, is a very small, brown beetle that can be found infesting a wide variety of products and is among the most common non-weevils. They have a worldwide distribution and can be more commonly found in warmer climates. They are similar in appearance to the cigarette beetle), but are slightly larger, adults can be over 2¼ -inches in length.

Drugstore beetles have antennae ending in 3-segmented clubs, while cigarette beetles have serrated antennae (notched like teeth of a saw). The drugstore beetle also has grooves running longitudinally along the body, whereas the cigarette beetle is smooth.

Their larvae are small, white grubs and they can be distinguished from the grubs of the cigarette beetle by their shorter hair.

The female is capable of laying up to 75 eggs at once, and the larval period lasts up to several months depending on the food source. It is the larvae that are responsible for most of the damage that this species can cause.

174

Drugstore beetles have a tendency to feed on pharmacological products, including prescription drugs. They will also feed on a diverse range of dried foods and spices, as well as hair, leather and books. They can bore into furniture, and in some cases tin foil or sheets of lead.

ELM LEAF BEETLE

General Information:

This is a small to ½ inch yellow and either black or brown beetle that may have yellow with green and black stripes. The adults may winter over in protected areas, tree bark or an old barn.

They may get into your house in the fall and return to the elm trees in the spring. They will feed on the foliage and leave tiny holes in the leaves.

The larvae looks like a small black caterpillar and changes to a dull yellow with black stripes when they mature. They love to eat the underside of elm leaves and will eventually skeletonize them. They will feed for several weeks before falling to the ground and pupate. Look for bright yellow pupae around the base of the elm tree and can produce 1-3 generations per season.

SPRAY THOSE TREES
One of the most effective methods to get rid of the beetle is to spray the trees with a mixture of pyrethrum according to the label on the container.

BENEFICIALS TO THE RESCUE
You can apply either Bacillus thuringiensis (BT) or tenebrionis to kill the larvae. You will need to apply them when the eggs hatch from late May to June. This is a safe and very effective method of eliminating the problem.

FLEA BEETLE

Identification:

This is a jumping beetle that is only ¼ inch in length. It is usually black with pale yellow stripes. It loves to consume young leaves and makes tiny holes in them.

General Information:

Their larvae feed on seeds and some roots. They will also feed on dichondra grass, cabbage, broccoli and cauliflower. In California there is a species of flea beetle that loves arugula. If you grow tomatoes the flea beetle may be found eating the early leaves but then leave before the fruit arrives. The damage they inflict looks like the plant was hit by a shotgun blast of small buckshot. Most plants recover, the only exception is eggplant.

FLEE BEETLE

The flea beetle loves cabbage leaves and will eat hundreds of holes in them, during their feast. To get rid of them, just use a garlic mixture. Just pulverize about 6 cloves of garlic with a hammer or run the car over them. Place the smashed garlic cloves in a glass jar and add1 tablespoon of cayenne pepper and 1 quart of warm tap water. Place a lid on and mix well, then allow the jar to stand in the sun for 2 days to steep. Spray the leaves with beetles, making sure you spray both sides of the leaves.

THESE BEETLES LOVE YELLOW

If you are having a problem with flea beetles, just purchase some yellow cards and place non-setting glue or Tanglefoot™ on them, then leave them in the areas you are having a problem.

They are attracted to the yellow color and will jump on the yellow and can't escape. This will get rid of a number of other flying pests.

KEEPS THEIR BREATH FRESH

Flea beetles do not like mint. If you want to keep them away from your cabbage, just plant some mint plants among the cabbage.

WORMWOOD WILL DO THE TRICK

2	Cups of wormwood leaves
2	Quarts of tap water
2	Cups of boiling water

Place the wormwood leaves in the boiling water and allow the leaves steep for 1 hour. Strain the mixture and add the 2 quarts of water and place into a sprayer for immediate use. This will eliminate the flea beetles and cabbageworms.

PLANTS THAT REPEL THE FLEAS

There are a number of plants that are capable of repelling the flea beetle. These include elderberry, catnip, marigolds, garlic, wormwood, tansy and mint.

THE FLYING FLYPAPER

Try waving strips of flypaper over the plants. This will disturb the flea beetles and make them jump into the air getting snared on the flypaper. This is one of the most effective methods of getting rid of them.

COFFEE TO THE RESCUE

Place old coffee grounds; around plants that are susceptible to flea beetles. This works very well!

CUT THE DECK

Flea beetles can be trapped using playing cards that have been smeared with a sticky substance like Tanglefoot™ or non-drying glue. You can place a small amount of beer in a shallow dish in the center of four cards placed around the dish to attract them. Flea beetles love beer, especially Coors™.

GETTING A BIT MISTY

You can dust your plants to keep the flea beetles off by using wood ashes mixed with lime, but be sure that you mist, all the plants first so that the dust will adhere.

FLEA RESISTANT VARIETIES

There are a number of plants that you can plant that are resistant to flea beetles. These include De Cicco, Atlantic and Italian green sprouting broccoli, Snowball cauliflower, Mammoth, Red Rock and Early Jersey Wakefield cabbage and Sequoia potatoes. Check with your local garden supply store for other varieties.

BEER TRAP

Place cheap beer in a shallow dish and bury it allowing the dish to just remain above ground making it easy for the beetle to get into the beer and drown. A number of bugs are attracted to beer. They are actually more attracted to malt liquor than they are to beer.

HIRE A TOAD

Toads love flea beetles and will eat all stages of this bug. Other ground beetles and wasps will also hunt them.

FLOUR BEETLE

General Information:

The flour beetle was found in the tombs of ancient Egypt and will consume a variety of foods. They love grains, beans, peas, candy, nuts and dried fruit. The most common of these beetles is the red flour beetle. They do not require water to survive and lay sticky eggs that hatch and crawl to the top of grains and look like small white pupae. Discard any food if you find any sign of this beetle or its offspring. They have the ability to excrete a bad smelling chemical that contaminates the foods they inhabit.

Freezing the foods will kill them but it is already too late

GETTING TO THE ROOT OF THE PROBLEM
Rhizomes, roots of turmeric have been used for centuries to ward off these bugs and works great when left on the shelves in the pantry.

Fenugreek placed out also works very well. These just repel the bugs and will not kill them.

HARLEQUIN BUG

Identification:
These bugs are either black and red or black and yellow and suck plant juices. They lay barrel-shaped eggs on the underneath side of leaves. Harlequin bugs: can be identified by the bleached areas they leave on the leaf when they feed.

General Information:
They spend the winter in old leaves and trash. Good reason to clean up the yard before the first snow. They are one of the prettiest bugs in the insect world. They love turnip seedlings and if they are not controlled you will never get a turnip. They also like to eat Brussels sprouts, cauliflower, kohlrabi, horseradish, broccoli and mustard.

ONE BUGGY, TWO BUGGY
Handpicking the bugs is one of the best methods to get rid of them. Handpick both the bugs and their eggs. If you can find a praying mantis you might ask for some assistance since they like to dine on these beetles. Insecticide soap sprays will also do the trick in short order.

PLANT BUG RESISTANT VEGGIES
There are a number of vegetables that have been developed that are resistant to this bug. They are Grande, Atlantic and Coastal broccoli; Copenhagen Market 86, Headstart, Savory Perfection Drumhead, Stein's Flat Dutch and Early Jersey Wakefield cabbage;

Early Snowball X and Snowball Y cauliflower; Vates, Morris Improved Heading and Green Glaze collards; Vale kale; and Red Devil, White Icicle, Globemaster, Cherry Belle, Champion and Red Prince radishes.

JAPANESE BEETLE

Identification:

This is a metallic green beetle with copper-colored wing covers. There are small tufts of short, white hairs under the wings and gray hairs on the underneath side. They are about ½ inch long and ¼ inch wide. The males are a little smaller than the females.

General Information:

The beetle is normally found in the eastern United States but is moving west. May be found almost anywhere in woods and gardens. They usually feed on only one plant and will not bother another one.
They like the sunlight and will feed more in temperatures between 83^0 and 95^{0}F. The beetle lays their eggs in early August, which is the best time to do some tilling.

AN UNWELCOME VISITOR

The Japanese beetle migrated to the United States around the turn of the century, probably in the root system of a plant. The beetle spends 10 months of the year in the ground in the form of a white grub.

Their white grubs feed on tender roots and grass and are the most common white grub in the eastern United States. Every species of white grub can destroy lawns and leave large brown areas. They winter in the soil until the spring and their period of greatest activity lasts from 4-6 weeks.

They are not fussy eaters and will consume almost any type of plant they come upon. Their favorites, however, are rose bushes, purple plum trees, cherry trees and myrtle. They will mass on ripening fruit and eat until nothing edible is left.

Most beetles will lay their eggs in the grass and one excellent method of reducing or eliminating the problem is to treat the grass with a killer in early spring before they hatch.

Japanese beetles are not fussy eaters and there are over 280 plants that they will dine on if given the chance. They leave the leaves of plants skeletonized.

THE ELIMINATOR
The following ingredients will be needed:

1	**Pound of hydrated lime (use with caution)**
5	**Ounces of alum**
10	**Gallons of cool tap water**

Place the water in a large bucket; then add the other ingredients slowly while stirring well. Place the solution in a sprayer and spray the tops and bottoms of the leaves.

This solution is poisonous and should be kept away from humans and animals. Use with caution and wear gloves.

SPRINGTIME WITH NC NEMATODES
If you spray the lawn with Nc nematode spray in the spring it will eliminate the problem of grubs munching on your grass stalks for lunch. You can also spray pyrethrums or use a garlic and onion spray.

TRAP THEM
There a number of commercial traps that work very well with Japanese beetles. Check with your local garden shop for trapping supplies. Use Geraniol oil, which is a rose scent to lure them into the trap.

FEED THEM FRUIT SALAD
Place a small can of fruit salad with the top removed in a safe location where neither animals nor insects can get to it and allow it to ferment. Use a large yellow bowl and place the can in the center raised up on a block of wood.

Fill the bowl with soapy water to below the top of the can and place the bowl in the garden about 20 feet from the plants that are infested with the beetle.

FEED SPORES TO GRUBS

One of the best remedies to control larvae of Japanese beetles is called "milky spores *(Bacillus popilliae)."* These spores can be purchased through a garden shop and are spread on the soil causing the grubs to contract a disease that kills them. The milky spores will not harm any beneficial organisms and only kills the grubs, thus eliminating the Japanese beetles. The milky spores will remain in the soil for many years just waiting for the grubs to appear. If you apply milky spore disease to your lawn and even fruit orchards it will eliminate the grub problem. The Japanese beetles can spend as much as 10 months every year as grubs in the soil.

LEAF BEETLES

General Information:

 There are many varieties of leaf beetles that attack the leaves on all trees. One of the best methods of eradication is to bring a beetle to your local nursery or garden store for identification and their recommended treatment. In most instances the best all-natural method will be to use a beneficial insect to control them such as BT.

MAY BEETLE

General Information:

There are over 100 species of May beetle and will cause damage by eating blackberry leaves. However, in the larval or white grub stage they will eat the roots of bluegrass, timothy corn, soybeans and other crops. They deposit their eggs one to eight inches deep into the soil during the spring and hatch about 3-4 weeks later. Keep an eye out for the white grubs in the spring.

ROTATION IS A MUST

Rotating crops is the best method of controlling these beetles, if you have the problem. Best to use crops; such as legumes, sweet clover or alfalfa, which they don't like. Legumes are your best choice.

MEXICAN BEAN BEETLE

Identification:

 These are light brown round beetles, about ¼-inch long with 16 black spots on their back. They are frequently mistaken for a ladybug (these are not ladies) and are a distant relative of them. The larvae are light yellow and covered with bristle hairs that are about 1/3 inch long.

General Information:

They will eat beans, pods, leaves and stems then lay their yellow eggs on the leaf underside. Their larvae will also eat the bean leaves when they emerge. The female is capable of laying 1,500 eggs if she is in rare form but usually lays about 500 on the lower surfaces of the bean plant.

As a grub it is a yellowish color and covered with spines. It will winter in the garden area usually under a woodpile or in some rubbish or debris. They have a peculiar craving for Lima beans and will go out of their way if any are in the vicinity.

They will totally skeletonize the leaves and the larvae will attach their hind ends to a leaf that is uninjured and pupate. If you see a skeletonized leaf, start looking on the underneath sides of leaves for yellow orange egg clusters.

NATURAL REMEDY

Release the parasite wasp, **Pediobius foveolatus** to eliminate the infestation in about 1 week or handpick the beetles and their eggs.

MORE ACUTE REMEDY

Mix up a batch of pepper, garlic and onion juice in 1 quart of water and spray them. Pyrethrum spray will kill them and soap and lime spray will cause them to vacate your premises in a hurry.

MIXING POTATOES WITH BEANS

If you plant potato plants among the bean plants chances are you will never see a Mexican bean beetle or the standard bean beetle. They hate potato plants and will avoid areas where they are planted.

PICK A BEETLE

The best line of defense is to just pick the beetles off the plants and drop them into a bucket of soapy water or water topped with kerosene.

POWDERPOST BEETLE

GET OUT THE PAINTBRUSH

 These beetles are commonly found in wood furniture and are brought into the house. They are also very common on posts around yards and cattle pens. Once they lay their eggs it is almost impossible to stop them. The best method is prevention, which involves placing a covering on the wood, so that when they land on the wood to test it for starch and sugar content, to make sure that there is enough to feed their young, they will reject the wood. Cover the wood with paraffin wax, varnish, shellac or just paint the surface to stop them.

ROSE CHAFER

General Information:

 This is a dark tan, long legged beetle that haunts rose bushes and skeletonize the leaves as well as leaving excrement on the leaves. It especially likes white roses and will feed on the petals. The larva is white with a brown head and likes to feed on the roots of grasses and weeds. It is mostly found in the northeastern states but has been found as far west as Colorado.

PICK-A-BUG

Since these bugs are easy to spot, the best method of eradicating them is to handpick them.

MAKE A BARRIER

You can make a barrier that will stop these bugs by using cheesecloth or mosquito netting.

Place the netting on poles covering the roses for the period of time that you notice they are bothering the roses. They cannot fly well and will leave the roses alone for greener pastures.

SAW-TOOTHED GRAIN BEETLES

General Information:

 These bugs have a saw-like projection at the midsection of their bodies that protrude on either side. The saw-toothed grain beetle and the merchant grain beetle are tiny, slender, flat, brown beetles that are about 1/10 inch long. Both beetles are similar in appearance, with six saw-like tooth projections on each side of the thorax. The saw tooth beetle can be found in warmer climates and does not fly, while the merchant grain beetle flies.

The saw-toothed grain beetle also has smaller eyes than the merchant grain beetle and a much larger area just behind the eyes. In both larval and adult stages, these beetles feed on all food of plant origin, especially grain and grain products like cereals, dried meats, breakfast foods, stock and poultry feeds, coconut, sweets and dried fruit; it is not uncommon to find these beetles infesting pet food, bird seed and rodent bait.

They are tiny enough to very easily penetrate tiny cracks and crevices in packages food products. The adult beetles live an average of 6 to 10 months, but some individuals may live as long as 3 years if they are not disturbed. The female beetle of both species drops her eggs among the foodstuffs or tucks them away in a crevice in a kernel of grain.

Eggs are laid either singly or in small masses in crevices in the food supply, or may be laid freely in items such as flour or cereal products. When the small, white eggs hatch, the emerging larvae crawl and feed on the food stuff. They become full grown in about 2 weeks during summer warm weather and then construct a cocoon-like covering by joining together small grains or fragments of foodstuffs with their sticky secretion.

Within this cell, the larva changes to the pupae stage. Development from egg to adult may take from 3 to 4weeks in summer.

BAY LEAVES TO THE RESCUE

These beetles do not like bay leaves. Place them around your pantry and even into some of the flour or grain products if they cannot be sealed up in a plastic container. A stick of spearmint gum in the product also works great.

SPIDER BEETLE

 The spider beetle is a scavenger and prefers stored food. The beetle's got its name from the shape of the adult beetle, which has long legs and antennae and when viewed from above, resembles a spider. It also has a "humped" appearance.

The adult spider beetle is shiny, reddish brown to almost black and its head and thorax are covered with small hairs. The head and legs are cream colored and the beetle is often confused with the shiny spider beetle, which is completely reddish brown. There are several species of spider beetles, including the golden, the brown, and the white-marked.

Adult spider beetles will deposit their eggs in the material that the larvae will eat after they hatch, which may be broken grain, flour or grain products. They also feed on human hair, feathers and even droppings from birds or mammals. They also seem to be attracted to moist, damp areas and will eat products that are moldy or products that have been stored too long to be usable.

They can live by scavenging and can survive in places like empty warehouses, feeding on old rodent droppings and other debris.

They are pests in mills, food processing facilities and museums and can infest bird and rodent nests. If the nest is in the attic or crawl space of a home, the beetles can easily move into the living space.

The larvae are curved and whitish in color and spin silken webbing on the surface of the food as they eat. They can also spin silken cocoons where they change to adult beetles. The adult beetles are active at night or in dark places, so they are difficult to see.

If you see holes in packages, webbing in food and silken cocoons, they are all signs of an American spider beetle infestation.

SQUASH BUG

Identification:

 This is a brownish-black, shield-shaped bug with long legs and antennae. They will suck the juices out of your plants and will be found on the leaves. They lay brown-gold shiny eggs on the underneath side of the leaves that change to reddish-brown. The adult will spend the winter in an old pile of leaves. The new hatchlings will have a reddish head and legs and green bodies.

General Information:

They feed by inserting their needle-like mouthparts into the plant tissue and drawing out the juices. They will also release a toxin that will cause the plant to wilt. If these bugs are disturbed or crushed they will release a foul-smelling odor.

They prefer to eat squash, pumpkins, melons and cucumbers. Vine crops; are easily killed by these bugs, especially during the early part of the growing season.

PRAY FOR A MANTIS

One of the best deterrents is to have some praying mantis around your property. If you don't have any and this bug is around it would be best to import some. They will eat the eggs as well as the nymphs.

PLANTS TO THE RESCUE

There are a number of plants that will ward off these pests if planted around your garden. They are the radish, nasturtium, onion, tansy and marigold plants. If you plant mustard greens near you garden they will go for that and leave all other plants alone. Planting peas in the rows will also deter them.

SOAP THEM UP

If you want to kill then, just use an insecticidal soap spray. You can also use a spray prepared from imitation vanilla extract and water.

HANDPICKING IS THE ANSWER

This is one bug that handpicking really works well. Wear gloves since they will release their foul-smelling chemical when you touch them.

PLANT BUG RESITANT VARIETIES

There are a number of bug resistant varieties that will fare better than most. These are Table Queen, Royal Acorn, Early Golden Bush Scallop, Early Summer Crookneck, Early Prolific Straightneck and Improved Green Hubbard squash.

TREE CRICKET

Identification:

Sometimes called the blackhorned tree cricket is a problem for raspberries and blackberries. It is a greenish-yellow bug with feelers projecting from the front of its black head.

General Information:

They will also attack a number of wild shrubs and love fruit trees when they can get to them. If you have a square field you will have less damage than if you have a long narrow field. The berry canes that are injured will show areas of split bark in an irregular line. If you look inside the splits you will see numerous small holes that will extend into the pith.

IT'S A PITHY

Since the damage extends into the pith it is best to remove all the injured canes and burn them.

The more numerous the rows of holes are the more likely that the canes will just fall over. Burning is the best method of eliminating the eggs. The chemical derris is also used successfully on these bugs.

WEEVILS

Identification:

This long snout beetle loves grains. They have a strong pair of mandibles at the end of their snout that is capable of opening most seeds, which they then lay their eggs in. The eggs hatch into larvae; that will eat the inside of the seed and allows the shell to remain intact.

General Information:

Weevils are one of the hardest beetles to control. They may also attack fruit trees, cotton, rhubarb and a variety of vegetables. The bean weevil loves beans and peas; however, if none are available they will eat almost any other vegetables.

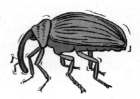

WORM THEM OUT

Best to eliminate them with Nc nematodes, which has been found to be one of the most efficient methods of controlling weevils.

GLUE THEM UP

Weevils normally crawl to your houseplants, especially vine weevils. However, the weevils can be stopped, by placing a thin bead of non-setting glue or Tanglefoot™ around the plants. This can get a bit messy but it does work well.

PEPPER THEM

Black pepper can be placed into foods that you ordinarily place it in to keep the bugs out. Even some beetles that will consume red pepper will not eat black pepper in most instances. Black pepper will actually kill the pests. The USDA found that 500 parts per million of black pepper will kill 97% of the weevils in wheat.

COWPEA CURCULIOS (BEAN WEEVIL)

These are small black or brown beetles that have a snout and have reddish legs and antennae.

They lay their eggs in holes that are chewed along the bean pod seams. The tiny white grub then feeds on the young seed and tends to come out when the beans are in storage and leave a small round hole when exiting.

They prefer southern peas and love Lima beans. Praying mantis, love to dine on these bugs! Spray the pods with a soap and pepper spray and they won't lay their eggs. Nc nematodes also will eliminate the problem. Stored dry beans; can be protected by heating them to 135^0F for 3-4 hours or suspending the seeds in a bag of tap water and heating it to 140^0F before drying them very rapidly.

SCARE THEM OFF

BOO!

Weevils tend to take up residence in dried beans and most grains. However, if you place a dried hot chili pepper in with the beans or grains you will never find another weevil or other insect in your beans and grains.
Placing the beans in the foods will not affect the foods.

LEAF NOTCHER

General Information:

The black or brown vine weevil is a very shy bug that only feeds at night and will munch notches around the edges of the leaves of the yew tree, rhododendron bushes, azaleas and most other ornamental shrubs. It will lay its eggs in the soil, which hatch into white legless grubs, which will feed on the roots of your plants. They hide in mulch and leaf litter during the day. Place Tanglefoot™ around the trunk of bushes and trees to keep them off. Rake in Nc nematodes to be rid of them permanently.

NUTTY WEEVILS

General Information:
These go by a number of nutty names such as the pecan weevil, chestnut weevil and the other nut weevil. All three are similar and have long snouts, which are actually as long as their bodies. The females use their snout to bite holes in developing nuts, which is where they lay their eggs.

The eggs hatch about the same time as when the nuts are ready to fall to the ground. If you spread Nc nematodes under the tree in the late summer when the nuts fall it will eliminate the problem.

STRAWBERRY ROOT WEEVILS ARE SHY

General Information:

These weevils feed on the upper parts of the plants and then lay their eggs in the soil. Their grubs feed on the plant roots and heavy infestations will easily kill the plant. Mulch containing Nc nematodes and a somewhat sandy soil around the plants will solve the problem. You can hand pick them, however, the adults only come out at night and are very shy.

SWEET POTATO WEEVIL

General Information:

This beetle looks like an ant and has a snout and a black body. They mainly eat foliage and lay their eggs on the stem and tubers of plants. When the grubs hatch they will eat down the stem into any tuber or potato that is available. These are normally only found in the southern United States. It also likes to eat stored sweet potatoes. If you get an infestation it would be best to burn the crop, however, Nc nematodes do work as a good preventive measure.

Sweet potato weevil is the most serious pest of sweet potato, not only in the United States, but worldwide. It causes damage in the field, in storage, and is of quarantine significance. It is inherently of interest to entomologists due to its strikingly colorful appearance and extremely long rostrum (beak).

Sweet potato weevil was first found in Louisiana in 1875, and then in Florida in 1878 and Texas in 1890, probably entering by way of Cuba. It is now found throughout the coastal plain of the Southeast from North Carolina to Texas. It also is found in Hawaii and Puerto Rico and widely around the world in tropical regions.

A complete life cycle only requires one to two months, with 35 to 40 days being common during the summer months.

The generations are indistinct, and the number of generations annually is estimated to be five in Texas, and at least eight in Louisiana. Adults never undergo a period of diapause in the winter, but will seek shelter and remain inactive until the weather is favorable. All stages can be found throughout the year if suitable food material is available.

Eggs are deposited in small cavities created by the female with her mouthparts in the sweet potato root or stem.

The female deposits a single egg at a time then seals the egg within the oviposition cavity with a plug of fecal material, which makes it difficult to observe the egg. Most eggs tend to be deposited near the juncture of the stem and root of the sweet potato.

Sometimes the female will crawl down cracks in the soil to access tubers for oviposition, in preference to depositing eggs in stem tissue. Duration of the egg stage varies from about five to six days during the summer to about 11 to 12 days during colder weather. Females apparently produce two to four eggs per day or 75 to 90 eggs during their life span of about 30 days.

When the egg hatches the larva will burrows into the tuber or stem of the plant. Those hatching in the stem usually burrow down into the tuber. The larva is legless and white in color. The mature larva creates a small pupae chamber in the tuber or stem. The pupa is similar to the adult in appearance, although the head and elytra are bent ventrally. The pupa measures about 6.5 mm in length.

Normally, the adult emerges from the pupation site by chewing a hole through the exterior of the plant tissue, but sometimes it remains for a considerable period and feeds within the tuber. The adult is striking in form and color and has a thin body, legs, and head. The head is black, the antennae, thorax and legs orange to reddish brown, and the abdomen and elytra are metallic blue. The snout is slightly curved and about as long as the thorax; the antennae are attached at about the midpoint on the snout.

The beetle appearance is smooth and shiny, but close examination shows a layer of short hairs. The adult measures 5.5 to 8.0 mm in length. Adults are secretive and often feed on the lower surface of leaves, and are not readily noticed. The adult is quick to feign death if disturbed. Adults can fly, but seem to do so rarely and in short, low flights

GETTING THEIR GOAT
Goatweed is a natural enemy of the weevils. You can powder the plant and place the powder in areas that you are having a problem in. You can also plant goatweed to protect plants from a number of pests.

FEED THEM THORN APPLES (Jimson Weed)

This is a very effective method of controlling seed weevils. Just dry the leaves and stems of the plant and use it as a dust to dust the crops that are affected. This plant can also be made into a spray by crushing a handful of the leaves in 4 cups of water and add 3 drops of liquid soap, strain and spray. ***This plant is poisonous to humans and animals and should be handled accordingly.***

PLAY DROPSY WITH THEM

The arbovitae weevil is a small black beetle covered with metallic green scales and emerges from the soil in early May. They like red and white cedar roots and the adults will eat foliage of adjacent plants as well. The best way to remove the beetles is to place a sheet under the plant or tree and shake for all your worth. They readily fall off and can be captured and disposed of with extreme prejudice.

REFRIGERATION WORKS

A number of large companies that sell and store grain in the United States found that they do not have any problems with grain beetles if they store the grain products at 40^0F. Most refrigerators maintain this temperature. Most companies now recommend that you store your grains in the refrigerator as soon as you bring them home from the store.

USE A COOKIE SHEET

If you are not sure if a problem exists in your flour or grain product, just spread out the product on a cookie sheet and place it in a 135^0F oven for 30 minutes. Check the oven with a thermometer since if you have a pilot light the temperature may be around the degrees you need without turning on the oven.

PEA WEEVILS PREFER THE WEST COAST

General Information:

The pea weevil is a coast-to-coast pest, however, they seem to prefer the states of Utah, Washington, Oregon and California the best. The adult beetle is a brownish color with scattered white and gray markings. It loves to feast on pea blossoms and lays their eggs on young pods.

The worms then burrow through the pod and into the pea flesh for their meal. Most remedies for weevils will work on this pest.

If you are going to use peas for seed it would be best to heat them to 125^{0}F for about 5-6 hours to be sure there are no eggs on the peas. This will not damage the pea for seed purposes. The weevils will settle when in flight as soon as they get the scent from pea blossoms and the edges of the fields are more susceptible to damage than the rest of the field.

CHAPTER 9

Lone Star Tick *(Amblyomma americanum)*

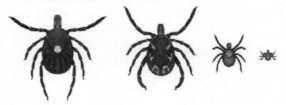

Dog Tick *(Dermacentor variabilis)*

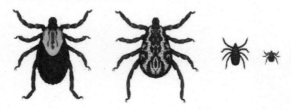

TICKS

TICKS THAT CAUSE DISEASE

American dog tick

These ticks are common on the east coast but can be found in most parts of the country. They are brown and have silvery-gray marks on their backs.

It normally prefers dogs but if none are available it will go to a human host. This tick can transmit tularemia and Rocky Mountain spotted fever and can cause a special tick paralysis in susceptible dogs and people.

Blacklegged deer tick

This tick loves deer and is usually found in the East. It prefers white-tailed deer as its source of food and transmits Lyme disease. In the Midwest the same tick is called the bear tick. It is a very small tick and the nymph is about the
size of a black pinhead. Because of the ticks size you will hardly know if you have been bitten. Males are black and females are reddish.

Blacklegged Deer Tick will feed on a variety of hosts including deer and people. The eggs will hatch in the spring and the very tiny larvae feed primarily on white-footed mice or other small mammals. The following spring, the larvae will molt into pinhead-sized, brown nymphs that will feed on mice, larger warm-blooded animals and people.

In the fall, they molt into adults that feed primarily on deer, with the females laying eggs the following spring. Adults are reddish-brown and about 1/8-inch long. These ticks are found mostly in wooded areas along trails. The larvae and nymphs are active in the spring and early summer; adults may be active in both the spring and fall. The blacklegged deer tick can transmit Lyme disease and possibly ehrlichiosis to humans.

Lone star tick

The lone star tick is usually found in Illinois, although it can occasionally be found further north. The larvae, nymphs and adults are not fussy and will feed on a variety of warm-blooded hosts, including people. The larva is very small, just a little larger than the period at the end of this sentence.

The nymph is the most common stage found on people and is about pinhead-sized.

The adults are about 1/8-inch long and brown. The adult female has a white spot in the middle of her back. The lone start tick is so similar in size it is sometimes misidentified by as the blacklegged deer tick. The lone star tick is more active from April through the end of July. Although it can transmit Rocky Mountain spotted fever, the lone star tick is not as likely to transmit the disease as the American dog tick.

This tick also may transmit tularemia and ehrlichiosis to humans. The lone star tick is not believed to transmit the bacteria that causes Lyme disease but may be associated with a bacteria species.

Rocky Mountain wood tick
Similar in appearance to the American dog tick and is usually found west of the Rocky Mountains. It transmits Rocky Mountain spotted fever, tularemia (rabbit fever), Colorado tick fever and tick paralysis.

Western black leg tick
This tick is found in the Western states and may be called the **"cowboy tick"**. It can transmit Lyme disease and is about the same size as the deer tick. It is reddish-brown and has black legs.

Winter tick

The winter tick is a species that feeds on larger mammals like deer, cattle, horses and an occasional person. It is different from the hard ticks since the winter tick attaches to the host as a larva and remains attached throughout its life. Because of this the tick is rarely encountered by campers or hikers. However, hunters may find the winter tick in large numbers on deer carcasses.

The winter tick may carry diseases to large wild mammals; however, it is not known to transmit disease to humans. The best way to protect yourself against tick-borne illness is to avoid tick bites. This includes avoiding known tick-infested areas. However, if you live in or visit wooded areas or areas with tall grass and weeds, follow these precautions:

- Wear protective clothing such as long-sleeved shirts, long trousers, boots or sturdy shoes and a head covering. (Ticks are easier to detect on light-colored clothing.) Tuck trouser cuffs in socks. Tape the area where pants and socks meet so ticks cannot crawl under clothing.
- Apply natural insect repellent to clothes and exposed skin.
- Walk in the center of trails so weeds do not brush against you. In camping areas, individuals who sit on the ground or disturb leaf litter on the forest floor may encounter ticks.
- Check yourself, your children and other family members every two to three hours for ticks. Most ticks seldom attach quickly and rarely transmit disease organisms until they have been attached four or more hours.
- If your pets spend time outdoors, check them for ticks, too.
- If ticks are crawling on the outside of clothes, they can be removed with masking tape or duct tape.
- A ring of tape can be made around the hand by leaving the sticky side out and attaching the two ends. Ticks will stick to the tape which can then be folded over and then placed in the trash.
- Remove any tick promptly. The mouthparts of a tick are barbed and may remain embedded and lead to infection at the bite site if not removed promptly.
- Do not burn the tick with a match or cover it with petroleum jelly or nail polish. Do not use bare hands to remove the tick because tick secretions may carry disease. The best way to remove a tick is to grasp it firmly with tweezers as close to the skin as possible and gently, but firmly, pull it straight out. Do not twist or jerk the tick. If tweezers are not available, grasp the tick with a piece of tissue or cloth or whatever can be used as a barrier between your fingers and the tick.
- Ticks can be safely disposed of by placing them in a container of soapy water or alcohol, sticking them to tape or flushing them down the toilet. If you want to have the tick identified, put it in a small vial of alcohol.
- Wash the bite area and your hands thoroughly with soap and water and apply an antiseptic to the bite site.
- If you have an unexplained illness with fever, contact a physician. Be sure to tell the physician if you have been outdoors in areas where ticks were present or traveled to areas where tickborne diseases are common.

FLANNEL COAT YOUR YARD

If you think that you have a bad tick or flea problem in your yard, just take a piece of flannel with a string on it and pull it around the yard. Fleas and ticks are attracted to flannel and will jump on for the ride. Turn the cloth over to check to see how many you have trapped. If there is a lot you will need to spray and disinfect the areas.

CHAPTER 10

FLIES

FLIES

GENERAL INFORMATION

There are over 100,000 species of flies. They are disease spreaders and should be eradicated whenever possible. An adult female housefly is capable of producing up to 2,400 eggs in her lifetime. In hot weather flies can multiply in 2-3 weeks, especially if they have a good supply of fresh warm excrement from a family pet. If you ingest fly eggs they can cause a stomachache. Flies have 4,000 faceted eyes and have ultra-sensitive hairs that can detect even the slightest change in air currents. Flies take off somewhat backwards and if you aim a flyswatter toward their back you will kill more flies.

When you see fly specs, the dark specs are excrement and the light specs are regurgitated food and saliva. A horsefly can actually bite through leather and can inflict a painful bite in humans. The stable fly has a proboscis like a hypodermic needle and draws blood, usually from a person's ankle, socks or no socks. Best to wear boots around stables!

Flies have three body parts: head, thorax, abdomen and one pair of fully developed wings. Their hind wings are reduced to small knob-like structures used to maintain equilibrium. Adult mouth parts are sponging, lapping, or piercing and all adults look like flies, but some may have a metallic color (blue bottle fly). Their antennae may be difficult to see.

Males and females may be hard to distinguish. Females are usually larger and can extend the tip of the abdomen to form an ovipositor, which is used to lay eggs. Sometimes males have enlarged eyes, which meet on top of the head. Flies have four distinct morphological stages; egg, larva (maggot), pupa and adult. After hatching from the egg, larvae molt twice as they grow and the molting of maggots is difficult to see.

Larvae are maggots with a legless soft body except for the dark mouth hooks. Pupae are dark, and look like a small barrel. Larvae will feed on decaying meat and feces. Adult flies will feed on sugary food of any kind, including nectar and rotting fruit.

Flies live in garbage and wherever animal feces are available. Dead animals attract flies within hours after death. Many birds, bats, spiders, and insects will eat the adults. Predatory and parasitic insects eat the larvae. The eyes of flies are among the most complex in the insect world. They are compound eyes with many individual facets, each representing a separate light-detecting unit. The light reflected from the eye of a horsefly can form a rainbow.

Flies taste, smell, and feel with the hairs that cover their bodies. The hairs on the fly's mouth parts and feet are used for tasting. Flies taste what they walk on. If they walk onto something tasty, they put down their mouth and taste it again. Flies use other hairs to tell them when they touch something. These hairs bend when touched. The eyes of a fly do not have eyelids, so flies rub their eyes with their feet to keep them clean.

Flies walk on smooth surfaces using sticky soft pads that act like glue. This allows them to walk on vertical glass surfaces and upside down. Flies and other insects, such as burying beetles, are very important in consuming and eliminating dead bodies of animals. Flies are also essential in the conversion of feces and decaying vegetation into soil. Flies serve as prey to many other animals. Some flies even aid in pollination.
Because of their habits of being attracted to feces and decaying meat, flies have been implicated in transmission of disease such as dysentery, typhoid fever, and cholera.

NATURAL METHODS OF ELIMINATION

WHY IT'S HARD TO SWAT A FLY

Houseflies have great all-round vision and can take off in any direction independently of how their body is aligned. This is one of the reasons why they are so good at evading an attack. In the instant between seeing a moving swatter and flying away, the fly's brain is able to calculate the position of the impending threat then place its legs and body in the perfect position that allows it to jump in the opposite direction.

All of the action is carried out within 100 milliseconds after the fly first spots the moving swatter, which shows just how rapidly the fly's brain can process the information.

The fly possesses an internal map within its brain which converts the position of the threat into the appropriate body motion that leads to successfully evading the swatter.

MAKING FLYPAPER WITH MAPLE SYRUP
The following ingredients will be needed:

1	**Tablespoon of brown sugar**
1	**Tablespoon of granulated sugar**
¼	**Cup of an inexpensive maple syrup**
1	**Brown paper bag**
1	**Cookie sheet**

Place all the ingredients in a small bowl and mix thoroughly. Cut 8-inch strips, about 2 inches wide from a brown paper bag and place them on the cookie sheet. Pour the mixture over the strips and allow the strips to soak overnight. Hang up the strips where needed.

GARBAGE CANS ARE A PROBLEM
Sprinkle dry borax into garbage cans after you wash them out, this will deter and kill them if they get it on them.

BLACK FLY

Some species of adult black fly females are fierce biters, whereas others are strictly a nuisance by their presence around one's nostrils, ears, arms, hands, and other exposed skin areas. Children are especially susceptible and may be severely bitten while adults in an area where they frequent are scarcely aware of the flies. Bites may appear where clothing fits snugly against the body, leaving a ring of bites just above or below the belt line.

When the black fly finishes feeding, bleeding may continue for some time. At first, the bite site appears as a small, red, central spot surrounded by a slightly reddened, swollen area. Next, the area becomes increasingly itchy, swollen and irritating, sometimes for several days. Some species of black flies readily attack people, whereas others prefer domestic animals or birds, often feeding during the daylight hours and sometimes into the night.

Black flies may become so abundant that they are drawn into the air passages of livestock, occasionally resulting in death. It is believed that allergic reactions to bites may be caused by histaminic substances in the fly's saliva.

These flies transmit a disease of filarial worms, onchocerciasis, which causes blindness in people in Mexico, Central America and Africa in addition to protozoan parasites, leucocytozoonosis to turkeys and wild birds.

They may also be potential transmitters of encephalitis and as with many aquatic insects, black flies are very sensitive to water pollution. Most species of adult black flies are about 1/8-inch long (2 to 5mm), black gray or even yellow colored, broad clear winged without hairs or scales with heavy veins near the anterior wing margin, have short 11 segmented antennae and large round eyes.

Black flies often occur in enormous numbers in the spring and early summer months, especially in the northern latitudes. Bites can be extremely painful, and their mouthparts are somewhat similar to those of a horse fly (bladelike and piercing) in the female. Mouth parts are rudimentary in the male.

When they get on people, they crawl into sleeves, under neckbands, around boot tops and other vulnerable places, especially favoring the head just beneath the rim of a hat. Bites can cause swelling and numb soreness for many days. There are records of both domestic animals and people being killed in a few hours through venomous bites and blood loss.

Death can result from suffocation as a result of plugged nasal or bronchial tubes and allergic reactions. Flies usually bite during the day in outdoor shaded or partially-shaded areas. They do not bite indoors or late at night. Some fly 7 to 10 miles from the breeding sites, or are blown by wind even further to feed on warm-blooded animals and people. Flies usually bite for about three weeks before they die. Dark blue cloth attracts more flies than white cloth.

Females deposit from 150 to 500 small, shiny, creamy-white eggs on submerged objects in the stream such as on water plants, rocks, twigs, leaves, etc. or simply scatter the eggs over the water surface. Eggs darken then hatch in four to five days at water temperatures of 70^0F.

Eggs deposited in the autumn do not hatch until the following spring when the water warms.

Young larvae attach themselves to submerged objects, molting six times as they grow. They are elongate with the hind part of their bodies swollen. A head fan sweeps food material into the mouth.

They retain their position in the water by means of sucker-like discs and tiny hooks at the tip of the abdomen. Also, they may spin a fine thread which aids in anchoring them. Winter may be passed as larva.

Pupation occurs in a cocoon, open at one end. Adults emerge in two to three days when the water is warm. They are capable of immediate flight and mating. The entire life history spans about four to six weeks, depending on species, water temperature, available food, etc. There may be four generations per year.

Black flies are attracted to mammals by the carbon dioxide and moisture in exhaled breath, dark colors, convection currents, perspiration, perfumes, toiletries, etc.

BLOW FLY

 Blow flies are so-called because the larvae develop inside the bodies of dead animals, causing the carrier to have a bloated appearance. They are attracted to garbage and about the size of house flies or slightly larger. They have been called "bottle flies" because their shiny blue and green color resembling colored glass bottles, although some species are shiny black or bronze.

If you find a large number of these flies indoors it usually indicates the presence of a dead animal such as a mouse or bird inside the house.

When huge numbers of flies suddenly appear inside the home, home-owners become very upset and often don't know what to do. The flies often look somewhat like houseflies, but may be shiny green, blue, bronze or black.

They congregate around windows and produce a buzzing sound and blow flies lay eggs in decomposing organic matter, like garbage, animal manure, decaying vegetables, grass clippings and poorly managed compost piles.

These flies are important in nature in the decay process of animal carcasses and are usually the first insects to arrive, within hours or even minutes after an animal dies.

During the summertime, flies will lay their eggs in meat and vegetable scraps in your trashcan and can go through an entire generation in less than a week. When fly maggots finish feeding, they will often crawl away and pupate in a dark, secluded place. Sometimes these maggots or pupae are seen by homeowners who do not know what they are. Best to vacuum them and discard the bag, however, those missed will emerge later as flies.

Bottle flies typically only infest "fresh" cadavers, but there are other insects that show up later, such as rove beetles, carpet beetles and hide beetles, but a cadaver is only a good food source for bottle flies for a short period of time.

The flies are attracted to the light from windows during the day so fly strips are a non-toxic method of capturing them. Make sure your draperies or window treatments are securely tied back so the fabric doesn't get "stuck" in the sticky tape.

CARROT RUST FLY

Identification:

This fly has a shiny greenish-black body, big red eyes and a yellowish head and legs. The larvae are yellowish-white maggots. The maggots will hatch from eggs that are laid around the carrots crown. After they hatch they burrow down into the roots. The tunnels they make are rusty in color from the maggot's excrement, which gives them their name.

Their damage leads to soft-rot bacterial problems.

General Information:
This is a sneaky little fly that damages the plants underground and the damage is not noticeable until it's too late. These flies love to munch on carrots, parsnips, celery, parsley, fennel and dill. The carrots will have minute tunnels with a light-colored fecal matter. These bugs hang out in the northeastern states, coastal Washington and parts of Oregon and Idaho. They will over winter in garden soil.

A SPOT OF TEA WITH YOUR SEEDS
Save your used tealeaves and place them into your carrot seeds when you plant. This will prevent any problems from carrot maggots.

PLANT REPELLANTS
There are a number of plants that when planted near the carrots and other similar vegetables will repel bugs. These include leek, onions, garlic, pennyroyal, rosemary, sage, black salsify and coriander.

DUST OFF THE PLANTS
If you prepare a dust composed of either wormwood or rock phosphate it will keep the flies from laying their eggs on the plants. The wormwood will mask the aroma of the carrots and the flies will avoid the plant.

TRAP 'EM
You can purchase some yellow sticky traps at a garden supply house and insert the stakes into the soil at a 45° angle.

GIVE THEM A CUP OF JOE
When sowing the carrot seeds, just mix them with some used coffee grounds, which will repel the rust fly and stop them from laying their eggs.

CLUSTER FLY

Custer flies are active in the fall when they fly to the sunny sides of homes in search of protected over-wintering sites and may be found flying about inside, often in great numbers all winter long. These flies do not reproduce within the structure, but become active on warm days and crawl out of wall voids and attics in a confused attempt to go back outside.

Cluster flies are thought to be native to Europe and may have found their way to North America in the ballast of ships containing soil and the cluster fly host, earthworms. Adult cluster flies are slightly larger than the common house fly but are dull-gray with black markings and have golden-yellow hairs on the thorax. The hairs are more numerous on the underside of the thorax between and near the legs.

The immature stages, egg and larva, are seldom seen as the eggs are deposited on the soil and the larva or maggots burrow into earthworms on which they feed. The maggots are cream colored and are an elongated wedge shape.

As a nuisance pest it joins the ranks of other over-wintering pests such as the multicolored Asian lady beetle, the western conifer seed bug and the boxelder bug. Cluster flies will not damage your home, however, the flies may leave small dark-colored spots of excrement on windows and walls, but they are not known to carry any diseases of medical importance to humans.

CRANE FLY

Crane fly adults are very slender, long-legged flies that may vary in length from 2–60 millimeters (0.079–2.4 in) though tropical species may exceed to 100 millimeters or 3.9 inches. The larvae can cause damage to lawns by feeding on the roots of grass plants. Numerous other common names have been applied to the crane fly, many of them more or less regional, including mosquito hawk, mosquito wolf, mosquito eater, soldier, gallon-nipper and golly-whopper.

In appearance crane flies seem long and gangly, with very long legs, and a long slender abdomen. The wings are often held out when at rest.

Unlike most, crane flies are weak and poor fliers and tend to "wobble" in an unpredictable pattern during flight, and they can be caught without much effort.

Female abdomens contain eggs, and as a result appear swollen in comparison to those of males. The female abdomen also ends in a pointed ovipositor that may look somewhat like a stinger, but is completely harmless. Adult mouthparts may occur on the end of the crane fly's long face, which is sometimes called a snout.

Larvae have a distinct head capsule, and their abdominal segments often have long fleshy projections surrounding the posterior that resemble tentacles. Adult crane flies do not prey on mosquitoes, nor do they bite humans. Some larval crane flies are predatory and may eat mosquito larvae but mostly feed on nectar or they do not feed at all. Once they become adults, most crane fly species exist as adults only to mate and die.

Their larvae, called "leatherjackets", "leatherbacks", "leatherback bugs" or "leatherjacket slugs", because of the way they move, consume roots and other vegetation, in some cases causing damage to plants. The crane fly is occasionally considered a mild turf pest in some areas.

DEER FLY

Deer flies (also known as yellow flies) can be pests to cattle, horses and humans. Distinguishing characteristic of a deer fly is patterned gold or green eyes. They are smaller than wasps and they have colored eyes and dark bands across their wings. While female deer flies feed on blood, males collect pollen. When feeding, females use knife-like mandibles and maxillae to make a cross-shaped incision and then lap up the blood.

Their bite can be extremely painful, and allergic reaction from the saliva of the fly can result in further discomfort and health concerns. Pain and itch are the most common symptoms, but more significant allergic reactions can develop.

They are frequently found in damp environments, such as wetlands or forests and lay clusters of shiny black eggs on the leaves of small plants by water. The aquatic larvae feed on small insects and pupate in the mud at the edge of the water. Adults are potential vectors of tularemia, anthrax and filariasis. Predators of the deer fly include nest-building wasps and hornets, dragonflies and some birds including the killdeer.

DOBSONFLY

Dobsonflies are found throughout the Americas and Asia, as well as South Africa. Both male and female dobsonflies can reach lengths up to five inches (12.5 cm), measured from the tips of their pincers to the tips of their four wings. Their wingspans can be twice as long as their body length and the wings are densely lined with intersecting veins. When not in use, the wings are folded along the length of their bodies. Dobsonflies also have long, multi-segmented antennae.

Both male and female dobsonflies have very sharp mandibles, those of an adult male dobsonfly are actually so big (up to 1 inch 25 mm) that they are unable to harm humans, as they have such poor leverage that they are incapable of breaking the skin. Their mandibles are used exclusively during mating, where males show them off and grasp the females during copulation.

Female dobsonflies, however, retain the short, powerful pincers they had as larvae, so they can inflict painful bites, which can draw blood. Both sexes will raise their heads and spread their jaws menacingly when they perceive danger. They are not venomous, but possess an irritating, foul-smelling anal spray as a last-ditch defense.

Dobsonflies spend most of their life in the larval stage, during which they are called hellgrammites and are familiar to fishermen who like to use the large larvae as bait. They live under rocks at the bottoms of lakes and streams and prey on other insect larvae with the short sharp pincers on their heads, with which they can also inflict painful bites on humans.

The larvae reach to 2" to 3" in length, with gills all along the sides of their segmented bodies that allow them to extract oxygen from water.

After a few years of living and growing underwater, the larvae crawl out onto land and pupate. They stay in their cocoons over the winter and emerge only to mate. Upon emerging, they live for only seven days.

FACE FLY

The face fly, which closely resembles the house fly, attacks livestock chiefly on the head and face. Face flies are of primary economic importance as an annoyance to cattle, horses and less frequently to swine. On cattle, a disruption of grazing, poor utilization of feedstuffs with subsequent weight loss or reduced milk production, and diseases can occur when fly populations are not controlled.

Face flies have been implicated in the transmission of conjunctivitis (pinkeye), infectious abortion and eyeworm in cattle. Beef and dairy cattle, horses and open-faced sheep are the principal animals bothered by this pest. They feed, without piercing the skin, upon the mucous secretions around the eyes, nose and lips and upon fresh wounds or saliva deposits on the shoulders, neck and legs.

Face flies are about 20 percent larger than house flies, being slightly longer and more robust. The adults are active from early spring to late autumn with only females normally being found on cattle and horses. Males frequent and feed on pollen produced by flowering vegetation. At night, both sexes are found resting on inanimate objects.

The face fly overwinters as an adult, hibernating in protected places such as building lofts and attics. Here, they can become a serious domestic pest by crawling on walls, windows and floors during winter warm spells and when they become active just before leaving the hibernation site. The flies mate shortly after becoming active in early spring. During this time flies congregate in sunny spots on high buildings near ventilator opening or cracks and crevices.

Adult face flies will feed on several kinds of large mammals, but do not lay eggs in or develop naturally in the manure of any animals except cattle. Furthermore, female face flies lay their eggs only in freshly deposited cow manure prior to crust formations, particularly that from animals on rangeland or pasture.

Face flies do not lay eggs in manure piles around barns and stables or in the disturbed, urine-saturated and trampled droppings usually associated with beef feedlots and dry lots.

In the manure, eggs hatch in about one day, and the larvae complete their development in 2½ to 4 days. As the larvae mature, they turn from white to yellow and move to the soil adjacent to the cow manure where they enter the pupae stage and in 5 to 7 days, they emerge as adults. The entire life cycle is completed in about 2 weeks, and numerous generations per year may occur, depending upon climate conditions.

FLESH FLIES

 Flesh Flies usually seek scraps of meat on which to lay their eggs. Similar to house flies, adult flesh flies are dark-colored (gray or black). Common species have three dark stripes on the thorax and are slightly larger than house flies with a checkerboard pattern on the abdomen.

Flesh flies are often mistaken for houseflies due to their coloration and markings. However, their gray-checkered abdomens are larger than those of the housefly. A flesh fly exhibits three dark stripes along the prothorax and four distinct bristles on top of the thorax. An extra row of bristles is also found beneath the flesh fly's wings and yet another can be found at each side of the thorax.

Flesh flies measure approximately ½-inch from end to end. Larvae are yellow in color, with pointed heads. Along with bottle and blowflies, flesh flies prove useful to forensic entomologists. These fly larvae may assist in pinpointing time of death. Flesh flies reproduce on decaying vegetable items, animal flesh, carcasses, garbage and excrement.

Although flesh flies do not bite and are not carriers of disease, their feeding habits can become a nuisance.

However, larvae can also prove beneficial to humans, as they prey on the eggs and larvae of other pests such as grasshoppers, blowflies, houseflies, spiders and snails. Flesh flies are rarely found in homes or restaurants. Infestations in these locations are most likely due to a different fly species.

FRUIT FLIES

General Information:

 If you see small flies or gnats in your kitchen, they're probably fruit flies. Fruit flies are a problem year round, but are more common during late summer and into fall because they are attracted to ripened or fermenting fruits and vegetables.

Tomatoes, melons, grapes and other perishable items brought in from the garden are often the cause of an infestation developing indoors.

Fruit flies are also attracted to very ripe bananas, potatoes, onions and other unrefrigerated produce. Fruit flies are very common in homes, restaurants, supermarkets and wherever food is allowed to rot and ferment. The adult fly is about 1/8 inch long and usually has red eyes. The front portion of the body is tan and the rear portion is black.

Fruit flies will lay their eggs near the surface of fermenting foods or other moist, organic materials. When the tiny larvae, emerges it will continue to feed near the surface of the fermenting mass.

This surface-feeding characteristic of the larvae is significant in that damaged or over-ripened portions of fruits and vegetables can be removed without having to discard the remainder for fear of retaining any developing larvae.

The reproductive potential of fruit flies is enormous; if given the opportunity, they will lay about 500 eggs and the entire lifecycle from egg to adult can be completed in about a week. They also will breed in drains, garbage disposals, empty bottles and cans, trash containers, and cleaning rags. All that is needed for development is a moist film of fermenting material.

Infestations can originate from over-ripened fruits or vegetables that were previously infested and brought into the home. The adults can also fly in from outside through inadequately screened windows and doors.
Fruit flies are primarily nuisance pests; however, they also have the potential to contaminate food with bacteria and other disease-producing organisms.

Once your home is infested with fruit flies, all potential breeding areas must be located and eliminated. Unless the breeding sites are removed or cleaned, the problem will continue no matter how often natural insecticides are applied to control the adults.

A LITTLE SQUIRT

If you own birds and feed them fruit you may develop a fruit fly problem. There is a pyrethrum aerosol spray that is safe to use around birds called Misty Miser XX™.

This will work as a short-term problem solver, but removing the food supply is the best answer. This spray is also one of the best methods of ridding your yard of flies.

FRUIT FLY LURE

Citronella grass is very effective in luring fruit flies into a glue-coated trap. If you have a problem with crops, just spray them with a diluted citronella oil spray.

GRAIN WILL KILL FRUIT FLIES

If you crush 1 cup of the grass-like grain called finger millet and place the powder in 1-quart of warm water then spray it works great for small areas or just a few trees.

MAKING FLYPAPER WITH HONEY

The following ingredients will be needed:

9	**Parts rosin**
3	**Parts canola oil**
1	**Part honey**

Place all the ingredients into a saucepan and melt together, stir well and apply to the paper while still warm. The paper should be prepared cutting strips of paper and folding them over and stapling them so that they will strong. Size the paper with shellac or varnish to prevent the mixture from spreading too far. **Keep away from children and pets.**

KEEPS THEIR BREATH FRESH TOO
Trying crushing some fresh mint and placing it into 1-2 sachets, then hang the sachets around the home or on the patio to repel flies.

HERBAL REMEDIES
Use bay leaves, pennyroyal, eucalyptus or cloves in a muslin bag and hang them around the house. Pound them to release the essence before placing them into a bag.

If you place some sweet basil in a small container in the kitchen or near a pets food dish it will repel flies. You can also plant sweet basil or rue around the doorways or place a cotton ball with a few drops of eucalyptus oil on it in a shallow container in the kitchen.

FLYPAPER 101
To make your own flypaper, just mix together:

¼	**Cup Karo® syrup**
1	**Tablespoon granulated sugar**
1	**Tablespoon of brown sugar**

Cut strips of brown craft paper and soak it in the mixture, then allow it to dry overnight. Place a string in a small hole on top and hang wherever you have a problem.

MAKE A FLY OMELET
Beat 1 large egg yolk with 1 tablespoon of molasses and add 2 pinches of finely ground black pepper, then place the mixture in a shallow paper plate.

DUST OFF THE DOO, DOO
If you don't want to pick up after the pet, then dust the pile with garden grade diatomaceous earth (DE). DE can be fed to your pet and the flies will stay away from their feces.

For cats feed ½ teaspoon every week, dogs should get ½ tablespoon each week and horses can get ¼ cup added to each meal. The flies won't even go near the horse manure.

SEND YOUR FLIES TO PEACEFUL VALLEY
This will be a permanent vacation for the flies. The trap is called the Peaceful Valley Fly Trap and is sold through most farm supply house. It will accommodate up to 25,000 flies. The trap used yeast and ammonium carbonate to attract the flies.

WHAT'S GOING ON DOWN THERE?
If you notice a number of very small flies and don't know where they are coming from it is probably from your kitchen drain. They are called drain flies and live in the drain on rotted foods. To trap them just place some duct tape over the drain at night, sticky side down. Pour vinegar down the drain and rinse out after a few minutes.

CARPET THE AREA
Cabbage root flies tend to lay their eggs close to young cabbage plants. To stop them from laying their eggs too close, just place a small circle of carpet with a slit so that it will wrap around the small plant and protect the base.

KEEP YOUR CAN CLEAN
Garbage cans and trash compactors can produce 1,000 or more fly eggs per week unless they are sealed tight. The problem can be solved with lavender oil. If you have a fly problem place a few drops of lavender oil on a piece of cotton and place it in the garbage can or an empty trash compactor bag before you start adding garbage.

You can also place a mint sprig in each can every week. Better yet just sprinkle the bottom of the can with insecticidal soap.

ESSENTIAL OILS TO THE RESCUE
There are a number of essential oils that will repel flies very effectively. The most effective are oil of peppermint and oil of cloves. If you place oil of lavender on a sponge and leave it in a room it will repel flies.

CLEAN UP AFTER YOUR PET
One of the preferred spots for flies to multiply on is your pet fecal material. It would be best to clean up after your pet daily to reduce the fly population around your home and garden area.

WHEN IS A FLY NOT A FLY?
When it is a whitefly, which is really a member of the insect family and not a "real" fly. They have four wings while flies only have two wings. They will suck the juices from plants and like to hang around greenhouses as their preferred residence. They lay their eggs on the underneath sides of leaves. They can be controlled in a greenhouse if you release the parasite *Encarsia formosa.* Also, ladybugs and lacewings enjoy munching on these bugs. A soap spray with a small amount of rubbing alcohol and coconut oil will dissolve the waxy coating on their larvae and kills them.

LEMON GRASS VERY PRETTY
If you have a problem, keeping flies away from your plants, just rub the leaves of the lemon grass plant on their leaves. By just rubbing the leaves on your plants it will provide the plant fly protection.

CAMPHOR TREE DOES THE JOB
If you plant a camphor tree near your kitchen it has the ability to repel flies. Chinaberry trees will also do the job.

FIGHT FLIES WITH FLIES
Wherever manure is you will find flies, especially around chicken ranches and stables. There a number of companies that sell fly parasites that can be released in these areas to control the fly population. The parasites deposit their eggs on the fly larvae or pupae in the manure and prevent them from becoming flies.

FLY MINTS

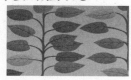

If you crush up some fresh mint and rub it on an animal, especially a horse it will keep the flies away for some time. The flies will not even land on them.

LITTLE GAME HUNTER

There are a number of commercial flytraps sold on the market. If you do purchase one be sure that it is not placed in direct sunlight, since filtered sunlight works best. Ripened fruit works best in the trap, but if that is not available a combination of cornmeal mixed with molasses works almost as well.

ZAPPERS DON'T WORK WELL WITH FLIES

Flies are unable to see ultraviolet light during the day so placing a zapper outside in daylight will not work well and at night flies are inactive. All you end up doing is killing the beneficial insects.

SOUTH OF THE BORDER

If you enter a dog kennel or stables and wonder what the plants are hanging from the doorways, it is probably Mexican marigolds. This plant has been used as a fly deterrent for hundreds of years and is still in use today.

GET A GIANT FLYSWATTER AND AIM FOR THEIR BACKSIDE
One of the best methods is still the good old flyswatter. For every fly that you kill, hundreds will not be born. A mesh flyswatter with a metal handle works the best. Be sure and wash the flyswatter in hot soapy water because of the bacteria and disease that they could harbor.

CHASE THEM WITH HAIRSPRAY
Better be sneaky and have a good aim, however, this works really well and is a bit challenging.

FAN THE FLIES
Flies do not like fast moving currents of air and will avoid them at all costs. If you have a fan over ever doorway that opens into the house, you will never have any flies in your home.

SPRINKLING MANURE
If you have areas with manure in piles it would be wise to sprinkle diatomaceous earth (DE) on the manure to reduce the fly population.

CITRUS REPELLANT
Scratch the skin of an orange and leave it out; the citrus acts as a repellent and will keep flies out of the room.

WON'T WORK LIKE MISTLETOE
If you hang a small sprig of ragwort over a doorway it will repel houseflies in the summer. Be sure that you are using the "real" thing.
Ragwort has the botanical name of **Senecio jacobeae** and is part of the family **Compositae.** Look for feathered leaves and clusters of bight orange flowers that look like daisies. Ragwort has a somewhat pungent smell, best to hang it just outside the door.

GREEN FLIES

 Green flies, or green bottle flies, are shiny and metallic green in color with large eyes that are compound and tinted red. Like other blow and bottle flies, these flies are commonly found on farms. Adults feed on pollen, serving as key pollinators for plants that mimic the smell of carrion.

Although painful, green flies are not known to transfer diseases through biting. Rather, the transfer of pathogens occurs when they land on food or food preparation surfaces after coming into contact with carrion or feces. Female flies choose dead and wounded animals, as well as feces, within which to lay their eggs.

Green bottle flies are particularly fond of dog feces and large populations may be found in dog parks and dog runs as a result. After hatching, yellow-gray larvae feed for two to 10 days, amassing enough body weight to last through their upcoming pupa stage. The scientific community has taken special interest in the larvae of these flies for their potential to treat necrotic flesh wounds in sanitized, controlled conditions.

ONION FLY

General Information:

 The onion fly can be a real problem if you are growing onions. The fly lays its eggs in an onion and the resulting maggot does a good job of ruining the onion. If you scatter wood ash around the base of the plant it will help keep their number down since the flies will shy away from wood ash.

ROOT MAGGOT FLY

General Information:

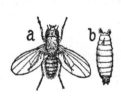 This fly looks like the common housefly but likes vegetables. There are a number of species all preferring their own veggie. The adult female lays her eggs on the roots of the vegetables and when the maggots hatch they proceed to live off the roots thus weakening the plant.

WOOD ASHES TO THE RESCUE

If you sprinkle a goodly amount of wood ashes around the roots it will keep these flies at bay and save your vegetables. Fireplace ashes will also do a very efficient job of keeping them away.

TAR PAPER WORKS
Place circles of tarpaper around the plants making a slit in each so that it will fit fairly snug around the plant.

DIG UP THE SOIL
One of the best methods of getting rid of root maggot flies is to dig up the soil in the fall and leave the pupae of the root maggots exposed to the cold of winter. This will also provide feed for hungry birds.

SAW FLIES

CALL IN THE WASP
One of the best methods of controlling sawflies is to use parasitic wasps.

ASHES AWAY
Dusting with wood ashes will usually get rid of sawflies.

SOLDIER FLY

This is one of the more unusual insects found around the home. It is the larva of the stratiomyid, or soldier, fly. The larval form of the soldier fly is a segmented, maggot-like creature that can be quite scary to someone not familiar with what it really is. However, both the larva and the adult are harmless.

The most common species of soldier fly is considered a filth fly because of its habit of breeding in manure and garbage.
The feeding habits of the larva, however, are not easy to classify since the larval stage of the soldier fly feeds on decaying organic material including manure and very moist, rotting vegetable matter. Since they like manure piles these insects are sometimes considered beneficial because they prey on other insects, like house flies.

They also like compost piles and are being sold by at least one manufacturer for use in specially designed containers to quickly decompose kitchen waste.

Soldier flies will on occasion infest animal carcasses. Problems in homes sometimes occur after a bee's nest has been exterminated in a wall since soldier fly larvae are one of several insects that may scavenge waste materials in bee combs.

Soldier flies are usually seen during their pre-pupal stage. Pre-pupal larvae are full grown larvae that have stopped feeding and begin a time of exploring before pupating (changing into an adult, or in this case the fly, form). During this exploring phase, larvae may travel several yards from the breeding site and may be seen crawling along a floor, patio, or fireplace hearth.

Soldier fly larvae are about one inch-long, have no legs, dark brown in color and flattened. The outer covering "skin" has a distinctive, leathery texture. Soldier fly larvae are also remarkably tough and are able to survive for weeks in a jar with no food or water.

The adult stage of the most identifiable species of soldier fly is about ¾ inch-long and black, with a translucent segment on the tail, or abdomen. Adult flies are rather lazy until induced to fly as well as being attracted to light, but do not seem attracted to food.

These flies are harmless to people and are beneficial in helping decompose garbage and filth. In some area they also help control more noxious insect pests, like house flies. They will frequent poorly maintained compost piles; wet grains or other decaying vegetable material, which may provide breeding sites for soldier flies. If you have a dead bird or rodent in an attic or chimney it may also be the reason for soldier fly or blow fly infestations.

STABLE FLY

Stable flies are not always found in filthy situations and both sexes feed on the blood of animals, including humans, usually biting around the ankles.

The bites are painful; however, they are not known to transmit disease to humans. Females will lay eggs in rotting straw and manure, moist piles of animal feed and yard waste.

The stable fly or dog fly is a blood-sucking fly which is of considerable importance to people, pets, livestock, and the tourist industry in Florida. Stable flies usually attack animals for their blood meal, but in the absence of an animal host will also bite man.

In its normal environment the stable fly is not considered a pest to man. However, certain regions of the United States have considerable problems with large numbers of stable flies attacking man. Areas hard hit are the coastal part of New Jersey, areas of Lake Superior and Michigan and the Tennessee valley. West Florida and along the Gulf coast to Louisiana are areas that historically have stable fly problems.

Stable flies like to breed in soggy hay, grasses or feed, piles of moist fermenting weed or grass cuttings, peanut litter, seaweed deposits along beaches and in soiled straw bedding. The female, when depositing eggs will often crawl into loose material.

Each female fly may lay 500-600 eggs in 4 separate batches. The eggs are tiny, white and sausage-shaped and will hatch in 2-5 days into larvae which feed and mature in 14-26 days.

Larvae are typical maggots and transform to small reddish-brown capsules (pupae) from which the adult flies will emerge. The average life cycle is 28 days ranging from 22-58 days depending on the weather! Adult stable flies can fly up to 70 miles from their breeding sites and as an adult is similar to the house fly in size and color. However, the stable fly has a long bayonet-like mouthpart for sucking blood. Unlike many other species of flies, both male and female stable flies feed on blood.

Stable flies will attack people, dogs, cats, and agricultural animals throughout Florida. Their bite is extremely painful to both man and animal. When hungry, stable flies are quite persistent and will continue to pursue a blood meal even after being swatted at. Although the bite is painful, there is little irritation after the bite, and few people exhibit an allergic reaction to it.

While one stable fly does not cause significant damage, 50-100 of these blood-sucking pests together with 500 horn flies cause a daily loss of blood. This can result in a loss of 10-20 percent in milk production and up to 40 pounds of beef gain eliminated per animal each year.

Stable flies also are known to transmit such diseases as anthrax, Equine Infectious Anemia and anaplasmosis to animals. In addition, bite wounds can be sites for secondary infection. Stable flies will feed mainly on the legs of cattle and horses and leave an animal immediately after feeding, which means that they may go unnoticed unless heavy outbreaks occur. They are inactive at night, roosting on fences, buildings, trees, and bushes.

The most practical and economical method for reducing stable fly populations is the elimination or proper management of breeding sources. It is important to remember that flies cannot develop in dry materials. Stable flies breed in the following types of material:

Green Chop or Silage - The stable fly maggot thrives in decaying plant material, such as old silage in and around feed troughs and trench silos. Silage probably has a greater potential for producing stable flies than almost any other material found on today's farms.
More than 3,000 stable fly maggots per cubic foot of silage have been found in mid-January on some West Florida farms, and 5 times that in number in late summer.

Crop Residues - Unwanted crop residues, such as peanut vines, discarded in piles during harvest are frequently very important sources of fly breeding. This material should be spread thinly for quick drying.

Hay and Grain - Accumulations of hay where animals are fed in the fields decay rapidly when exposed to the elements and may produce flies in tremendous numbers. To prevent this source of fly breeding, cattle should be fed at a different place in the field each time so that accumulations of old hay do not occur. Spilled grain around feed troughs or storage bins likewise may provide the stable fly with a moist, favorable breeding medium and should be cleaned up immediately.

Animal Manures - When handled properly manure need not breed stable flies at all. It should not be allowed to accumulate for more than a week before spreading thinly on the fields, where quick drying eliminates stable fly breeding.

Stables - The recent popularity of pleasure horses has created a staggering number of new fly breeding sources. However, proper care and management of waste feed and manure can greatly reduce or eliminate fly populations in these areas. Stalls should be cleaned of droppings daily and the manure spread thinly (not more than 1-2 inches deep). The choice of bedding is also very important. Hay or straw absorbs urine and decomposes rapidly and unless it is changed every few days will produce flies by the thousands. A far better material is wood shavings, which, when cleaned of manure daily and changed approximately every two weeks, does not normally breed flies.

Other Sources - Any pile of moist, decaying organic matter should be considered a potential source of stable flies that can cause serious damage to farm animals.

YELLOW FLY

Yellow flies are biting flies and similar to the common mosquito. Females feed on blood to trigger egg production and both male and female yellow flies eat plant nectar and pollen for energy. Males do not bite and yellow flies are found extensively throughout Latin America and tropical regions of the United States.

The true yellow fly is believed to have migrated into the United States through Mexico. Yellow flies prefer hot, humid weather; they do not like sunlight and are most active during the hours just before twilight. They are also attracted to water, where they lay their eggs, and are frequently found at the edges of forest lakes and streams.

Adults measure approximately one centimeter in length, with one pair of black front legs and two pair of yellow back legs. Their abdomens are yellow and furry.

Yellow fly eggs measure approximately 1/16-inch. Initially white, these eggs quickly darken and turn black, at which point they are commonly mistaken for feces. Larvae are semi-aquatic, feeding on decaying organic matter found on water banks.

They molt approximately 10 times before burrowing into the ground for winter. After emerging, they locate a dry location within which to pupate. Female yellow flies are fierce biters. Traps may help reduce populations near gardens or swimming pools.

CHAPTER 11

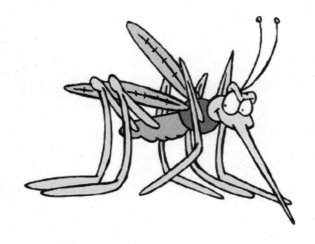

MOSQUITOES

MOSQUITOES

KILL THOSE LITTLE BLOOD SUCKERS

Luckily, only 50% of the mosquitoes worldwide suck human blood. The female mosquito needs the protein from human blood to develop her eggs and lay them. When they don't get the blood meal they have to consume their own wing muscles. There are 2,500 different species of mosquitoes worldwide and they only weigh in at $1/25,000^{th}$ of an ounce. They are so light that they are able to walk on water. The mosquito saliva, which they leave when they bite you, is what causes the itching.

In the United States alone there are over 150 species of mosquito and most can mature from an egg in one to two weeks. Mosquitoes need water to reproduce and they can usually find some standing water in pets dishes, drainage ditches, fishponds, old tires, damp mulch, rain gutter lines, sewers, planters, leaks around spickets, etc. Mosquitoes like to live near your home and are smart enough to know that there are plenty of free meals there; you and your family.

During the day they will seek shelter from the sun and are more active when it cools down or in a shady spot. They will never go too far from water. Getting rid of any location that has even the slightest amount of standing water should help to eliminate the problem. They don't like windy condition and prefer still air areas. Using a fan in the home will keep them out as well.

The female mosquito eats a blood meal and then lays an egg on the surface of water. The water must be still so keep this in mind regarding mosquitoes on your property. If you have any standing water and there are mosquitoes in the neighborhood you will have eggs hatching in your backyard. They prefer very shallow water so it doesn't take much to make them happy. They will feed on bacteria in the water after they hatch then they will turn into pupae. It only takes several days for mosquitoes to turn into an adult and go looking for you.

It only takes 1 pint of water to nurture 500 mosquito larvae.

Your best protection against mosquitoes is to be sure that they do not have a point of entry into your home. Be sure and seal off any openings and especially holes in screens.

Types of Mosquitoes: Aedes, Anopheles, and Culex
There are approximately 2,700 species of mosquito in the world; the three most significant genera are the Aedes, Anopheles, and Culex, as these types of mosquitoes are responsible for transmitting various diseases that are hazardous to mankind.

> **Since mosquitoes can be a pest both indoors and outdoors, the information and identification will be found in both books.**

ASIAN TIGER MOSQUITO (AEDES)

 The Asian tiger mosquito (Aedes Mosquito) is one of the most dangerous types of mosquito, the Aedes, as it is more commonly known, feeds on the blood of humans. However, only the female mosquito bites. It transmits among humans diseases such as yellow fever and dengue fever and can also cause lymphatic filariasis, an illness that can trigger elephantiasis in certain cases.

Most species of Aedes can be found in the tropical and subtropical zones of the world. Recently, the genus has been discovered in more temperate regions, and its presence can now be anticipated on every continent except Antarctica. The female Aedes mosquito lays its eggs on the surface of water; adulthood is reached within approximately six to seven days.

The mature mosquito breeds, feeds, and dies within a week or two, which is the life cycle of most mosquitoes. This mosquito is the primary and secondary vectors for dengue fever. Aedes is the most important vector in the tropics and subtropical regions such as the southern United States.

Eggs of these mosquitoes; typically are laid singly or in rafts and although they may stick to the surface, they may sink if the water is disturbed. They prefer clean water for the development of the larvae and in tropical areas they will develop in water pots and tanks on roofs and in rain butts.

Feeding is described as endophagic because the mosquito prefers to feed in and around structures and the mosquito then rests in cool damp spots within structures while the meal is digested (endophilic behavior). A blood meal takes 2-7 days to digest and 1-3 meals are needed to complete development of clutch of eggs. Transmission between humans comes from repeated biting when the mosquito injects saliva that acts as an anticoagulant.

ANOPHELES MOSQUITO

 The Anopheles Mosquito is different from other types of mosquitoes as it is the genus most accountable for spreading malaria to humans. Malaria can be fatal; its typical symptoms include fever, headaches, chills, and general flu symptoms. The species of Anopheles known as Gambiae is infamous for transmitting plasmodium falciparum, the most threatening form of malaria in the world.

The Anopheles mosquito is generally located near bodies of water, such as ponds, swamps, marches, ditches, and rain pools. The Anopheles female favors laying its eggs in fairly still water that is oxygenated, and where there is an abundance of wild plant life. Some species enjoy the shady areas, while others prefer sunlight.

Malaria is transmitted between people by female Anopheles mosquitoes, and more than 60 species have been incriminated in the transmission of infection (there are about 430 species of Anopheles and about 3500 species of total species of mosquitoes).

Some species are more significant than others as vectors because of variations in susceptibility to the parasite or the propensity of the mosquito to bite humans and to enter houses when looking for a blood meal.

Females lay their eggs in batches of 70-100 on the surface of water at night. The type of water used for egg laying is indicative of the mosquito species and includes irrigation channels, a pool of water in a tree trunk, and sewage effluent. In tropical temperatures the eggs hatch after two to three days.

The larvae lie just below the surface of the water and feed on algae, and after 7-14 days turn into pupae during a five-minute process. The pupa is comma-shaped and is the least active stage of the Anopheles lifecycle. After two to four days the pupa metamorphoses into an adult mosquito. The adults emerge during late evening and are able to fly within minutes.

CULEX MOSQUITO

The Culex Mosquito can be considered the least dangerous of the three major types of mosquitoes due to the fact that humans are not their preferred blood meal. Instead, most species of Culex are partial to biting birds rather than humans. Despite this inclination, the Culex female mosquito is nevertheless recognized as spreading diseases such as the West Nile virus, malaria, filariasis, and encephalitis.

The Culex, like the Anopheles, tends to favor standing water to lay its eggs; however, unlike the Anopheles, it does not necessarily opt for plant and wild life surroundings. Instead, it often breeds in the outdoor objects on your property, such as barrels, cans, garden pots, used tires, as well as other places where stagnant water can collect.

NATURAL METHODS OF ELIMINATION

NUMERO UNO MOSQUITO KILLER

If you don't have a cat this is the best mosquito killer that is available. Catnip placed in a sachet and placed around the home will deter any and all mosquitoes in short order. Catnip contains the essential oil nepetalactone, which is at least 10 times more powerful than any commercial mosquito killing solution. A tea made from catnip can also be placed into a spray bottle and sprayed anywhere you have a problem.

MOSQUITO REPELLANT 1
The following ingredients will be needed:

1	**Ounce of oil of citronella (from health food store)**
1	**Drops of corn oil**

Place the ingredients in a small bowl and mix well. Rub the mixture on your skin before going into mosquito-land.

SOLUTION FROM INDIA
A natural vegetable oil that is extracted from an Indian tree called the "Neem tree" is very effective in repelling mosquitoes. The seeds and the leaves contain the chemical sallanin, which has been used for hundreds of years in India to repel flying insects. It is natural and more effective than any commercial product on the market. One Internet site to get the product is www.nutraceutic.com.

HERBS 101
To get rid of flying insects, just place some fresh basil in a muslin bag or two and hang them around the house or on the porch. Flying insects do not like the smell of basil and it will repel almost every flying insect.

MOSQUITO REPELLANT 2
The following ingredients will be needed:

3	**Cups of rubbing alcohol**
1 ½	**Cups of red cedar wood shavings**
½	**Cup of eucalyptus leaves**
1	**Spray bottle**

Place all the ingredients in a large bowl and mix well. Cover the bowl and allow it to stand for 6 days before straining the solution through a piece of cheesecloth. Place the liquid in a small spray bottle and spray on skin as needed.

MOSQUITO REPELLANT 3 FOR ARMS AND LEGS
The following ingredients will be needed:

| 4 | **Parts glycerin (from pharmacy)** |
| 1 | **Part eucalyptus oil** |

Place the ingredients into a small bowl and mix thoroughly. Place in a well-sealed container. Rub a small amount on arms or legs to keep mosquitoes from biting.

WATER, WATER, EVERYWHERE
Be sure that there is no standing water anywhere on your property. Mosquitoes like pets, water dishes and birdbaths. If you sprinkler system is leaving a puddle that does not dry up in a short period of time, be sure and fix it.

REPEL MOSQUITOES WITH YOUR BARBECUE
It doesn't matter if you use real charcoal or artificial charcoal, just place a few sprigs of rosemary or sage on top of the coals and you won't see a mosquito for some time.

GETS RID OF VAMPIRES AND MOSQUITOES
Mix 1 part of concentrated garlic juice with 5 parts of water and place it in a spray bottle. Spray in any area that they frequent. This treatment will be effective for 5-6 hours and you will have great smelling mosquitoes.

A GRASS THAT REPELS MOSQUITOES
A very effective substance that repels mosquitoes is citronella. Citronella can be found in lemon grass and in the natural oil form, found in the grass, which is even more effective than the citronella that you purchase from the store. It is also called Thai grass and is available at most garden stores.

Use the scallion-like stem of the plant, crush it and use it on your arms, legs and neck to repel mosquitoes. You can also make a spray by making a tea from the stem.

SCARE THEM AWAY WITH BEANS
If you want an easy solution to ridding your home and garden of mosquitoes, just purchase some castor bean seeds and grow a few plants. Castor bean plants grow like weeds and will repel mosquitoes. The chemical in the castor bean is ricinine and when extracted it is a deadly chemical.

GROW SOME BAMBOO PLANTS
Dragonflies are attracted by bamboo plants and are safe around people. They like to live among the long bamboo shoots in warm and sunny areas of your yard. One dragonfly will consume at least 100 mosquitoes in 30 minutes and will eat their larvae as well.

They can spot a mosquito 25 yards away and go after it at 60 miles per hour. Dragonflies can be found in most areas of the United States.

GET BATS IN YOUR BELFRY
If you don't have bats in your neighborhood you might consider purchasing a bat house. Most garden supply stores will sell a bat house for about $25.00.

This will eliminate thousands of unwanted insects every night. Bats will not bother people; however, if you have a pool or birdbath they will swoop in for a drink occasionally.

MOSQUITOES VS ZAPPERS
Studies have shown that electric bug zappers have no effect on mosquitoes. They seem to have a special sense that keeps them away from electrical magnetic fields.

BIRDS LOVE INSECTS
If you place a number of birdhouses on your property to attract birds it will decrease your insect population significantly. To be sure that the birds don't eat your plants you will need to have a few bird feeders around with birdseed and keep them filled.

NATURAL REPELLANT PLANTS

There are a number of plants that will repel mosquitoes very effectively. They are tomato, basil, germanium, citrosa, lemon thyme, citronella grass and eucalyptus. These plants tend to give off oils that repel mosquitoes. You can crush up most of these plants and make a natural mosquito repellant, but be sure and try a small area of your skin to be sure that you do not have an allergy to that particular plant.

A LITTLE BOUNCE™ WILL DO YA

Florida's state insect is the mosquito or at least should be. When you are in Florida and see people with a Bounce™ fabric softener sheet sticking out of their clothing, they are wearing them to repel mosquitoes. This seems to be a very effective method of keeping them away from you.

POSSIBLE REPELLANTS

Rumor is that rubbing apple cider vinegar, peppermint, bay cloves, vanilla bean, sassafras, cedar, eucalyptus or parsley on your skin will repel mosquitoes for a short period of time.

CLEARING THE ROOM

If you open a bottle of pennyroyal or citronella oil and leave it open it will eliminate all the flying insects in the room. Just be sure and leave them a way out.

MOSQUITO REPELLANT 4

The following ingredients will be needed:

1	**Cup peanut oil**
½	**Cup dried chamomile**
½	**Cup of dried nettle**
½	**Cup of dried pennyroyal**
¼	**Cup of sweet basil**
½	**Cup of sweet orange oil**
1	**Teaspoon of boric acid**

Place all the ingredients in a double boiler and crush the herbs into the oil, then heat, stirring occasionally for about 45 minutes. Cover the mixture and remove from the heat and allow it to cool. Strain the mixture through a fine sieve, mashing the herbs to acquire the most fluid possible.

Store in a well-sealed container in the refrigerator until needed! It will not take very much to do the job when rubbed on exposed areas.

THE MOSQUITO HUNTERS
Both toads and bats consume thousands of insects. Mosquitoes are one of their delicacies and they can consume thousands of mosquitoes every night. If you live in an area where toads live and want them in your yard, just build them a "toad house."

They like to live in clay flowerpots so just place a flowerpot upside down and break a hole near the top (which is the bottom now) and they can easily jump in. They like cool, dark homes to get away from the heat of the day.

JUST ONE LITTLE CANDLE
Candles will attract mosquitoes and will kill them when they get too close. Just don't use citronella candles inside the home since the fumes are harmful to your health.

THE NEW MAGNET
There is a new device on the market called the Mosquito Magnet®. This device employs propane and in a Florida swamp test no one had a single bite.

THE YOLK IS ON THEM

If you break open a few egg yolks and allow them to spread over the surface of water or a pond it will suffocate the mosquito larvae and last for several days.

Looks yummy

THE MOSQUITO FISH

If you have a pond or small lake on your property you may consider stocking the lake with *Gambusia affinis*. These fish thrive on mosquito larvae.

PAMPER THE MARLINS

Purple marlins love mosquitoes and will consume a great amount of the adult mosquitoes. They like apartment-style birdhouses and make the entrances 21/8 to 2½ inches and allow the depth from the hole to the bottom of about 6 inches. They are very fussy where they live. Make sure that you drill a small drainage hole in the bottom.

TINY MOSQUITO HUNTERS

Minnows can make excellent mosquito larvae and pupae hunters and finds them one of their favorite foods. They will also catch a female while they are laying their eggs on the surface of the water.

CHANGE THE SURFACE TENSION

Mosquitoes like water and if you spray the surface of the water with Safe Solutions, Inc. Enzyme Cleaner with Peppermint (from garden supply store) it will make it almost impossible for the mosquito larvae and pupae to survive. The adult mosquitoes cannot maintain surface contact if the spray is used. Another chemical, which will change the surface tension of the water, is "*isostearyl alcohol ethoxylate*" **(use with caution)** It is a non-irritating alcohol that comes from plants and has no odor. It is commonly used in the cosmetic industry.

FLOAT THE KILLER

If you float rings of Bti, which is a special strain of Bt it will kill only the mosquito larvae in your pond or small lake. The crotches of trees that extend into the water are especially a problem area in which Bti will do the job. Soap spray is very effective as well and changes the surface tension of the water.

BURNING GRASS?

If you place some lemon grass in a safe metal container and burn it, it will repel mosquitoes. If mosquitoes are frequenting a plant and you don't want them, just rub some lemon grass on the leaves.

OIL THE WATER

If you spray any aerosol oil on any standing water you must have on your property it will kill the mosquito larvae and pupae by suffocating them.

BARBECUE THEM

Next time you barbecue and want to keep the mosquitoes away, just throw some sage or rosemary on the hot coals. Both of these herbs work great on the barbecue and will keep all flying insects away.

ITALIANS RARELY GET BITTEN

People, who consume garlic on a regular basis, rarely get bitten by a mosquito. Mosquitoes hate garlic flavoring in your blood.

One of the best biological control of mosquitoes utilizes garlic oil emulsion. The active ingredient **allyl sulfide** is a known mosquito killer.

CHAPTER 12

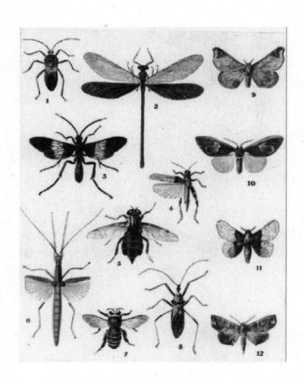

MISCELLANEOUS FLYING INSECTS

GNATS

Identification:

The adult gnat is about 1/8th inch long and is a grayish to black, with long legs and one pair of wings. The larvae or maggot is legless, white with a black head and about ¼ inch long. The larvae, is transparent and food in the gut can be observed through the body wall.

General Information:

Gnats, also called, fungus gnats or no-seeums are small, black, flying insects, similar to mosquitoes but much smaller. They don't buzz, and they don't bite humans, they're just an annoyance. Gnats often show up at the most inappropriate times, usually when you have company over for dinner and they will hover around your face and head. Gnats are drawn to light, so you may notice them first in bright rooms, near a window or on a mirror.

Gnats love fungus, and fungus loves moisture! Fungus and moisture can come from: Overripe peaches, bananas or tomatoes that have been sitting on your counter for a couple of days, softening potatoes stored under the cabinet for a few months or over-watered indoor potted plants.

Getting rid of the gnats is not that easy since gnats have a total life span of about four months and a female can produce as many as 300 eggs, in small batches, in fermenting or decaying organic matter. This means that if you notice that you have a gnat problem but don't know where it's coming from, several dozen females can each lay a few hundred eggs in the time.

HIDE THE PRODUCE

Keep fruits and vegetables in the refrigerator or throw them away if you aren't going to eat them and they're "past their prime." Don't over-water your plants since not all plants need to be watered weekly (or even monthly). Drain excess water from your plant containers a few minutes after you do water them. Poor drainage leads to plant rot, and both the moisture and the rot attract gnats.

Indoor gnats, which are also known as fungus gnats, are not only annoying. Their larvae feed on plant stems and roots and can cause considerable damage to seedlings and small plants. Luckily, you can get rid of these obnoxious little pests without using harsh chemicals.

Tips for preventing an Infestation
> Select healthy, bug-free plants for your home. Avoid the problem in the first place by keeping them away from your home.
> Isolate new plants from your existing houseplants and keep an eye out for signs of insects and diseases. If you don't notice any problems after two weeks you're in the clear to move the new plants to their permanent locations. This is a super easy way to prevent spreading problems to your healthy plants.
> Fungus gnats thrive in warm, moist environments. Allowing the soil to dry between watering kills gnat larvae and makes your plant less hospitable to adult gnats looking for a place to lay eggs.

Natural Solutions
> If your plant does develop a fungus gnat problem, the first thing you should do is isolate the affected plant so the problem does not spread to healthy plants.
> You can then trap and drown adult gnats by placing apple cider vinegar or wine in a small bowl near the problem plant.
> Remove 1/4 inch of topsoil and replace with sand. Fungus gnats prefer moist soil with a lot of organic matter and will avoid plants top dressed with sand.
> If you can't get the gnat population under control you will need to repot the plant in sterile potting soil. Gently remove as much of the original soil from around the roots and trim out any diseased or rotting roots prior to repotting in fresh soil.

BAIT & TRAP
Gnats are easy to trap and eliminate from your home using a vinegar and water trap. Just fill a small jar about ¾ full of water and add 1 tablespoon of apple cider vinegar. Place the jar on your kitchen counter near a ripening fruit or even better an overripe fruit. The gnats will investigate the jar and will be killed. To control the gnat larvae in the soil use a natural organic product called Neem™. Neem™ can be purchased in any garden shop.

MOTHS

General Information:

Never use mothballs in your closets: or even have them around the house, they are very poisonous and many pets have died from eating them and they have made hundreds of children very sick.

The adult moths are not the guilty ones when it comes to eating your clothes and leaving holes, however, it is their larvae; that actually do the damage. The female moth lays her eggs on fabric and if the fabric is moved will easily dislodge them. The larvae, uses any stains that contain food, urine or sweat to get their vitamins.

If you leave sweaty clothing in a closet the moths will find it and set up housekeeping and lay eggs.

MOTH ORCHID TO THE RESCUE

The moth orchid or Phalaenopsis is a wonderful indoor plant because of its beauty. It has pink and white blooms that resemble a flying moth. Moderate lighting conditions make this an easy plant to grow. Moth orchids need warm temperatures but shouldn't be in direct sunlight. Keep the soil slightly moist all the time. This plant will grow better if a small amount of water is kept in the planter. Replant moth orchids every one to two years.

I love moths!

THE FEMALE TEMPTATION ALWAYS WORKS

In the late spring, try hanging pheromone traps in the apple trees. They contain sticky paper and a capsule of the female hormone to attract the male. If you trap the males then they cannot fertilize the females and no eggs.

Let's have some fun

CABBAGE MOTHS

Identification:
These very small pale purple moths kill young sprouts.

TAR PAPER TRAPPER

Roofing felt or tarpaper can be very effective against cabbage moths. Make a slit in the paper and place it fully around the plant. This will stop the cabbage moths from laying eggs around the base of the cauliflower; cabbage, broccoli or Brussels sprout plants. The plant will open the slit more and more as it grows.

CLOTHES MOTHS

Identification:

The adult moths are gold colored with reddish-gold hairs on top of its head. Their wings have a span of about ½ inch with rows of golden hairs. They like the dark areas of closets and are not attracted by light.

Clothes moths have been of great economic importance in the past but are rarely a problem today. Almost all insect-related clothing damage results from carpet beetles. Most clothes moth problems probably originate on imported woolen goods that are infested.

The webbing clothes moth generally is light in color and small (about ½ inch from wing tip to wing tip). There are also reddish, fluffy hairs at the top.

Female moths rarely fly until they have laid most of their eggs, so simply killing flying moths will not control them. Although clothes moths are no longer abundant, do take preventive measures for more expensive woolen or fur articles. Dry cleaning kills all stages of the insect.

Place the articles in airtight containers to prevent re-infestation. Cedar chests and moth balls do repel some moths, but will not consistently kill existing insects.

PHERMONE MOTH TRAPS TO THE RESCUE

The key to trapping moths with a pheromone moth trap is that the pheromone lure makes male moths think a female moth is nearby. The male moth follows the scent of the moth pheromone lure, and gets caught in the moth trap's sticky glue board.

MOTHS ARE ATTRACTED TO YELLOW

To trap moths, mix 1 part molasses with 2 parts white vinegar and place in a yellow container to attract moths. Clean regularly.

INDIAN MEAL MOTH

 Indian meal moth is a small moth that will reside in your home for periods of about three weeks. Indian meal moths are small (wing spread of about 5/8 inch) and have a broad, grayish band on their bronze-colored wings. Adult moths do not feed, but immature meal moths are capable of developing on almost any dried food product in the home.

This general feeder has been found on grain, grain products, dried fruits, dried vegetables, seeds, nuts, graham crackers, powdered milk and dog food. There usually is some webbing on the infested product, which identifies the moth. Most household infestations originate from purchase of infested foods, but some movement of the moths from outdoors is possible in warm weather.

Control of Indian meal moths requires a thorough search of all dried food, including things like dog food and bird seed that often are overlooked.

The problem will more likely have developed in foods that have not been used for some time. Small, white worms and webbing indicate sources of the problem. Discard infested foods if possible and examine the remaining food to kill any insects that are left.

The easiest way to kill Indian meal moths is to place the food package in the freezer for several days. Warming the infested food in an oven or microwave also can kill insect eggs and larvae. Temperatures of 125^0F to 130^0F maintained for three hours should be adequate.

Because of the potential hazard of food contamination, natural methods are not for control of Indian meal moths in houses. After treating or discarding all potential food for the moth, keep everything stored in tight containers, outdoors, or in the refrigerator for a couple of weeks. After adult moths are no longer observed, food can be returned to storage areas because the source of the infestation should be eliminated.

MILLER MOTH (Army cutworm)

 Miller moths (Army Cutworms) are the most common nuisance moth. These moths can be extremely annoying when they get into homes and cars, but they do not breed indoors and die within a few days. Army cutworm moths, more commonly known as a Miller moth are about 1 inch long and variable in color. Usually they are gray or brown with two characteristic light spots on each wing.

Miller moths have an unusual life cycle. The caterpillar stage (larvae), overwinter in the soil, primarily in alfalfa and wheat fields. In the spring, they feed and complete their development, causing some economic damage to Crops. Moths usually emerge in May or June, with the majority emerging during a short period.

Very soon after emergence, the moths migrate to higher elevations in the mountains to feed on flowering plants, crossing the heavily populated areas of the state. During this migration, some of the moths move into buildings, causing nuisance problems. They stay in the high elevations until late summer to early fall, when they return to the plains. Fall migrations are smaller and less frequently observed. Upon returning to the high plains, the moths lay eggs in the soil. Larvae begin to feed before overwintering.

During periods of heavy moth flights, seal any openings, reduce evening lighting (which attracts them), and watch the door as you enter the house at night to prevent moth entrance.

The few that enter can be controlled with fly swatters or vacuum cleaners, or you can wait for the insects to die on their own in a few days.

The problem will decline as the continued migration moves the moths through the area to the mountains.

LIGHT 'EM UP!
Moths can be trapped by keeping a light suspended over a bucket of water during the night.

HIT THEM WITH A CHILI POD

To prepare a potent spray for moths, just follow the recipe. Grind up 2-3 handfuls of ripe hot peppers then allow them to soak in 1½ quart of water for 24 hours. Mix well, strain and add 3 quarts of water and 3-4 drops of Ivory liquid soap. Strain again and place in sprayer. This is meant for the outside, do not use in the home.
Before you spray all the plants check and be sure that the mixture is not too strong and will damage the plants.

THE VINEGAR TRAP
If you are curious as to what kind and how many moths you have, just place a shallow dish or bowl with white vinegar in it on the shelf to trap them.

WAX THOSE MOTHS
To make moth repellant paper, just mix together 4 parts of naphthalene and 8 parts of paraffin wax. Melt both together and paint it on a piece of thin white cardboard while the solution is still warm.

HERBS TO REPEL MOTHS
The following herbs can be placed in your closet to repel moths. Try using pennyroyal, wormwood, sage, santolina, lavender and mint.

CLOTHES DRYER WILL HELP
Just run your clothes through a warm cycle in the dryer to kill off any moths and eggs.

CEDAR CHEST NO HELP
Since cedar loses its oils and effectiveness after 2-3 years don't expect much protection from cedar for any extended length of time.

KILLING THE EGGS
If you are worried that you may have moth eggs in your woolens, just place the garment in a plastic bag and place it into the freezer for 24 hours. This will kill the eggs permanently.

WHOOOOSH
If you vacuum your clothes it will eliminate the problem, however, you should do the carpet as well while you are at it.

SKIP THE MOTHBALLS
You will never have a moth problem if you place one hedgeapple in every closet and change them about every 2 months. They work better than mothballs without the offensive odor.

GIVE THEM THE COLD SHOULDER
If you have a problem with moths it would be best to place the suspect garment into a plastic bag and freeze it at -4^0F for 7 days to kill off all eggs and larvae.

TURN UP THE HEAT
Heat can disinfect your clothing and kill all stages of moths. If the clothes are exposed to 122^0F for about 12 minutes or 140^0F for 1 minute that should do the trick and the clothes will be free of moth problems. Woolens, however, may not take the heat well and would be better in the cold.

MOTH REPELLER
The following ingredients will be needed:

All herbs may be purchased at a health food store

4	**Teaspoons of orris root powder**
1	**Cup of wormwood**
½	**Cup of lavender**

1 ½	Cup of yarrow
1	Cup of mint
10	Drops of oil of cloves
1	Cup cedar chips
10	Bay leaves
1	Tablespoon whole cloves
3	Clothespins or bag clip
	Stainless steel fork

Place the orris root powder in a small bowl and add the oil of cloves, then mix well (crush any lumps) with the stainless steel fork. Place all the other herbs in a brown paper bag and shake to mix. Add the oil and orris root to the bag and shake well to mix. Seal the bag with the clothespins or a bag clip and place the bag in a dry, cool location for 2 weeks.

After the herb mixture has mellowed, place a portion in a number of old socks and hang them up in the closets. You will never see another moth they will be fighting to get in next door.

A LITTLE HERE, A LITTLE THERE
Diatomaceous earth (DE) powder sprinkled in the corners of shelves. To make the DE more effective mix half pyrethrum and half DE.

HANG UP A SACHET OR TWO
Make a sachet to hang in the closets using dried mint, peppercorns, rosemary, lavender, bay leaves, whole cloves and cedar chips.

KILLING CLOTHES MOTHS
These moths are rarely seen since they only come out at night to feast on your clothing. They prefer protein-based fibers such as woolens, carpets and furs, which are a delicacy, pet hair and even your hairbrush hair.

SEND THE MOTHS TO THE CLEANERS
Dry cleaning will kill the moths as well as their larvae but will not stop other moths from attacking the clothes after you wear them and the chemicals wear off. After you dry clean them, place them into a plastic bag and place them into cold storage for safe keeping if you are not going to wear them for a while.

NATURAL ELIMINATION, TOGA PROTECTION

Place cedar chips in a porous cloth bag; then hang it in the closet. Moths do not like the aroma of cedar.

You can also place cedar oil on a piece of absorbent cloth and hang that in the closet. Cedar oil tends to work better since cedar chips will lose their effectiveness after several months and the oil dries out.

The Romans used oil of cedarwood placed on backs of parchment to get rid of the moths that were eating their togas.

PUT A SUNLAMP IN THE CLOSET

Moths hate the sunlight! If you bring your clothes outside when it's sunny for 30 minutes you will eliminate the problem. Best to give them a little beating to be sure they all fall off, including the larvae and eggs.

HERBS VS MOTHS

Make a sachet using a combination of rosemary, lavender and rose petals and hang in the closet. Dried lemon peels also do very well to deter moths just placed in the closet.

HOW TO PREVENT THEM

Meal moths are a problem when food is stored in moist areas or the humidity is high. They normally reside in grains or grain products such as cereals.
Exposed grains attract them.

They love cookie crumbs and especially dry dog food. Toasters are their favorite place to hangout especially when they are not used for a while.

They will come for a visit in loose grains that are purchased in markets or health food stores.

They will chew their way into cardboard boxes without any trouble. Best to inspect boxes every once in a while for holes.

If you have rodents that steal pet food the moths will find it. Be sure and vacuum all cracks and crevices in food areas regularly.

TRAPS WORK GREAT
Pheromone traps are available through garden or agricultural supply stores and work great. However, don't expect immediate results since it will take about 2 years to get rid of the pests.

DON'T CODDLE THEM
About mid-summer, scrape off an area on your apple trees and wrap the area with a piece of burlap (tie it down good). When the caterpillars climb up the tree to pupate they will hide in the burlap. The burlap can then be removed and discarded.

TRICHING CODDLING MOTHS
If the trichogramma wasp is released at the beginning of spring it will eliminate or at least, greatly reduce the infestation. Also, spraying with an Nc nematode solution in late winter will make a big difference.

WRAP THE TREES
In early summer you can wrap the tree trunks with a sticky paper or use Tanglefoot™ and trap the caterpillars as they go down the tree. Best to keep them wrapped all summer if you have this problem.

DIAMOND BACK MOTHS

WILD SUNFLOWER VS DIAMOND BACKS

To eliminate diamond back moths, just use wild sunflowers. Pound the leaves and extract the juice and use as a spray diluting the juice of 1½ pounds of leaves with 4 cups of water, strain and spray.

GYPSY MOTH

General Information:

These were brought to the United States by a Frenchman hoping to breed them with silkworms.

The northeastern Unites States is the hardest hit by gypsy moths attacking oak, birch, willow, linden, basswood and apple trees.

They tend to defoliate trees and have become a major pest. The adult moth hardly eats anything and the female cannot fly. The problem is, however, the larvae is a voracious eater and is very mobile. The larvae, eats at night, most of the time and is difficult to spot.

The female moth lays her eggs in large clusters that can reach up to 1,000 eggs, under stones or on tree trunks. You can even find the eggs on patio furniture or on your car. The caterpillars can travel as far as ½ mile on a strong current of wind. For some reason when the moth population, builds up too high, they are killed off by a virus.

NATURAL ENEMY
A ground beetle called **Calosoma frigidum** eats the caterpillar and hunts it down. The beetle has a black and greenish shine and is a night hunter. Another beetle that goes after the gypsy moth larvae is the **Calosoma sycophanta** and is another excellent caterpillar hunter.

CALL FOR REINFORCEMENTS
One of the best methods is to call for a professional if the infestation is a major one. If not spraying with Bt or Neem™ will solve the problem without the use of pesticides or harmful chemicals.

USE THE SEX ATTRACTANT
Pheromone traps have been very effective in catching these pests. They should be coated with Dispalure® or Gyplure® (Gyptol) to lure in the male moths.

JAPAN HAS THE ANSWER
Biological control of this moth has been very successful. The Japanese insect **Oercyrtus kuvamai** is now produced by the USDA labs and has been released in several states including New Jersey, New York and Pennsylvania. The female of this parasite lays her eggs, in the eggs of the moth and destroys the majority of them.

DRIVE THEM CUCKCOO
If you have a black-billed or yellow-billed cuckoo living in your neighborhood, it would be wise to entice them to your property since they are the number one bird predator for gypsy moths. There are many other birds that like the moth for dinner but the cuckoo has a real thing for them.

FOREST SERVICE USES NPV
The U.S. Forest Service uses a Nuclear Polyhedrosis Virus (NPV) and marketed as Gypchek®. This spray is non-toxic to all other insects and animals but kills the gypsy moth. The forest service recommends two spraying to eliminate the problem.

STALK BORER MOTHS

GUMMING THEM UP
If you have a problem with stalk borer moths all you have to do to control them is to grind some young leaves from the gum tree into a fine powder and use it for dusting. You can also crush some young leaves and allow them to soak in water and add a few drops of a liquid soap. Soak the leaves until the water is green then use the water as a spray. Best to use the spray when the moths are active and be sure and test an area of your plants since this mixture may burn the plants.

WASPS/YELLOW JACKETS/BEES

Identification:
The adult wasps are about 1-inches long and a bright yellow and black or sometimes have white and black patterned bands on the abdomen depending on the species. Their wings are clear and folded neatly back when not flying. The queens are twice the size of the workers.

General Information:
Wasps are beneficial insects that will not bother humans unless agitated. They consume insects that are pests and should only be eliminated from your immediate environment when they are pesky. Wasps are active in pollinating a number of crops including melons and spinach. Stay as far

from their nesting places as possible since they will attack you if you get too close. If you see more than one wasp in your home they may be making a nest and you need to investigate thoroughly.

Only 50 species of wasp out of about 2,500 species will sting you

Yellow jackets are wasps that are very aggressive and feed on sweets and meats. Their nests, usually only lasts for 1 year then the queen flies away to start another nest and the workers die off. A nest that is left over will not be used again.

REMOVING A STINGER
When you get stung by a bee, yellow jacket or wasp be sure that you do not pull the stinger out. When you try and remove it you may cause more venom to enter the body by squeezing it. The best method of removal is to use a credit card and scrape it off at an angle until it is dislodged. This will stop the poison from entering the skin.

HAIRSPRAY TO THE RESCUE
Hairspray will give you some temporary relief if you have bees or wasps hovering around your lawn eating area.

Just spray them with hairspray and it will coat their wings so that they can't fly. However, eventually it will wear off and you do not want to be around when it does.

LEAVE THE VIBRATOR IN THE HOUSE
Wasps and yellow jackets are very sensitive to vibrations such as running, yelling or any other fast movement anywhere in the vicinity of their nest. They will investigate and take action if they feel threatened.

ZIG-ZAG PATTERN
If bees are chasing you it is best to run in a zig-zag pattern to confuse them. This may save you from getting stung too many times.

WASPY FACTS
> Wasps will be attracted to protein foods and they love being a guest at barbecues
> A dish of pet food outside will attract them.
> Wasps imprint foods and even when they are removed they will return to that same area.
> In late summer and early fall wasps like sweets and are more aggressive.
> If you step on a wasp and kill it they release a pheromone, which attracts other wasps.
> Rotting fruit will attract wasps.
> Bright clothing attracts wasps.
> Perfumes should not be worn if wasps are present in the area.
> Wasps are attracted by yellow light.
> Remove nests at night only. Place a cloth over the entire nest and seal it.
> Burning a nest will make them very mad at you.

DON'T USE A BRIGHT LIGHT

If you decide to eliminate the wasp or yellow jackets nest at night when they are dormant, be sure that you do not use a flashlight or cast a shadow on the nest. Best to place some red cellophane paper over the lens since red light does not bother them.

PUT THEM IN A FISHBOWL

If you locate a nest on the ground, try covering it with a large glass bowl and allow it to remain for 2 weeks to kill off the nest.

ICE THEM

Placing dry ice around a ground nest will eliminate the nest by putting carbon dioxide gas into the nest. The CO_2 is heavier than air and will enter a nest that is partially underground.

INSULATE THEIR NEST

If you inject aerosol foam insulation into their nest at night (using a red light) this will eliminate the nest. This method is frequently used in tree cavities or logs.

BAIT THEM

Sweet attractive bait can be prepared by using a 5% food-grade DE or sodium borate (borax) and honey or jelly. Form small balls and leave it in areas that they frequent.

Make sure it is not near any pets or children since it is not safe for them. They also love soda cans that are left around by the kids.

USE A FIRE EXTINGUISHER
CO_2 fire extinguishers work great for getting rid of stinging insect nests. Use it at night for the best results.

CALL FOR PEPE LE PEW
Yellow jackets frequently make their nest in the ground. There are two animals that love to dig up these nests; they are skunks and raccoons. They will prey on the yellow jackets when they can find them.

BOTTLED YELLOW JACKETS
If you place some sweet soda pop in a tall plastic soda bottle and leave it out the yellow jackets will go in get confused and will not be able to get out. A piece of fresh liver or ham placed away from your area helps as well.

WHITEFLIES

Identification:

These are moth-like flies that are milky white and covered with a waxy powder. Their eggs are laid on the underneath side of the leaves. The eggs are yellow and will turn to gray as they mature. If you shake a plant that you think has been infested with whiteflies, these tiny moth-like bugs will fly up from underneath the leaves. They look like **"flying dandruff"** and multiply very quickly.

General Information:
Whiteflies excrete sticky honeydew that will also damage a healthy plant. These are a real pest in greenhouses or on indoor plants since they like warm, sheltered areas. They are more prevalent in the southern United States. They are not fussy eaters and will damage almost any plant, especially if a plant is deficient in magnesium and phosphorus.

DOCTORS ANSWER TO WHITEFLIES
Try using 10 tablespoons of Dr. Bronner's Peppermint Soap™ to 1 gallon of water and add 1 tablespoon of pyrethrum and 1 tablespoon of sunflower oil to the mixture. This spray is usually only used for a serious infestation. For a minor infestation use Jungle Rain™.

Remember if you don't control the ant population you can't control the whiteflies since their favorite food supply comes from aphids, which are herded by ants and produce honeydew.

WHITEFLIES LOVE YELLOW

Whiteflies will damage your tomato plants unless you protect the plant. All you have to do is to place a small can (vegetable can) that has been painted yellow over the top of the stake that supports the tomato plant then place a small baggie over the can and rub Vaseline® on the baggie. This will eliminate the whitefly problem.

BIO-CONTROL TO THE RESCUE

The parasite *Encarsia formosa* will attack the larval stage of the bug and eliminate the problem. Ladybugs and lacewings find them a tempting dish to dine on.

WHOOOOOSH

If you have a portable hand vacuum it will come in handy. Just vacuum the plant and you will eliminate the whiteflies. Be sure that the vacuum is not too powerful that it will damage the plant when you try this.

COLD KILLS THEM

In the north, freezing temperatures will kill greenhouse and silverleaf whiteflies.

ISOLATION IS A MUST

Whenever you bring new plants home, be sure and quarantine them for a few weeks to be sure they are not infested.

CHAPTER 13

MISCELLANEOUS INSECT PESTS

BED BUGS

What Are Bed Bugs?

General Information:

Bed bugs are insects of the order Hemiptera, the true bugs. Like all insects bed bugs have six legs. They are wingless insects but do develop wing pads. Bed bugs have piercing sucking mouthparts. Their needle like proboscis is inserted into the host to take a blood meal. Bed bugs feed exclusively on blood. Entomologists believe that bed bugs are evolved from nest parasites that fed on cave nesting birds and bats. When early man or hominids became cave dwellers bed bugs began to feed on man. Bed bugs develop from eggs through gradual metamorphosis where the immature bed bugs resemble the adults. The common bed bug is the most troublesome bed bug encountered within human dwellings. The scientific name of this pest is *Cimex lectularius Linneaus*.

Bed bugs do not fly and while their preferred primary hours of activity are from approximately midnight to about five in the morning, bed bugs may adapt to the hours of their host. Bed bugs do not fly and crawl from their hiding places to take a blood meal from their sleeping hosts.

WHERE DO BED BUGS COME FROM & HISTORY

The short answer is that bed bugs come from their parental bed bugs. However, bed bugs are transported from place to place by man and our travel habits. Bed bugs are efficient hitchhikers and are usually inadvertently picked up by people who visit places where bed bugs are.

Bed bug experts tell us that the increase in international travel these past many years has helped bed bugs cross borders and travel broadly across the globe. Business, travelers, vacation travelers, shipping, immigration and other factors have all served to facilitate the spread of bed bugs.

Bed bugs have been known as human parasites for thousands of years and over millions of years bed bugs have evolved as nest parasites living in the nests of birds and the roosts of bats.

Bed bugs, however, have learned to adapt to the human environment and live in our homes and mainly our mattresses.

Before the mid-twentieth century, bed bugs were a very common annoyance and according to a historical report by the United Kingdom, in 1933 it was thought that all the houses had some degree of bed bug infestation.

Bed bugs became a serious problem during World War II. In fact, General MacArthur made a comment that bed bugs are the "greatest nuisance insect problem at all military bases in the United States. However, with the arrival of powerful pesticides, especially DDT in the 1940s, bed bugs were almost eradicated in Western countries.

Bed bugs may have originated in the Middle East, in caves inhabited by bats and humans thousands of years ago. Bed bugs were even mentioned in ancient Greece writings as early as 400 BC and were also mentioned by Aristotle. Pliny's Natural History book that was first published around 77 AD in Rome, stated that "bed bugs had medicinal value in treating ailments" such as snake bites and ear infections.

This belief in the medicinal use of bed bugs curative properties persisted until the 18th century, when they were recommended for use in the treatment of hysteria. Bed bugs were also mentioned in Germany during the 11th century and in France in the 13th century.

They were mentioned in writings in England in 1583, though they remained relatively rare in England until 1670 when they became more of a pest. It was thought that in the 18th century bed bugs were brought to London with supplies of wood to rebuild the city after the Great Fire of London in 1666.

The traditional methods of that time to repel and/or kill bed bugs included the use of plants, fungi and insects (or their extracts), as well as black pepper, eucalyptus oil, henna, fly agaric, tobacco, heated oil of turpentine, wild mint, narrow-leaved pepperwort, bayberry, geranium, the herb and seeds of cannabis, maple or European cranberry bush and masked hunter bugs.

During the mid-19th century, smoke from peat fires was used as well as dust from grain storage. Other deterrents used for centuries included, plant ash, lime, dolomite, certain types of soil, and diatomaceous earth (DE), which has seen a revival as a nontoxic (when in food grade form) residual pesticide for bed bug control. Insects exposed to diatomaceous earth may take several days to die as the tiny spicules go deeper and deeper into their bodies.

One of the more interesting methods of ridding a bed of bed bugs was to place basket-work panels around beds then shaken out in the morning. This method was especially popular in the United Kingdom and France in the 19th century. Another favorite method was to scatter leaves of plants that had microscopic hooked hairs around the bed at night then sweeping them up every morning and burning them. This was also popular in southern Rhodesia and in the Balkans.

Why Are Bed Bugs a Problem Now?
By the late 1960s bed bugs were nearly eradicated from the United States. They were still here but in such low numbers that nearly no pest professionals were called about bed bugs. Veteran pest professionals report that bed bugs were rather easy to take care of years ago. This was so because there were many effective pesticides available to kill bed bugs with and the techniques used were more suited to kill bed bugs then.

Pest professionals report that calls about bed bug infestations first began in the early to mid-1990s. These calls came in from major cities and with time became more and more frequent. In subsequent years pest management professional associations have reported that the incidence of bed bugs has continued to grow each year. While bed bug calls would be viewed as uncommon by most by the year 2000, by 2010 the majority of pest control companies are fielding bed bug related calls on a regular basis.

In addition to this, while bed bugs have been in the news in the recent past the general lack of public awareness has contributed to their continued recent resurgence as a pest.

Bed Bug Development, Recognition & Identification

Bed bugs hatch from eggs and develop to adults. Bed bug eggs are oblong cylindrical shaped eggs with one end rounded and the other end with a flattened round hatch. They appear pearly white and are about one millimeter in length. The immature bed bug emerges from the round flat hatch like end which flips open when the egg hatches. This round flat cover may remain attached or may fall off during the hatching process. Once the immature bed bug has emerged from the egg the empty egg appears hollow or empty and may take on a yellowish translucent appearance.

The newly hatched immature bed bug will be a translucent yellowish in color and slightly larger than the egg it emerged from. Immature bed bugs are called instars by entomologists. Bed bugs go through five instar stages prior to becoming adults. An immature bed bug must take a blood meal in order to molt to the next instar stage of development. A freshly fed immature bed bug will take on a bright red color. As bed bugs get older they begin to take on a darker color with adults having a rusty red appearance.

Once an immature bed bug takes a blood meal it retreats back to its harborage or hiding place to digest and continue the development process. After the food resource has been sufficiently digested the immature bed bug molts into the next stage of development. As a result of the molting process the developing bed bug sheds its skin and emerges as a larger bed bug with a yellowish translucent appearance. The bed bug abdomen may contain a small dark area which is the remainder of the previous meal.

This feeding, hiding, development, molting process repeats itself five times as the immature bed bug develops through the five instar stages to become an adult reproductive bed bug.

Bed Bug Feeding

Bed bugs feed exclusively on blood. Developing bed bugs must take a blood meal in order to successfully grow to the next level of development and adult bed bugs must take a blood meal in order to be able to successfully reproduce. Generally, bed bugs spend the significant majority of their time hiding. They are aptly named as they hide on or near a bed and emerge to feed when their host is sleeping.

Generally the host does not feel a bed bug bite. Bed bugs prefer to not climb on a host to feed if it can be avoided. Doing so may alert the host should a bed bug inadvertently bump into a hair as it crawls. Bed bug bites may appear to be in a line because a number of bed bugs may be lined along the host's body as they rest on the bed or sheet while feeding. It is a myth that bed bugs bite in a line along a blood vessel. It is also a myth that bed bug bites appear in groups of three.

To feed, a bed bug raises its rear and lowers its head whilst forcing its needle like mouthparts into the host's skin. The mouthparts are so fine that the sleeping host normally will not feel the insertion. While this is occurring the bed bug simultaneously injects an anticoagulant and antihistamine so that the host's blood flows freely and area is numbed so the host does not feel the bite occur. While a bed bug may move to another suitable feeding spot they usually feed in one spot until fully engorged.

Bed bugs have piercing sucking mouthparts and pierce the skin of its host with a structure called a stylet. Similar to a mosquito's mouthparts, the stylet is composed of the maxillae and mandibles, which have been modified into elongated shapes. Their right and left maxillae are attached at their midline with a section at the centerline forming a large food canal as well as a smaller salivary canal.

The entire maxillary and mandibular bundle is capable of penetrating the skin. However, the tips of the right and left maxillary stylets are not similar: the right is hook-like and curved, while the left is straight. The right and left mandibular stylets extend along the outside of their maxillary stylets and never reach near the tip of the fused maxillary stylets.

The stylets are stored in the labium and during feeding they are released from the groove as the jointed labium is bent out of the way. The tip never enters the wound. The mandibular stylet tip has small teeth and by alternately moving the stylets back and forth, the bed bug is capable of cutting a path through tissue to allow the maxillary bundle to reach an acceptable sized blood vessel.

Feeding time may vary from about three minutes up to about ten minutes per feeding depending upon the individual bed bug. Feeding times may vary for a variety of reasons but the bed bug will grow many times its size and weight when fully engorged from feeding.

The younger the individual bed bug the more times its original size it will grow from feeding. Immature bed bugs may grow as many as six times their original size while adults may grow almost three times their original size after feeding.

After feeding bed bugs retreat back to their hiding places or harborage. Along the way and in the harborage areas bed bugs will excrete fecal matter. This fecal matter emerges from the bed bug as a dark liquid which very much appears as an ink droplet. These droplets vary in size with the individual bed bug and appear dark or nearly black in color. The appearance of these fecal stains may vary depending upon the porosity of the surface upon which the fecal droplet is deposited.

Fecal stains are a telltale sign of a bed bug infestation and may appear as small as a pepper like black dot up to a larger black spot about the size of a BB. Fecal liquid deposited on a sheet or mattress fabric may spread further than fecal liquid deposited on a wood or metal bed frame. Fecal stains may appear in great number and concentration in advanced or long established infestations.

Generally speaking bed bugs may be recognized by their characteristic rusty red color, oval round shape and flattened body. Adult bed bugs are about one quarter to five sixteenths of an inch long. Immature bed bugs range in size from about one millimeter or about one twenty fifth of an inch long up to adult size.

Bites and Detecting Bed Bugs

Bed bugs are difficult to find and detect but their presence may be determined by the outward or telltale signs they leave behind. Telltale signs of bed bug infestation include the presence of fecal stains, bed bug egg, shed skins, live bed bugs and carcasses. It cannot be determined if bed bugs are actually present based upon the presence or symptoms of bite evidence alone.

It is estimated that from about thirty to thirty five percent of the population may not react to bed bug bites at all. In additional to this, there may be some folks who are not as attractive to bed bugs as are others. This means that there may be some folks who are either not bitten or simply may not yet know that they being bitten.

Reaction to bed bug bites may vary by individual and usually does. Some people may have severe reactions while others may have a minor reaction. Still, others may be bitten and display no reaction at all. And, there are many stimuli to which a bite like reaction may result. For these reasons reliance upon bite reaction alone is not a dependable indicator of the presence of bed bugs and bed bug activity.

Bed Bug Inspection
Ranging in size from as small as one millimeter up to just about five millimeters, bed bugs are capable of hiding in the smallest of places and cracks and crevices. While we know that bed bugs may prefer to harbor or hide nearby their potential hosts however, it is also possible that bed bugs may crawl or travel undetected and finds their way into many areas within a home away from the bed.

When inspecting for the presence of bed bugs we need to search those areas where bed bugs are commonly found including but not limited to: the mattress, box spring, internal box spring frame, bed frame, head board, foot board, night stand, the couch, couch frame, upholstered chairs, chair frames, other furniture, wall hangings, wall outlets and utility penetrations.

When inspecting for bed bugs it is wise to use a good flashlight such as an LED type flashlight that provides suitably bright light. And, because bed bugs are so small, using a magnifying glass may enhance your ability to find bed bugs and your inspection results.

When conducting bed bug inspections we are looking for the telltale signs of bed bugs as previously mentioned. One of the easiest of the telltale signs of bed bugs to find are fecal stains. These fecal stains may be deposited on various surfaces by bed bugs where they crawl and harbor. Bed bug fecal material is evacuated from the bed bug anus as a dark ink like looking liquid. These dry deposits may run or smear when cleaned or touched. In severe infestations the wall and ceiling junction may appear to be badly stained such that residents of these infested homes think that these stains are mold growing on the wall. However, these areas are in fact badly stained by bed bug fecal matter.

Bed bugs eggs may be present and found during an inspection but may be difficult to find or detect sue to their small size at just one millimeter long. Viable eggs are pearly white in color.

Hatched empty eggs may take on a yellowish color and non-viable eggs, that are those eggs that have died without hatching, take on a yellow to darkened yellowish brown color. The manipulation of a flashlight at a low angle may help to reveal eggs during an inspection as the glossy egg surface may reflect the light making the eggs more readily detectable.

Shed skins are also a telltale sign of bed bug infestation. These shed skins take on a translucent yellowish color and may be readily seen once the inspector has gained experience. From a distance, some shed skins may appear to be live bed bugs but closer inspection will quickly reveal that they are just hollow husks.

The presence of live bed bugs may be difficult to find and confirm in low level infestations because bed bugs are crypto-biotic creatures that are best served by remaining hidden from their hosts. At the early stages of an infestation it may take a significant amount of inspection time to find just one bed bug present. Bed bug carcasses may be found in similar areas as are live bed bugs. This is especially so when an infestation has become more advanced or mature.

Bed Bug Facts

> - Bed bugs are small, oval-shaped insects
> - All stages of bed bugs feed exclusively on blood.
> - The common bed bug, *Cimex lectularius*, prefers to feed on humans but may feed on other animals as well.
> - Bed bugs hatch from an egg and go through five instars or stages to become an adult.
> - Bed bugs develop through gradual metamorphosis.
> - Immature bed bugs molt to develop into the next stage of development.
> - Bed bugs must take a blood mea in order to develop to the next stage of development.
> - Under ideal conditions an adult bed bug may survive up to eighteen months without feeding.
> - Newly hatched first instar bed bugs may expire in about ten to fourteen days without feeding.
> - Bed bugs can reside in any area of the home and can live in tiny cracks in furniture as well as on textiles and upholstered furniture.
> - Bed bugs tend to hide most where people sleep or rest.

- Bed bugs are most active at night.
- While bed bugs are most active at night they can feed on a sleeping or resting host at any time during the day and will adapt to their host's daily routine as needed.
- Bed bugs may bite any area of the body but the face, neck, hands, arms and legs are common sites for bedbug bites.
- Not every person reacts to bed bug bites.
- A bed bug bites are painless and may go unnoticed for a period of time.
- Small, flat, or raised bumps on the skin are the most common sign; redness, swelling, and itching commonly occur.
- The necessity of treatment for bed bug bites is dependent on the individual reaction. In severe cases, medical care may be indicated.

Bed Bug Biology

An adult bed bug female may lay up to as many as twelve to eighteen eggs per day. These eggs are coated with a sticky substance. When this substance dries the eggs become glued in place where deposited. Eggs hatch in from three to ten days depending upon local conditions. Hatching may take longer under cooler conditions.

Depending upon where the egg was deposited, the newly emerged first instar nymph bed bug must find a suitable hiding place and host from which it will feed. To assure their survival first instar nymphs must feed within about two weeks or may perish. Immature bed bugs are translucent yellowish in color but take on a red color upon feeding.

A first instar nymph is a small bed bug being just about one and a half millimeter long or about one twenty fifth of an inch long. When fully engorged from a blood meal these tiny bed bugs may grow up to about six times their original size. To accommodate this growth the abdomen enlarges many times its size as it fills with blood. When the meal is completed the bed bug simply stops feeding and crawls off to hide in a suitable harborage.

Whilst hiding, the bed bug digests its meal and utilizes the food resources to fuel its development. Entomologists tell us that much of the food resource is used up by the development, metamorphosis and molting process.

Once development has been completed the first instar is ready to molt and shed its skin to become a second instar bed bug nymph. After the development has been completed and the skin is shed through molting the cycle repeats itself and emerged bed bug is now in need of its next blood meal. The freshly molted immature bed bug returns to the yellowish color until it feeds again.

Immature bed bugs or nymphs must go through this development process five times in order to become mature reproductive adult bed bugs. Adult bed bugs may reach from 5 mm to7 mm in length. When viewed from the side bed bugs are built very flat which enables them to hide in small places. Adult bed bugs are rusty red in color, appearing more reddish after feeding on a blood meal.

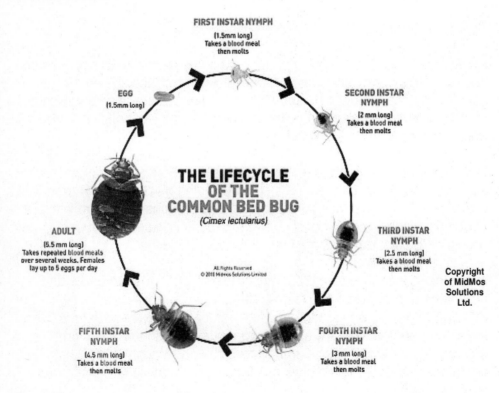

FIRST INSTAR NYMPH
(1.5mm long)
Takes a blood meal
then molts

EGG
(1.5mm long)

SECOND INSTAR NYMPH
(2 mm long)
Takes a blood meal
then molts

THE LIFECYCLE
OF THE
COMMON BED BUG
(Cimex lectularius)

All Rights Reserved
© 2018 Midmos Solutions Limited

THIRD INSTAR NYMPH
(2.5 mm long)
Takes a blood meal
then molts

ADULT
(5.5 mm long)
Takes repeated blood meals over several weeks. Females lay up to 5 eggs per day

FIFTH INSTAR NYMPH
(4.5 mm long)
Takes a blood meal
then molts

FOURTH INSTAR NYMPH
(3 mm long)
Takes a blood meal
then molts

Bed bugs can live for months and if conditions are ideal, can live for over a year without feeding, they can also be found in vacant homes and apartments waiting for these locations to be inhabited again.

Bed bugs are most active at night and may bite any exposed areas of skin while an individual is sleeping.

Bed bugs are active at night and most active between midnight and about five in the morning. Some experts are researching the various sleep phases with regard to bite activity and indications are that most biting occurs during REM (rapid eye movement associated with deep sleep and dreaming). However, bed bugs may feed at any time of day or night if they are hungry and a suitable host is available.

Bed bugs are not interdependent upon each other except for mating purposes. They aggregate in populations but do not live in colonies. In the United States bed bugs were very common in the early 1900s, through the World War II era and into the 1960s being found in homes, hotels, furniture and boardinghouses. Bed bugs were virtually eliminated with the use of pesticides including DDT, cyanide and other pesticides that are no longer used today. Bed bugs have been making resurgence in the United States since the 1990s and have become a global pest since about 2000.

However, since the mid-1990s bed bug infestations have come back with a vengeance for reasons which are not clear, but contributing factors may be our complacency regarding the insect, increased resistance to pesticides, changes in pest management methodologies and increased international travel. There is a current wave of bed bug infestations all across North America, which has spawned an industry for bed bug prevention, eradication and the reporting of infestations. The most significant organization is the **National Bed Bug Resource Authority**.

NATURAL ENEMIES
Bed bugs do have some natural enemies; however, you probably do not want them in your home. These include the masked hunter (also known as "masked bed bug hunter"), cockroaches; most species of ants, spiders, predatory beetles, mites, millipedes and centipedes. The Pharaoh ant's venom is lethal to bed bugs

Biological pest control by other insects is not very practical for eliminating bed bugs from human dwellings however.

WHAT YOU SHOULD LOOK FOR
One of the easiest things to identify is bed bug fecal matter, which sometimes looks like mold, blood stains on sheets, castings of nymph growth or a peculiar odor. Since they may be in different stages during your investigation from larva to one of the 5 stages of growth, don't be discouraged.

If a person is getting bit by bed bugs and it is probably safe to assume that the bed bugs will be found in the bedroom where the person sleeps or relaxes, which could include the den or family room. Never stop your inspection thinking that you will find them only in the bedroom. Keep searching and inspect every room carefully as if you suspect them to be everywhere. Remember, that they are "hitchhikers" and will use clothing, shoes and just about anything they can to move easily from room to room.

Start with the bed:
1. The first thing you should do is to check out the bed. Pull back the blanket or comforter, lift the bottom sheet away from the corners of the bed and check the seams thoroughly. Open the seam as wide as you can to see deep into the crevice. Use a powerful flashlight and magnifying glass to check close. Look for possible signs of adults, fecal matter, castings of nymphs and possibly white larva (eggs).

2. If you locate anything, that even slightly resembles bed bugs or evidence of them you will need to check the entire mattress from top to bottom and all around the outer perimeter. Once you have completed an inspection of the upper mattress, remove the top mattress and set it aside.

3. Next examine the box spring, corners and seams in the same method. Especially, search where the fabric is attached to the box spring, usually with staples. Remove the box spring and then check the frame.

4. Don't forget to check the mattress tag and plastic protectors around the edges since this a favorite hiding place of bed bugs.

5. Move on to the headboard and check all areas of the wood, metal or fabric for very small black spots, which are usually smaller than the size of poppy seeds. Examine behind the headboard and the feet for, translucent skins, eggs or actual bed bugs. Remember bed bug spots (fecal matter) will be dark brown to black and the eggs may stick to the surface. If you spot something, try taking a moist paper towel and wiping the spot to see if it smears and if it does, it may be fecal matter.

6. Be sure and continue to look at the night stands, radios, telephones, backs of mirrors and dressers alongside the bed. You need to remove all drawers and contents. Check all corners and especially the seams inside and out and even underneath.

7. Remove any pictures or wall hangings near or alongside the bed then examine all corners, seams and folds of the items. Best to use a magnifying glass since even the most trained inspectors find it difficult to find eggs or nymphs.

8. Check any luggage when you arrive home from a trip, including the contents.

9. Be sure and check the wall sockets by removing plates, spaces around the edges of the carpet, baseboards, drapery folds, artificial flowers and pots.

10. If you have a chair or dressing stool, turn it over and remove the cushion then check all the seams. If you locate any bed bugs or signs of bed bugs, remove the legs from the furniture and check the areas. Rough surfaces or raw unfinished wood are favorite hideouts of bed bugs but can be found just about anywhere.

11. Don't stop with the bedroom and continue your inspection with every bedroom and make notations for every room. Be sure and check any room that is adjacent to the bedrooms and continue with your inspection thoroughly.

Always remember single homes vs. apartments. When bed bugs are found in a single family home and it is isolated from the home next door, chances are the infestation will not affect the neighbor (unless you are close to your neighbor and visit each other often).

Apartments are another story and it is safe to assume that the bed bugs have moved into the walls and crawl spaces and will travel to nearby apartments above, below, next to and across very easily. Your apartment neighbors need to be notified if bed bugs are found.

ACCURATE IDENTIFICATION

If you locate any findings, use sticky tape or glass bottle to contain your finding. Label where you found the suspect material and if it is alive capture your findings for proper identification, making notations on an inspection ledger.

Use a camera to document any bed bugs or findings and note location of each picture. These pictures will be useful especially if you are renting the property.

> - If you do see them, be sure and follow them to where they are living since you need to eliminate their home base and all their family members.
> - You need the Sherlock's Holmes approach and use a big magnifying glass and look for very small, thin, flat beetle-like insects on your mattress or couches.
> - A bed bug that has just had a blood meal and is full of blood is dark red and will actually ooze blood if you squeeze them. Resources to the problem will be found at www.nbbra.org

If you capture a bed bug, you need to positively identify it since other insects look similar. You may possibly be able to do this yourself, but if you aren't sure you can check with your local County Health Department or University Extension Agent. Be sure and use a sealable container or zip lock plastic bag to trap bugs near your sleeping areas.

There have been no known cases of the transmission of any infectious disease that have been reported, however, bed bugs are known to carry at least 28 different human pathogens. It also has been found that bed bugs may be able to transmit Hepatitis B, since the virus has been found in bed bug droppings. Bacterial infections are also possible if the bite creates an open sore, which could be the result of itching then scratching.

CLEAN UP THE CLUTTER

Be sure and never leave any clutter where bed bugs can hide such as unused luggage, furniture, clothing and bedside clutter. It is also common for bed bugs to make a home near animals that have nested within a dwelling, such as bats, birds or rodents. The eggs of bed bugs can be found in similar locations where the bed bugs themselves are found and will be attached to surfaces by a sticky substance they excrete.

DISPOSE OF BED BUG INFECTED ITEMS SAFELY

The very first thing that people do when they find out they have bed bugs is panic and throw things out of their homes. What they don't realize is that by doing this it may cause more harm than good. To make sure that your infested items do not become a source of contamination for others, items must be disposed of in a responsible way. Some states now fine people for leaving bed bug infested items on the curb.

If you have any bed bug contaminated items **_DO NOT_** just toss items into a garbage can or on the street or alley. Most people are grossed out by the very thought of bed bugs and tend to want to throw everything away. This is unnecessary and could possibly make the problem worse. When you disturb bed bugs and carry items through the home, bed bugs can fall off the item causing them to spread throughout the home to uninfected areas.

Also, discarded items are frequently picked up by other people (maybe even your next door neighbor), spreading the problem to new areas. If you must discard an item it must be wrapped and sealed in plastic so that the bed bugs cannot drop off during transport.

DO NOT leave infected items curbside as they can be picked up by unsuspecting people.
DO NOT remain in denial about bed bugs if you discover that you have them. If you should experience bed bugs, or suspect that you have them, let people know that you have them so that they do not come over and pick up a few to take home with them.
_DO_ pay attention to where you go and how you place your purses, luggage, backpacks or anything that could possibly "pick up" the hitch hikers.

NO VISITORS
You will be doing friends or neighbors a great service telling them **NOT** to come over until you have the problem taken care of. If your friends have been to your home and then you discover you have bed bugs call them immediately!

NOTE:
While moving the furniture through the home, bed bugs can fall off on an area where it is clear of bed bugs thus creating a new infestation area. Innocent people may become victims to bed bugs when they see a perfectly good mattress, dresser or couch, grab it up and take it home with them only to cause an infestation in their own homes.

Depending on the extent of the infestation people need to recognize that it is not always necessary to throw out items because they can be treated and replacement cost is very high. Some bed bug specialists are capable of decontaminating an infestation.

If you have infested furniture follow the **National Bed Bug Research Authority** www.nbbra.org advice in safe and effective treatments.

If you insist on getting rid of the items that are infested, make sure that they are 100% properly contained and wrapped in plastic, taped and boldly marked *CAUTION - BED BUG INFESTED before* you move them through your home or out on to your sidewalk or lawn for proper disposal.

If you do call a disposal company to remove infested items let them know that what they are picking up is infested with bed bugs.

What NOT to do:
Think *safety first and foremost* when seeking solutions for bed bug elimination. Mistakes lead to re-contamination and possible damage to you or your home.
DO NOT use excess amounts of foggers or aerosol type of insecticides. These can cause explosions and fires!
DO NOT place items in the microwave – Again extremely dangerous!
DO NOT use a conventional oven – FIRE RISK!
DO NOT use a hair dryer. This will blow them all over the place!

DO NOT Send your infested clothing to a dry cleaner! You could spread the infestation to others.

Please act responsibly by identifying items and spreading the word about bed bugs.

THEY LOVE TO BE A STOWAWAY
Used furniture needs to be checked and cleaned thoroughly before placing it in your home. They may also be hiding in a suitcase, pillow or other item that may be carried on a trip or into a hotel room. They can survive for many months without feeding and if you wake them with a move they will become active and go looking for a meal. They can even go from apartment to apartment through small crevices in the walls.

HERE A BITE, THERE A BITE
If you are complaining of a bite, you should suspect bed bugs, especially since they only infest a small area of a house or apartment and usually the bedroom. If you wake up with a bite or two in the morning, you had better start investigating the bed area and take action immediately. They can be anywhere in the bedroom such as the springs, baseboard, mattress, box spring, wicker furniture, behind cove molding or even in the laundry.

SCRUB-A-DUB, DUB
If you do identify a problem, start cleaning immediately. Scrub all infested area that are suspect with a stiff brush to dislodge any eggs and use a vacuum cleaner to clean up the area. Remove drawers and clean inside the tracks, which is one of their hiding places. Dismantle the bed frame to expose any hiding areas. Once you clean the mattress and box spring, enclose them is a special cover to stop the bugs from getting back in. Be sure that the blankets do not touch the floor.

SURVIVING COLD CLIMATES
Prolonged exposure to sub-freezing temperatures is necessary to successfully destroy 100% of bed bugs treated. Professionals report that infested items must remain frozen for several weeks in order to deliver 100% control.

SEARCH & DESTROY

If you think that you have a problem but are not sure, just use a flashlight at night and search the area. You can find out where they are and eliminate their home base.

THEY DON'T LIKE HEAT

Bed bugs do not like excessive heat. Experts report that 122^0F for about one minute will kill all life stages of bed bugs. Professionals use steam and heat treatments to kill bed bugs. Steam cleaning a mattress will kill bed bugs on contact.

TREAT THE MATTRESS

One solution is to treat the seams, folds and especially the button areas if your mattress has some.

Special thanks to Paul J. Bello, Entomologist for assistance with the bed bug information.

For Additional Bed Bug Information:
NBBRA- National Bed Bug Resource Authority
6 Hutton Centre Dr. # 600 Santa Ana, CA 92705
www.nbbra.org   Email to info@nbbra.org 1-888-9-NOBEDBUGS

BLACKBERRY PSYLLID

General Information:

 This is a jumping pest that will injure cultivated plants, but is usually found on wild blackberries. The adult is yellow-brown and has three yellow bands on each wing. They will lay their eggs on the stems of the leaves and young shoots. The nymphs and adults will puncture the leaves and stems resulting in stunted or distorted growth patterns. Ladybugs like to feast on these bugs.

DUST THEM
A good dusting with diatomaceous earth (DE) will eliminate these pests if they do leave the blackberry patch and head for your garden.

CABBAGE ROOT MAGGOT

General Information:
These are legless white maggots that have a black hook on their heads and prefer to feed on cabbage, radish, turnip, broccoli and cauliflower roots.

They will kill a plant if not stopped and are capable of producing two generations every year. Their eggs are laid in the soil and the adult flies hatch in early spring.

WORMS WIN AGAIN
One of the best methods of eradication is to use Nc nematodes when planting in seed furrows or around areas that you are transplanting. You can also use soap and lime spray to stop them from laying eggs.

CELERY LEAFTIER

General Information:

Found throughout North America this bug will do a lot of damage to vegetables and ornamentals. They are pale green in color and have a white stripe running down their back.

Eventually as they mature they will turn yellow.

The worms will eat holes in the leaves and stalks and will fold the leaves together and tie them with their web material. Their eggs look like fish scales and are laid on the underneath side of leaves.

BUG ELIMINATION

There are a number of methods of eliminating these bugs that work well. These include handpicking, using Bt and if the infestation is really bad you will have to use pyrethrum.

Pyrethrum is a natural botanical poison that will make the larvae so sick that they will leave their webs, pack up and head for greener, safer pastures.

CENTIPEDES

General Information:

These creepy crawlers can actually have as many as 346 legs and sometimes as few as 30, which will depend on the species. They have a pair of claws that are venomous and can paralyze their victims. These are good to have around the garden, (but will occasionally frequent the house) since they eat snails, slugs, grasshoppers and many other pests. When you find them in the basement or house they are looking for cockroaches, flies and moths.

The very small centipede-looking bug, that you may see in your garden resembles a white centipede but are really "symphylan." These can do a great deal of damage to plants and are mainly found in greenhouses in the southwestern states. There is also a species called the "house centipede."

The house centipede is believed to have originated in the Mediterranean region and was introduced into Mexico and the Southern United States and has increased its distribution. The first observation of the centipede was first recorded in Pennsylvania in 1849 and today, the house centipede can be found in many buildings throughout the United States. It does not survive winters outdoors in Pennsylvania, but readily reproduces in heated structures.

They are very secretive, have a scary appearance and darting motions, homeowners typically fear the house centipede. The adult centipede has 15 pair of legs with the last pair (on adult females) nearly twice the length of the body, which is about one to one and one-half inches in length. This gives the centipede an overall appearance of being from three to four inches in length (including legs and antennae).

The house centipede's legs are banded light and dark, and the body is a dirty yellow with three longitudinal, dark stripes. Newly hatched larvae have four pair of legs. During the next five larval molts, the centipedes will have a different number of legs.

On the sixth molt the centipede is considered an adolescent and will have 15 legs during each of the next four molts then becomes an adult.

Females have been known to survive for several years and produce numerous offspring (maximum of 150). During the daytime, the centipedes like a dark, damp locations in the home and come out at night to forage for prey. House centipedes will feed on silverfish, carpet beetle larvae, cockroaches, spiders and other small arthropods. When you see a centipede frequently, this indicates that some prey arthropod is in abundance, and may signify a greater problem then the presence of the centipedes.

Their favorite hiding places are, beneath concrete slabs and they enter the house through expansion cracks, around sump pump openings or other breaks in slab integrity and inside cement block walls.

REMEMBER, USE FOOD GRADE DE
Dusts are either boric acid or diatomaceous earth, both of which are inorganic insecticides and have very low risk to mammals. Sprays or dusts should be applied to sites where centipedes are suspected such as cracks and crevices in concrete slabs, block walls, etc.

CHIGGERS

General Information:

Chiggers; are a relative of spiders that attach themselves to our bodies and proceed to feed. They can cause itching, illnesses and can even kill you if the infestation is not controlled. Chiggers can also inject an enzyme that will cause healthy cells to disintegrate. Baby chiggers will attack any warm body that gives off carbon dioxide. Their favorite method of getting on people is to jump on your feet and work their way up till they are right at home.

OUCH, OUCH
To get rid of the discomfort of chigger bites, try using a paste made from crushed aspirin and warm tap water.

SULFUR TO THE RESCUE
Chiggers can be eliminated with the use of powdered soil sulfur. Just place the sulfur in a broadcast spreader and spread the sulfur on your lawn early in the morning when the lawn has dew on it. Be sure and wear rubber gloves and a mask when working with powdered sulfur. Use an oscillating sprinkler and water the lawn good for about 15-20 minutes after the treatment. It takes about 5 pounds of sulfur to treat 100 square feet of lawn.

SPRAY THE YARD
Prepare a mixture of 4 tablespoons of dishwasher soap and 4 teaspoons of canola oil in 1 gallon of cool tap water. Spray the entire yard to kill off the chiggers.

CHINCH BUG

Identification:

These small black bugs with white, red or brown wings bugs tend to damage grasses by sucking the fluids from the blades of grass and replacing the fluid with toxic saliva, which interrupts the water conduction system of the grass and kills the blade.

General Information:
They are usually found in lawns that lack proper watering or have had too many chemicals used on them. If not removed, they are capable of wintering over in the grass. If your lawn is developing a bad odor you probably have a chinch bug problem. When the bugs are crushed, by stepping on them they give off a foul odor. These bugs like hot, sunny lawns like a schoolyard or football field.

THIS IS A CINCH FOR FINDING A CHINCH
If you want to find out if you have chinch bugs in your lawn, just use a tin can and cut out both ends then push the can into the lawn. Pour soapy water into the can and allow about 10 minutes.

Check the area and if you have chinch bugs they will come to the surface since they hate a soapy bath. This method is also used for grubs.

WORMING YOUR WAY OUT

One of the best methods of eliminating chinch bugs is to introduce Nc nematodes into your lawn areas. They will eliminate the problem in short order.

GIVE THEM THE OLD PEPPER SPRAY

A spray that combines onion, garlic and hot pepper will eliminate these pests in very short order. If you are doing a large lawn area a soap spray will work best.

¼	**Cup Tabasco Sauce™**
1	**Medium onion**
4	**Cups of warm tap water**
7	**Cloves of garlic**
1	**Teaspoon of Ivory Liquid Soap™**

Place the garlic, peppers or Tabasco Sauce™, onion and 2 cups of water into a food processor and blend well. Allow it to stand for 24 hours, strain and add the balance of the water and the soap. Spray both sides of the leaves.

THERE'S A CHINCH FUNGUS AMONG US

A new strain of fungus in now available commercially called **Beauveria bassiana** that will kill the chinch bugs.

CRICKETS

General Information:

Crickets are a member of the cockroach family, the noisiest member. They will look for a warm location when the weather starts to get cold and can be a real pest. However, in many societies around the world they are considered lucky and are never killed or disturbed.

Gryllus campestris

BAITS DO WORK

Place some molasses balls containing 5% food-grade DE or use borax or Comet®. This will kill them without a problem. *Make sure all baits are out of reach of pets and children at all times.*

A LITTLE SQUIRT WILL DO YA

You can prepare a spray that will kill the crickets in about 30 seconds if sprayed on them. Just mix 1 ounce of dishwasher soap in 1 quart of water. If you prefer to use vinegar use 4 ounces in 1 quart of water and it will kill them in about 60 seconds.

MOLE CRICKETS ARE SNEAKY

Mole crickets fly into the garden at night usually on very cloudy days and are drawn to light. These are large crickets and are about 1¼-inches long with sturdy shovel-like forelegs for digging into the soil. The northern mole cricket is a brownish-gray and the southern ones are usually more pinkish. They are most active in moist, warm weather and their tunnel tends to cut off the roots of seedlings. All deterrents that work for grasshoppers should be used.

EARWIGS

General Information:

Earwigs; are a relative of the cockroach with over 1,000 species known worldwide. They love to feed on plants and can be a real pest in greenhouses. They do feed on aphids and are sometimes considered a beneficial insect.

Earwigs are among the most frequently recognized insect pests in home gardens. Although they can devastate seedling vegetables or annual flowers and often seriously damage maturing soft fruit or corn silks, they also have a beneficial role in the landscape and have been shown to be important predators of aphids.

Although several species occur, the most common in California gardens is he European earwig, which was accidentally introduced into North America from Europe in the early 1900s.

The striped earwig occurs in southern California and can annoy residents when it is attracted to lights. It has a very disagreeable odor when crushed. However, the striped earwig does not damage plants.

The adult earwig is readily identified by a pair of prominent appendages that resemble forceps at the tail end of its body. Used for defense, the forceps are somewhat curved in the male but straighter in the female. The adult body is about ¾-inch long and reddish brown.

Many species have wings that are under short, hard wing covers, but they seldom fly. Immature earwigs are similar to adults except are smaller and lack wings. Earwigs do not attack humans!

Earwigs feed mostly at night and seek out dark, cool, moist places to hide during the day. Their favorite hiding places are under loose clods of soil, boards, dense growth of vines or weeds, or even within fruit damaged by other pests such as snails, birds, or cutworms.

Female earwigs dig cells in the ground where they lay masses of 30 or more eggs. Eggs hatch into small, white nymphs and remain in the cell protected and fed by their mother until their first molt. Later nymphs are darker and forage on their own.

Generally there is one generation a year, but females produce two broods. Part of the earwig population hibernates during the winter as pairs buried in cells in the soil. In milder California climates, some remain active all year.

Earwigs may seek refuge indoors when conditions outside are too dry or hot or cold. Large accumulations of earwigs can be annoying but present no health hazards. Sweep or vacuum them up and seal entry points. Earwigs eventually die indoors because there is little for them to eat.

Management of earwigs requires an integrated program that takes advantage of their habitat preferences. As moisture-loving insects, earwigs would not normally thrive in California's arid climate without the moisture and shade provided by the irrigated garden. Where earwigs are a problem, consider reducing hiding places and surface moisture levels.

EARWIGS LOVE TUNA

A key element of an earwig management program is trapping. Scatter numerous traps throughout the yard and in the house if a problem exists. Traps can easily be hidden near shrubbery and ground cover plantings, or against fences.

A low-sided can, such as a cat food or tuna fish can, with ½-inch of oil in the bottom makes an excellent trap. Tuna fish oil is very attractive to earwigs or vegetable oil with a drop of bacon grease can be used.

A TUBULAR EXPERIENCE

Save your paper towel and toilet paper cardboard tubes to use as traps for earwigs. Stuff them with straw and the little pests will hide there and make it easy for you to locate and dispose of them. If you spray areas where they frequent with a soapy solution you can get rid of them that way as well.

SHOOT THE LITTLE DEVILS

A dishwasher detergent soap mixed with water in a spray bottle will kill earwigs upon contact. Use 1 ounce per spray bottle of water. To find them go looking after dark with a flashlight and the spray bottle in your holster.

TRAPS WORK GREAT

If you plan on trapping the earwigs, place a shallow dish or tuna can that is buried so that it is level with the ground, they are real lazy and will not work too hard for a meal. Place some honey and peanut butter laced with borax in the dish. You can also use food-grade DE if you have some handy.

STICKY-SIDE UP
Earwigs will not cross a piece of tape with the sticky side up or Vaseline®.

HEAVY DRINKERS
Earwigs love beer and if you leave a shallow dish around in the evening where they frequent, you will find the dish full of earwigs in the morning.

HERE LITTLE EARWIG
Chickens love to eat earwigs and will snoop all over the place looking for them. If you have a few chickens you will never have an earwig problem.

GRUBS

GARLIC VS GRUBS

Finely mince 5 garlic cloves and allow it to dry then crush into a powder. Place the powder in 2 teaspoons of water and allow it to stand for 2 hours.

Add 2 quarts of water mix well, strain and place into sprayer. Test an area first in case the mixture is too potent for plant leaves. Spray the area where the grubs have been found. Use only glass spray jars, never metal since metal may react with the chemicals in garlic.

HEAD LICE

General Information:

This is a wingless blood, sucking parasite that is only about $1/10^{th}$ of an inch long. It bites and will suck blood from the scalp of the person it gets attached to. It causes itching, swelling and lays eggs called "nits" on strands of hair. There are thousands of species worldwide in both the sucking and biting types. These bugs can only live for a few days when they are away from a human body. A female louse can lie about 8-10 eggs a day and only lives for a month.

Lice are able to take on the color of the hair that they infest. If you are a blond, the lice will be light-colored and if you are a brunette they will be darker.

A growing louse will keep feeding over and over every 2-3 hours and making a new puncture every time. This results in itching and discomfort. Its specialized anticoagulant saliva is what causes the itching and burning, which tends to force you to scratch your head. The scratching will then cause more bleeding and possibly and infection.

If you get a bad cold with a fever it will kill the lice since they cannot tolerate high temperatures. Adult lice and nymphs (baby lice). The adult head lice (louse), is no bigger than a sesame seed and is grayish-white or tan.

Nymphs are smaller and become adult lice about 1 to 2 weeks after they hatch. Most lice feed on blood several times a day, but they can only survive up to 2 days off the scalp.

With lice bites cause itching and scratching, which is actually due to a reaction to the saliva of lice. However, the itching may not always start right away and depends on how sensitive your child's skin is to the lice.

It can sometimes take days or weeks for kids with lice to start scratching. They may complain, though, of things moving around on or tickling their heads.

For some kids, the irritation is mild; for others it is a more bothersome rash. Excessive scratching can lead to a bacterial infection (the skin would become red and tender and may have crusting and oozing along with swollen lymph glands). Best to see your doctor and if your doctor thinks this is the case, he or she may treat the infection with an oral antibiotic.

You may be able to see the lice or nits by parting your child's hair into small sections and checking for lice and nits with a fine-tooth comb on the scalp, behind the ears and around the back of the neck. A magnifying glass and bright light may help. But it can be tough to find a nymph or adult louse — often, there aren't many of them and they're able to move fast.

SEE THE DOC OR PHARMACIST

If you feel that you have contracted lice it would be best to see your doctor of pharmacist for medication that will remove them safely. There are a number of shampoos and medications that work well.

KILL THE BUGGERS

Use a coconut-based shampoo specifically designed for head lice. Drug stores sell lice combs that will comb-out the nits. Shampoos with pyrethrums also work very well. Check with the pharmacist for any new treatments. Keep repeating the process daily until the lice and their nits are 100% gone.

LEAFHOPPER

Identification:

These are slender wedge-shaped bugs that suck juices from the plants and kill the leaves as well as spreading viruses and bacteria to other plants. Some are green, while others are green with some red and white markings. They will fly off when disturbed and will usually be found on the underneath side of the leaf.

General Information:

Leafhoppers tend to frequent apple trees, beet plants and potatoes. The dragonfly will eat them, when they can find them.

The most common leafhopper is the "aster," which has six spots over a greenish-yellow area on its back, the beet leafhopper, the potato leafhopper and the red-banded leafhopper.

KILL THEM IN THE MORNINGS
The best method of killing them is to spray them early in the morning with an insecticidal soap solution. The leafhoppers are less active in the mornings. The only bug that seems to like these insects is the lacewing, which will eat their eggs. Of course, the lacewings will eat almost any insect eggs.

A GOLDEN CURE
Marigolds will eliminate the leafhoppers. Just crush 6 ounces of the leaves, roots and flowers then pour 4 cups of boiling water over it and allow it to soak for 24 hours. Add 4 more cups of cold water, strain and use as a spray.

THEY HATE PETUNIAS
If you plant petunias or geraniums in areas where you suspect trouble it will repel the bugs.

SPRAY THEM
Any liquid soap spray will eliminate the bugs in short order. Also Diatomaceous earth (DE) will also work great at keeping them at bay.

LEAFHOPPER (GRAPE)

General Information:
Both the adults and nymphs feed on the underneath side of the leaves resulting in spots that will turn brown. If there is a bad infestation the fruit will be affected.

LEAFHOPPERS KILLED BY WASPS
The grape leafhopper: can be controlled by releasing the parasitic wasp called **Anagrus epos** in the early part of the growing season. These wasps are capable of producing three generations in one summer.

During the early part of the summer the wasp prefers to feed on leafhoppers that frequent blackberries and it would be wise to plant some around the edges of the grape vineyard. When summer arrives the wasps will head for the vineyard and eat the grape leafhoppers.

ZAP, BLUE-LIGHT SPECIAL
A special blue-light insect electrocuting light trap is available that will make short work of these pests.

LEAFHOPPER (POTATO)

General Information:
In the southern states this bug is called the "bean jassid." It is a small wedge-shaped green leafhopper with white spots on its head and thorax. The nymphs have an odd habit of crawling sideways like a crab.

The leafhopper causes a condition on the potato plants known as "hopperburn" in which the tips and sides of the potato leaf will curl upward, then turn yellow or brown and become brittle. They will lay their eggs in the main veins of the leaves.

CANOPIES WORK
Leafhoppers prefer open areas where they can easily move on if necessary. If you plant the potato plants in a sheltered area they will probably not come around. If this is not practical then you may need to protect the plants with a netting of cheesecloth, muslin or other type of netting material.

KILLS THE BUGS AND INCREASES GROWTH
A dusting of pyrethrum will eliminate the leafhoppers as well as act as a growth stimulant for the plants.

LEAFMINERS

Identification:

These maggots are green or black and about 1/8th of an inch long. They actually tunnel between the upper and lower leaf surfaces and leave a white trail behind for you to follow.

The adults are flies that are half the size of a housefly, black with yellow markings and hairy.

General Information:
Three or four generations of the fly can hatch every year. They prefer to feed on spinach, berries, potatoes, peppers and cabbage. They will also feed on columbine, roses, nasturtiums and chrysanthemums.

DINNERTIME
Ladybugs and lacewings are an excellent deterrent to these maggots. If you can't get them try purchasing other parasites such as **Diglyphus begini** or **Diglyphus isaea**.

PEPPER THEM GOOD
Pepper spray is highly recommended as a spray treatment that usually works every time. When the plants are wet try dusting them with lime and this will repel the flies and stop them from laying their eggs.

CROP ROTATION WORKS
It is best to rotate your crops so that the leafminers in the soil gets confused and are unable to find the plants every year in the same spot. If you till in the fall it will also destroy the pupae.

THESE LEAVE YOUR PLANTS TIPSY
The arborvitae leafminer causes browning at the tips of the leaves. Spray plants and trees in late June or early July if you have the problem with a soap spray. Shaded plants are usually more heavily infested.

EGG CRUSHER
Leafminer eggs can easily be seen on spinach plants and can be crushed. If the leaves are heavily infested, it is best to pick them off and dispose of them.

LYGUS BUG

General Information :

These bugs are not too fussy what they eat but do prefer beans, strawberries and most orchard crops. The adults may be green, yellow or brown with a yellow or green triangle on their backs.

When they are on beans they attack the buds and flowers causing them to fall off. If they attack tomatoes and fruit they will cause discoloration, bumps or depressions. If you disc or rototill the area and especially the weeds, it will reduce the infestation.

DAISY'S TO THE RESCUE

If you border your strawberry patch with Shasta daisies it will keep the lygus out of the strawberry patch. They will eat the daisies as long as they are flowering and leave the strawberries alone.

MEALYBUG

Identification:

They are elliptically shaped and have short spines. They have piercing/sucking moth parts and are cottony-looking. The females do not have wings. They prefer soft-stemmed plants and suck out their juices eliminating the plant's nutrients. Mealybugs love orchids and other exotic plants. They will thrive indoors and like a warm, dry environment. They are capable of producing several generations in a year.

- To identify a mealybug look on the underneath side of a leaf and around the leaf joints. They look like miniature balls of cotton. The plant will also look withered and have a sticky sap on the leaves and stems.
- If you find a problem, move the infested plant and isolate it from any other plants. They are very invasive and will eventually move to all the plants.
- One of the easiest methods of control; is to just spray a forceful stream of water at the bugs and just wash them off the plant.
- If the water spray is not working then try a spray made from a soap/oil mixture. Prepare a solution of ½ teaspoon peppermint soap, ¼ teaspoon of a horticultural oil (garden supply) and 1 quart of tap water.

General Information:
They are a problem for citrus crops and a number of solutions will kill them and their relatives. They excrete honeydew, which makes them a friend of the ants.

They can usually be picked off the plants with a long tweezers and look like small tufts of cotton on the underneath sides of leaves. In the northeastern United States mealybugs are indoor pests as well.

THE DOUBLE WHAMMY
You can make a spray that is two killers in one by mixing 1 gallon of cool water with 2 tablespoons of canola oil and 2 tablespoons of dishwasher liquid soap. Place the mixture in a power sprayer and spray your plants in the area where the problem exists. The dishwasher liquid soap will kill most of them on contact and the oil will penetrate their skins and eventually suffocate them.

THE MEALY MASSAGE
If you only have a small number of mealy bugs, just keep a spray bottle around with rubbing alcohol in it and give them a squirt. You can also dip a paintbrush in the alcohol or use nail polish remover and paint them; however, be very careful not to touch the plant or the alcohol will cause damage.

PARASITES TO THE RESCUE

There are two parasites that are very effective in controlling mealybugs. They are *Cryptolaemus ladybug* (not the one we are used to) and *Pauridia*. Both of these should be available through a garden supply or agricultural house.

MEALYBUG KILLER SPRAY

The following ingredients will be needed:

3	**Tablespoons of light corn oil**
2	**Tablespoons of liquid dish soap**
2	**Gallons of cold tap water**

Place all the ingredients in a medium bucket and mix well. Place a small amount in a sprayer and spray the plants that have the mealybugs on them. Give the bugs a good squirt or two.

POKE THEM WITH A TOOTHPICK

Use a toothpick or the point of a knife to pick off mealybugs and scale from a plant. These tools should easily dislodge them without damaging the plant.

PINEAPPLE MEALYBUG

General Information:

 The bug is a whitish/gray insect that is covered with a white, waxy excretion. This bug is the number one pest of pineapple plants. However, the insect has also been known to infest nutgrass, panic grass, Spanish needle, caladium, avocado, citrus, mulberry, royal palm, hibiscus, sugarcane and some ferns. They are known to be the cause of pineapple wilt disease, which results in stunted plants that have leaves of reddish yellow with light green spots.

The leaf tips of the plants will look dead or are in the process of dying. Fire ants are a real friend of these bugs and will even carry them from wilted plants to healthy plants to get the honeydew they excrete.

PARASITES DO THE JOB

A tiny wasp called **Habletonia pseudoccina** will sting the mealybug and lay her eggs in them. Using a dormant oil spray or sprinkling crushed bone meal around will also help do the job.

PILLBUG (SOWBUG)

General Information:

These bugs are actually related to lobsters and crayfish and have seven pairs of legs and segmented bodies. They are sometimes called "rolly-polies" since they will roll up in a ball when disturbed. They like moisture and will normally be found in moist areas. If the area becomes dry they will move on. They like to eat ground cover, especially if the ground cover has a good amount of moisture in it. Their favorite home is a corncob and they are also fond of potatoes.

Sowbug

Pillbugs and sowbugs are somewhat different, but will be found in the same area. They are hard to tell apart, but the easiest way is to know that the pillbug will roll up in a ball and the sowbug will end up with a "hump" and not be as round. Sowbugs also have gills and need constant moisture conditions to survive. They always feed at night and like decaying leaf litter and vegetable matter.

GET OUT THE MAGNIFYING GLASS

When you get new potted plants it is very important to quarantine the plants for about 30 days and be sure and examine them frequently for mealybugs.

THE BARKING PILLBUG

Pillbugs love dry dog food and if you sprinkle some dry dog food around the base of the plants they are bothering they will eat the dog food and stay away from the plants. Cat food may work as well.

ONION SPRAY

3	Onions
¼	Cup Ivory Liquid Soap™
4	Cups of cool tap water

Slice and peel the onions then place them in a food processor and cover them with water. Blend very well then allow them to stand for 24 hours before straining and adding the liquid soap.

THE POTATO TRAP

Cut a raw potato in half and scoop out part of the insides then place it just below the surface of the ground where the pillbugs frequent. The pillbugs will congregate in the potato and can be discarded very easily.

CORNCOBS ATTRACT THEM

These bugs really like corncobs and if you just leave some corncobs in the areas you see them; they will find them and not bother other vegetation. If you get out real early in the morning or the very late night hours, you can retrieve the corncobs with the bugs on them and drop them into a pail of soapy water to kill them.

SPIDER LOVES PILLBUGS

A small spider named **Dysdera crocata** loves pillbugs and will hunt them. The spider is only ½ inch long with a brown rear body and a reddish front body with prominent fangs. It is harmless to humans and will run and hide when disturbed. The spider feeds almost exclusively on pillbugs and is usually found under rocks feeding at night.

ROOT MAGGOTS

Identification:
These look like houseflies and will lay their eggs in the soil. When they hatch the white maggots emerge looking like a grub with a pointed head.

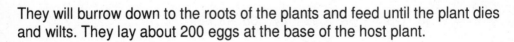

They will burrow down to the roots of the plants and feed until the plant dies and wilts. They lay about 200 eggs at the base of the host plant.

General Information:
If you think that root maggots are your problem, just pull up the plant and see if there are little white maggots on the roots. The two most common root maggots are the cabbage and onion root maggots.

They prefer young seedlings. Their pupae spend the winter 1-6 inches into the soil then the flies come out in the spring and lay their eggs, immediately producing white maggots.

SERVE THEM TEA
Save all your used tea bags and place the loose tea in your planting mix or mulch. This acts as an excellent deterrent for maggots. Coffee grounds may work almost as well as the tea.

IT'S DARK IN HERE
Place old pieces of carpeting or pieces of tarpaper with slits cut around the base of the plants will stop the root maggots from getting to the roots. Cover the slits with a good waterproof tape. Maggots do not like the smell of tar, which is an excellent repellent.

MAKE A BARRIER
Try and acquire large quantities of eggshells from a local restaurant. Crush the eggshells and mix it in with the soil. You can also use DE or plain sawdust mixed in with the soil. This will stop them from burrowing in. Wood ashes can also be sprinkled around the base of the plant with good results.

REPELS 100% OF THE TIME
Prepare a mixture of equal parts of lime, rock phosphate and bone meal. Mix well then add an equal measure of wood ash. Place some of this mixture in the hole that you are planting in.

PARASITE KILLERS
You can order Nc nematodes or Chalcid and trichogramma wasps and release them as well as rove beetles.

ONION MAGGOT

General Information:
These maggots are more common in coastal areas. The maggot tapers to the head similar to the cabbage maggot. They damage the onions by feeding on the lower areas of the stem or bulb.

A single maggot is capable of destroying a number of seedlings by eating their underground parts. Several maggots will ruin a large onion by attacking the onion through its base where they enter the root and burrow upwards. If the damaged onions are placed into storage they will readily decay.

THEY LOVE ONIONS
These bugs love onions with the exception of yellow onions. Yellow onions will usually repel the bugs, however, red and white ones will not.

SPACE OUT THE PLANTS
Since home gardens are arranged in rows the maggots find it easy to go from one plant to another. You can stop this pest by scattering the onion plants all over the garden. Every maggot needs several young seedlings to survive or they will die after they eat one. If they can't find the next seedling, they literally starve to death after their first meal.

ASHES TO ASHES
If you add sand or wood ashes to the top layer in planting rows it will stop the maggots and kill them.

SCALE

General Information:
Scales have similar biology to mealybugs but with a white waxy covering and a hard shell of a variety of colors. There are about 1,700 species. Most do not lay eggs but bear live nymphs.
They will reproduce faster indoors, which may be as little as a month while outdoor scales may take up to a year. There are soft scales and hard scales and it takes different methods to get rid of them so identification is a must.

SOFT SCALE VS HARD SCALE
To get rid of soft scales or black scales a wasp parasite, **Metaphycus helvolus** will solve the problem. To get rid of the hard, red scales call in the parasite **Aphytis melinus** to kill off the scale.

Another, good scale eradicator is the ladybug **Chilococorus nigritis**. Actually, almost any ladybug beetle will be glad to eat your scales.

SWAB THEM
Scales can be removed from the infected plants if the areas where they reside are swabbed with isopropyl alcohol. This application must be repeated on the affected areas every 3-4 days until the scales die.

THE EARLY SPRING SOLUTION
In the early spring before the buds of the plants open, try spraying the plants with a solution of soap and lime, as long as the particular plant will tolerate the spray. Most plant will tolerate this spray very well and it will eliminate the scale problem.

A STICKY WICKET

3	**Cups of warm tap water**
1	**Tablespoon of liquid paper glue**

Mix the two items together and place in a sprayer. This will make the plant leaves inedible and the glue will coat the bug's bodies and suffocate them. The spray will flake off the plant. Do not use a spray-on adhesive from an aerosol can since this will work but is not environmentally safe.

DON'T CRY FOR ME..............
To get rid of scale, just crush up 1 pound of white onions and place them in 3 pints of water then allow it to stand for 24 hours. Strain the mixture and use in a sprayer in areas where you have a scale problem. Test a leaf first to be sure that you will not damage any plants.

GET OUT THE OIL CAN
In the late winter before any new growth starts you will need to spray the plants with horticultural oil spray. This will suffocate any scale that is on the plants.

LADYBUG, LADYBUG WHERE HAVE YOU BEEN......
Ladybugs are one of the best methods of controlling scale.

BLACK SCALE

General Information:
The female is a dark brown or black color and will have ridges on her back that form the letter "H." It is usually found on twigs or leaves and occasionally fruit. Black scale; can be controlled by using the parasite ***Metaphycus helvolus***, which is commercially available. Good identification is a must so call on your local gardening or agricultural supply house to assist you. They prefer citrus and olive trees.

BROWN SCALE

General Information:
These scales will attack avocados and citrus and are soft brown oval scales. They are usually found on leaves and young twigs and will rarely bother the fruit. Heavy infestations will leave honeydew, sooty mold and ants that are attracted to the sweet honeydew.

BEETLES AND PARASITES DO THE JOB
The parasite ***Metaphycus luteolus*** and the lady beetle ***Chilcorus cacti*** will make short work of this brown scale.

CALIFORNIA RED SCALE

General Information:
This is an armored scale with no visible egg stage. Crawlers are usually light yellow and the adult is a tiny yellow-winged bug. It is almost always found on fruit and fruit should be inspected at regular intervals.

PARASITES AND PREDATORS
There are a number of parasites and predators that will easily take care of any California Red Scale problem. These include the wasps *Aphytis melinus, Aphytis lingnanensis, Encarsia perniciosi* and *Comperiella bifasciata*. The predators are the small black ladybeetle *Lindorus lophanthae*.

CITRICOLA SCALE

General Information:
This scale can produce honeydew, which will cause a sooty mold to grow on fruit and plants. Specific parasites are very effective and it is best to check with your garden supply store. They prefer citrus, walnuts and pomegranate and luckily only produce one generation each year. The parasites *Metaphycus luteolus* and *Metaphycus helvolus* should take care of the pests.

COTTONY CUSHION SCALE

General Information:
This scale prefers citrus trees and excretes a large amount of honeydew, which pleases the ants to no end. They will be found mainly on twigs and leaves and rarely on the fruit. The nymphs are red and have black legs and antennae. The females lay a cottony-looking egg sac, which will remain attached to their bodies.

NATURAL ENEMIES TO THE RESCUE
The natural enemies include the vedelia beetle and the parasite fly *Cryptochetum iceryae*. The beetle will usually be hanging around if you have any cottony cushion scale in the area.

PURPLE SCALE

General Information:
This scale is found on leaves, twigs and some fruit. The scale produces a toxic substance that can kill the more heavily infested areas of trees and plants. You will easily be able to spot the dead areas. The female has an oyster shell shape that is purple.

OYSTERSHELL SCALE

General Information:
This armored scale attacks most fruit and nut trees and is shaped like a mussel or oystershell. It only feeds on bark and will leave the leaves and fruit alone.

It will be more of a pest if the fruit trees are located near a poplar, willow or walnut tree, which are the preferred host trees. Dormant sprays are not affective since it winters in the egg stage and is protected by the old female covers. It is best to locate the scale and prune the limbs or twigs.

RED SCALE

General Information:
Found on twigs, leaves and fruit and will produce a toxic substance that will kill the leaves, twigs and fruit it inhabits.

The scale is reddish-brown and round. If it is found on green fruit is will appear as a yellow spot that will go through to both sides of leaves. Most chalcid wasps will eliminate this pest.

SAN JOSE SCALE

General Information:
This scale attacks most fruit and nut trees. The adults are gray-brown with a tiny white bump in the center of their bodies.
These scales should be found during the dormant season and destroyed. They will be found on the top of trees as well as the limbs and twigs.

ELIMINATING THE PROBLEM
Pheromone traps work very well on this scale as well as releasing a natural enemy the twice-stabbed lady beetle *Chilocorus orbus*.

WALNUT SCALE

General Information:
This is an armored scale that lays tiny eggs all together on a chain. They hatch into yellow worms within 3-4 days. The adult males are very small yellow-winged bugs. This bug will blend in very well with tree bark and are hard to locate. It is best to spray supreme or superior-type oil: at the end of the dormant season to control the walnut scale.

WASP FOR CONTROL
The tiny parasitic wasp called **Aphytis melinus**; does an excellent job of locating and destroying the walnut scale.

SCALES FOUND IN ORCHARDS

SCALE	PRINCIPAL HOST
Brown Soft Scale	Citrus, avocado, stone fruit
Calico Scale	Walnuts, pear, stone fruit
California Red Scale	Citrus, grape & olive
Citricola Scale	Citrus & walnuts
Cottony Cushion Scale	Citrus, other trees
European Fruit Lecanium	Walnuts & almonds pears , grapes
Frosted Scale	Walnuts
Italian Pear Scale	Walnuts, apples, pears
Olive Scale	Olive trees, almond trees
Oystershell Scale	Apples, nuts & pears
Purple Scale	Citrus
San Jose Scale	Fruit & nut trees
Soft Scale	Citrus, olives, nut trees, fig, apple, pear
Walnut Scale	Walnut trees

SCORPIONS

HIRE A CHICKEN
Chickens like to dine on scorpions and will hunt them out. However, I don't think you want a bunch of chickens walking through the living room so best to let them remove the scorpions that are outside.

HERE KITTY, KITTY

Cats are very effective in catching and removing scorpions, especially ones that do not like catching mice. We haven't figured out the reasoning for this one yet.

LIGHT 'EM UP

Scorpions tend to fluoresce under ultraviolet or black light and can easily be found at night. They are unable to jump and can easily be killed or captured. If you carry a hand vacuum with you, you can just vacuum them up and dispose of the bag.

BAIT THEM

A shallow plate with water and boric acid will work great at getting rid of them and their relatives. *Be sure that there are no pets or children around.*

TRAP THEM

If you dampen an old burlap bag or any heavy piece of cloth and leave it on the ground at night, the scorpions will crawl under making it easy for you to find and kill them.

SILVERFISH

General Information:

Silverfish do not have wings and are silvery to brown in color because their bodies are covered with fine scales. They are generally soft bodied and the adults can be up to ¾ inch long, flattened from top to bottom, elongated and oval in shape, have three long tail projections and two long antennae.

A relative of the silverfish is the firebrat, which is quite similar in habits but is generally darker in color. The firebrat prefers temperatures over 90°F but has a similar high humidity requirement. It is common near heating pipes, fire places, ovens and other heat sources.

Female silverfish lay eggs continuously after reaching the adult stage and may lie over 100 eggs during her life. Eggs are deposited singly or in small groups in cracks and crevices and hatch in 3 to weeks.

Silverfish develop from egg to adult within 4 to 6 weeks and continue to molt throughout their life. Immature stages appear similar to adults except they are about 1/20 of an inch long when they first hatch and generally whitish in color, taking on the adults' silver coloring as they grow. They are long-lived, surviving from two to eight years.

Silverfish are chewing insects and general feeders but prefer carbohydrates and protein, including flour, dried meat, rolled oats, paper and even glue. They are capable of surviving long periods, sometimes over a year, without food but are sensitive to moisture and require a high humidity (75% to 90%) to survive.

They also have a temperature preference between 70 and 80°F. They move fast and are mostly active at night and generally prefer lower levels in homes, but may be found in attics. It is primarily a nuisance pest inside the home or buildings and can contaminate food, damage paper goods and stain clothing but is medically harmless. Many of their habits are similar to cockroaches and they appear to be more common as household pests in drier parts of the state. Occasionally they damage book bindings, curtains and even wallpaper.

These bugs have no odor and will not harm you. They also love to eat very young termites if there is a nest in the vicinity.

SETTING A STICKY TRAP
Take a piece of light cardboard and place some Tanglefoot™ on it, then place some oatmeal in the center. The Tanglefoot™ is very sticky and they can't escape. They will never even make it to the oatmeal.

BE SWEET TO SILVERFISH
To get rid of silverfish, try mixing 1 part of molasses in 2 parts of white vinegar, then apply the mixture to any cracks or holes where they tend to reside. Make sure that you treat the baseboards and the table legs as well.

THEY LIKE HIGH HUMIDITY
If you keep the humidity low in the house with a dehumidifier chances are that you will never have to worry about silverfish.

You can also keep packets of silica gel around your bookshelf. These gel packets are available in most hardware stores.

PROTECT YOUR BOOKS
If you set out some of the herb santolina (lavender cotton) around your bookshelves it will repel silverfish. You can also sprinkle some diatomaceous earth (DE) around the books. *If you use DE be sure and wear a mask and eye protection.*

THE GLASS TRAP WORKS GREAT
Use a jar and butter the inside 1-2 inches. Wrap the outside with masking tape and give them a tongue depressor ramp. Bait the trap with some wheat flour or sugar and in the morning it should be filled with silverfish. Pour soapy water in to drown them.

SYMPHYLAN

General Information:

This bug is often confused with the centipede and is called the "garden centipede." It is not a good bug to have in the garden.

It has a body that is broken up into 14 segments and moves around on 12 pairs of legs.

They will eat young plant roots and are voracious eaters. To check to see if you have this pest doing damage, just dunk a root ball in a bucket of water and wait for the pest to rise to the top.

THEY DON'T CARRY FLOOD INSURANCE
If you have a field that is infested the best method is to flood the area and drown them. This is not a good method if all you have is a small garden.

INVITE THEM TO TEA
Preparing a tea with garlic and tobacco will do in the bugs in short order. Just drench the area to kill them.

TARNISHED PLANT BUG

General Information:

These are brown and black bugs with nymphs that love to suck up plant juices. The areas on the affected plants will be a dark color. They lay their eggs on the leaves and will also feed on weeds and grass. They will hibernate in the winter in cracks or in trash.

TOUGH CRITTERS
There are no known good controls for these bugs. You can try the typical bug removal methods of picking them off and using Nc nematode mulch around the base of the plants. The soap and lime spray will irritate them and they may move on.

CHAPTER 14

BENEFICIAL
INSECTS

BENEFICIAL INSECTS

Your garden and yard contains millions of insects and small creatures, some good and some bad. There are on the average 1,000+ insects in every square yard of your yard. Only about 1% of all insects can be considered a pest and will do damage in your yard. The beneficial insects can do a great job of reducing the number of bad insects providing you do not kill them off while hunting down the bad bugs.

If you do order beneficial insects to assist in keeping the bad bug population down, be sure not to use and harsh chemicals or pesticides for at least 2 months before they have been released.

ANTLIONS

General Information:

 These look a lot like damselflies and have been called **"doodle bugs."** They can dig small pits in dry earth or sand and then just wait for their victims to fall in. They then throw sand in the air to confuse the prey, jump on them, paralyze them and suck out their fluids. They will them throw what's left of the bug out of the pit and wait for the next victim to come along.

ASSASSIN BUG

General Information:

  These bugs resemble spiders and stab their victims, injecting a dissolving fluid before sucking the liquids out of them. They love to feed on leafhoppers, bed bugs, caterpillars and an assortment of other bad bugs. There are hundreds of species in the United States and Canada. These bugs have very broad bodies, sturdy front legs, a long beak and large eyes.

Drop that leaf!

These are good bugs to have around the garden; however, if you bother them they will bite you.

BIGEYED BUGS

General Information:

These bugs love to live in weedy areas and eat aphids, leafhoppers, Mexican bean beetles and insect eggs. They need meat to reproduce and will only occasionally consume plant juices. They have large "bug eyes" are oval in shape and usually gray to tan in color.

BEETLES

General Information:

There are about 3,000 species of beetles worldwide. Many are good and some are bad and sometimes it is difficult to tell the good guys from the bad guys.

Professional gardeners will tell you that if the beetle is slow moving kill it and if it is moving fast it is probably in pursuit of another bug. All beetles have a straight line running down its back where its wings join.

BLISTER BEETLE

General Information:
The only good thing about this beetle is that its larvae, consumes grasshopper eggs. If you touch this beetle it will give you a painful blister. Spanish fly is produced from this beetle.

CHECKERED BEETLE

General Information:

Bright-colored beetle: that is covered with a thick coat of short hairs. The larvae are usually yellow or red and have a horn. Most have a checkerboard pattern and prey on woodborers; however, their larvae will kill many pest larvae and the eggs.

FIREFLY

General Information:

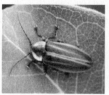

These beetles are also referred to as *"lightning bugs"* and have a luminous area near the end of their abdomen. They use this light to signal for a mate so they will not be too happy when you catch them and interrupt their mating ritual. The larvae eat cutworms and many small insects. They love to eat snails and inject them with their digestive juices and then drink the liquefied tissue.

GROUND BEETLES

General Information:

These night-hunting beetles can boast over 20,000 species worldwide and are rarely seen, making it hard to identify them. They are black and somewhat iridescent with bodies that are shaped like a shield. They may go by the name **"caterpillar hunter."** Their favorite foods include ants, cutworms, termites, spider mites, gypsy moths, mosquitoes, snails and slugs.

They may even be seen climbing a tree to get to their prey. Some of these beetles will expel a foul-smelling gas if you go to pick them up.

ROVE BEETLES

General Information:

This beetle looks more like an earwig (without the pincers) than a true

beetle. It tends to prefer scrounging around in decaying material looking for prey and is especially fond of cabbage beetles, mites, bark beetles and cabbage maggots.

SOLDIER BEETLES

General Information:

These beetles have a long rectangular body that is brownish in color. It looks like a firefly but without the taillight. The larvae enjoy feasting on many of the bad insects; however, the adults love an easy life of retirement and just hang around on a flower with their legs up taking it easy. The adult beetles will feed mainly on aphids and grow to about ½ inch in length.

TIGER BEETLES

General Information:

These are the professional hunter beetles that are a pretty iridescent blue, green and bronze. They are speedy, large beetles that can grow to ¾ of an inch long. It prefers aphids and caterpillars but will not turn down other pests if they are readily available. This species is only found in the western United States. They usually lie in wait at the bottom of tunnels and wait for an insect to fall in for dinner.

CENTIPEDES

General Information:

These creepy crawlers can actually have as many as 346 legs and sometimes as few as 30, which will depend on the species. They have a pair of claws that are venomous and can paralyze their victims. These are good to have around the garden since they eat snails, slugs, grasshoppers and many other pests. When you find them in the basement or house they are looking for cockroaches, flies and moths.

The very small centipede-looking bug, that you may see in your garden resembles a white centipede but are really "symphylan." These can do a great deal of damage to plants and are mainly found in greenhouses in the southwestern states.

COUNT THEIR LEGS

Centipedes are good for the garden and consume many of
the garden pests; however, millipedes are not very good
to have around.

Millipede

MILLIPEDE TRAPPER

Find a tall can of any type, preferably one like a large tomato juice can and
punch holes in both sides as well as the bottom of the can. Fill the can with
some carrot and potato peelings. Once a week check the can and empty
the millipedes into a bucket of soapy water then reset the trap.

DAMSEL BUG

Identification:

These bugs are only about ¼ quarter
inch long and have a body that narrows
toward the head and have large front
legs for grabbing small prey. They eat aphids,
leafhoppers, treehoppers, psyllids, mites and small
green caterpillars.

DAMSELFLIES

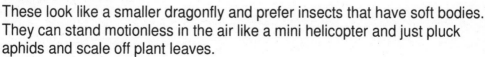

General Information:

These look like a smaller dragonfly and prefer insects that have soft bodies.
They can stand motionless in the air like a mini helicopter and just pluck
aphids and scale off plant leaves.

They normally only look for prey during the day and like to look for their meal near a body of water. If they find an area that has mosquito larvae they will literally gorge themselves.

DECOLLATE SNAILS

SNAIL HUNTER

 There is a small snail that will hunt other snails and kill them. The decollate snail is somewhat smaller than the average snail and has a shell that resembles a seashell. It is a natural enemy of the brown garden snail and has the same habits as the brown snail. When it runs out of snails it will eat decayed leaves and help clean up the garden. It does need a source of moisture to survive. Poisons will kill this snail so try and avoid them, if you have a number of these snail hunters in your garden.

DRAGONFLIES

General Information:

 Dragonflies may be called by a number of different names such as horse stingers, darning needles or mosquito hawks. They are very fast and few prey, can avoid them when they are chasing them down. They grab their prey by using their hairy legs and look like they are carrying a shopping basket.

They cannot wait to dine and eat their victims while they are flying by sucking the fluids from them. They have been known to eat their own weight in 30 minutes or less. Their leg baskets are capable of carrying up to 100 mosquitoes, which is one of their favorite meals.

The dragonfly begins its life under water and then enters the air world for the majority of its life. It has an insatiable need for flying insects almost as if it a challenge for it to catch them. If you have them in your yard just hope that they remain!

EARTHWORMS

General Information:

These are really one of the best good guys. They eat through the earth digesting organic matter and some minerals and turn them into better, more usable soil. The worms can also attract birds, which consume insects. If you don't have earthworms it would be best to order some. If you use chemical fertilizers or pesticides that are used to kill snails or slugs, they will also kill the earthworms.

EARWIG

Identification:

They are about ¾ inch long, brownish-black with a pincer on their rear end. They have very small wings that are almost useless and will lay white round eggs in the soil.

General Information:

They are fairly beneficial since they enjoy feasting on aphids and many other pest bugs. They clean up a lot of decayed materials and are active at night. When they are cleaning up the leaves and such, they find pests and kill them. If you don't want them around they can be eliminated using one of the following methods.

Rumor is that earwigs will crawl into your ear while you are sleeping. This is not true and they will not harm you even though they look menacing.

SAFETY FIRST
If they get into the house, one of the best repellants is to use diatomaceous earth placed around baseboards and windowsills. This will last a long time and still be an effective natural killer.

DAILY NEWS TO THE RESCUE
If you want to trap earwigs, just lightly spray a newspaper with water and then roll it up loosely and place it near an area that you have earwig activity. Allow it to remain overnight, then remove it and place it into a well-sealed container for disposal. Since they are beneficial this is only used inside a house.

OILING AN EARWIG
To make an earwig trap, just use a straight-sided container and fill it half full with canola oil. Leave wherever the problem exists and clean out whenever it has sufficient earwigs in it. The oil can be re-used. Use only if you are overrun with them.

GIVE THEM A HOME
If you place a small amount of dry moss in a few matchboxes and hang them from sticks around the plants they will climb up in them to spend the night and you can dispose of them every morning.

Yummy!

BANTAM HENS LOVE EARWIGS
Bantam hens will hunt for earwigs all day and will consume large quantities of them as well as other pests. They may peck at a few pieces of veggies or fruit but they do more good than harm.

FLIES

The following flies are not available through mail order insect houses. However, you may want to be aware of them so that you will leave them alone and allow them to do their job.

HOVER FLIES (SYPHID FLIES)

General Information:

 These are very colorful flies that are yellow-striped and somewhat resemble bees or certain wasps. This weird appearance keeps them safe from birds; who tend to confuse them with bees. They are relatively harmless to humans and animals and can hang motionless in flight similar to a hummingbird. They prefer to feed on aphids, scale, thrips and leafhoppers. You may spot one on rose bushes that look like a tiny green worm.

They are attracted to yarrow, goldenrod, asters and Black-eyed Susan's and will sip their nectar. Chances are if you plant these you will find that the flies will arrive if they are in the neighborhood. They will not sting you, however, they do resemble a wasp.

ROBBER FLY

General Information:

 These flies resemble bumblebees and can act very ferocious when attacking wasps and bees. They can be seen even chasing their prey when they are after small grasshoppers. Their larvae will feed on other larvae in the soil.

TACHNID FLIES

General Information:

This bug looks like a large black housefly that needs a haircut.
They can also be found in yellow, red or brown and are usually seen around leaves and flowers. They attach their eggs to caterpillars or on the plants that they consume.

They do an excellent job of controlling the caterpillar population and especially European corn borers and gypsy moths. They prefer nectar or honeydew secreted by aphids and other insects.

There are over 1200 species in North America. The adult bugs like buckwheat and if you plant some you will have these flies in your garden.

FLY PARASITES

General Information:

These are mainly livestock parasites that kill flies that frequent cattle and other livestock. People hardly ever even notice these flies. The fly parasites lay their eggs inside of fly pupae and kill them before they can ever emerge. They look for their prey around manure piles in stables, kennels, barns and feedlots. Commercial composting operations are one of their favorite hangouts.

GREEN LACEWINGS

HERE, PRETTY BUG

General Information:

The lacewing has long wings that look like a piece of old fashioned lace and very long antennae. They dine on aphids and their larvae as their favorite meal as well as other insect pests. They will be attracted to yarrow, Black-eyed Susan's, goldenrod and the aster family.

The larva of the green lacewing also loves to feast on aphids and have been called **"aphid lions".** The larva of the brown lacewing dines on aphids and also many soft-bodied insects such as the red spider mite, thrips, mealybugs, scale and will eat the eggs of many pest worms. The lacewing larvae, is very cannibalistic and if they are near each other eggs they will eat their own eggs.

They can be ordered and will arrive with the eggs packed in feeding material such as rice hulls. This is done in case some hatch while in transit and hopefully will eat the rice hulls instead of the other eggs. They are so minute that 1,000 of them would fit in a small thimble.

If you do see any movement you will need to disperse them immediately. Just sprinkle the eggs on the plant foliage, preferably on a warm day. If you want to keep them around they require some honey or sweet nectar.

BRRRRRRRRRRRR

If you do buy lacewings don't refrigerate them, just keep them at room temperature. Watch the bottom of the container in case some of the kids hatch and start looking for food.

LADYBUGS

Identification:

 These are round beetles that are about ¼+ inches long and are bright orange to red with a number of black spots and white markings on the thorax. They will consume about 400 aphids a day and an adult can eat thousands of aphids and scales during the season. The ladybug can produce 4-5 generations of offspring in one summer under ideal moisture conditions.

General Information:

There are almost 400 species of ladybug worldwide. The **convergent lady beetle** is one of the best predators and their favorite meal is aphids but won't turn down a good tasty meal of scales. They will also eat leafhoppers, thrips, and a variety of eggs and moths. In the late 1880's one of the ladybugs relative the **Vedalia beetle** was imported from Australia and became famous for saving the California citrus crop from the cottony cushion scale.

LADYBUG, LADYBUG WERE HAVE YOU GONE

Ladybugs are a common insect that enjoys munching on aphids, mites, scales and whiteflies. They love daisies, tansy or yarrow and will frequent gardens that have these plants.

If you do purchase ladybugs there are a few important facts you should be aware of:

- Make sure that the yard is well watered before releasing the ladybugs or they may fly away looking for a more, moist location. They must have water droplets to live.
- Handle them very gently or they will get scared and fly away.
- Be sure and place them at the base of the plants but don't place too many in one location.
- They can be stored in the refrigerator (not the freezer) for up to two weeks and released gradually.
- Make sure you have food ready for them when you release them. Spray the plants with a 10% sugar or honey solution. You can also use a commercial food such as Control™, Honeydew™ or Wheast™.
- If a plant has an aphid or scale infestation, place the ladybugs on the plant and cover the plant immediately.
- Ladybugs: are easily killed by pesticides.

MEALYBUG DESTROYER

General Information:
These bugs are related to the ladybird beetle and destroy mealybugs. In fact in its larval stage it even resembles a mealybug.

They will eat other garden pests; however, they need to be kept away from ants. Do not use any pesticides for at least a month before releasing these good guys.

MITES (BENEFICIAL)

General Information:

The majority of mites are real pests; however, there are beneficial mites that will eliminate the bad mites. They are available commercially and shipped as adults and should be scattered by hand in the garden areas as needed.

The adults that you are releasing will then lay their eggs next to the pest mite on the underneath sides of the leaves. The beneficial mites will sometimes feed on nectar but will not harm the plants. The mites will not feed on aphids, whiteflies or scale and only feed on the bad mites.

Pesticides and fungicides will kill the beneficial mites so care needs to be taken if you are going to use them. It is best to catch the problem early if you expect good results. The minimum order by one mite sales company is 300 predatory mites, which will guard 15-20 plants that are lightly infested.

PREDATORY MITES COMMERCIALLY AVAILABLE

PREDATORY MITE	DESCRIPTION
Metaseiulus occidentalis	The most commonly released mites are very effective at temperatures over 90^{0}F.
Phytoseiulus persimilis	They like mild humid conditions, especially in greenhouses up to 80^{0}F. Higher temperature strains are available if needed.
Amblyseius californicus	Used in greenhouses and outside. Used at temperatures up to 85^{0}F.
Amblyseius (Euseius)	Species will feed on all types of mites but is mostly effective against the citrus red mite on citrus trees in Southern California. They will not go into areas that are heavily infested with spider mites.

Nc NEMATODES

WORMING THEIR WAY IN

These beneficial nematodes are microscopic roundworms that are recognized as one of the safest methods of eradicating a number of pests.

The bugs that respond well to **"death by nematode"** are wireworms, cutworms, Colorado potato beetle, Japanese beetle, grubs and June beetles.

The beneficial nematodes will kill more than 200 species of pest insects. However, they will not harm earthworms, which make them a preferred method of control. They are capable of living in the soil for 2-3 months.

Nc nematode eggs can be purchased in most garden shops and usually come in a small sponge with about 1 million eggs. They hatch quickly and grow to adults in a very short period of time. Nc nematodes are harmless to pets and humans.

Nematodes enter their victim through any bodily orifice and most will introduce deadly bacteria into the victim or just eat their tissue. Never spray nematodes in direct sunlight or you may kill them.

PARASITIC WASPS

General Information:
These wasps are one of our best insect hunters and eliminators. They will eat the pest's eggs and larvae and lay their eggs in the pests. The pest then acts as an incubator for the wasp eggs. They are available through many mail order companies.

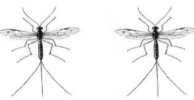

BRACONIDS
These wasps look like small white rice-like drops that attach to the backs of caterpillars. These are actually the cocoons of the future wasp generation. The larvae, spends a small amount of time inside the body of the caterpillar before leaving and making their cocoon. It actually consumes some of the caterpillar's tissue without killing it.

They then hatch and go looking for aphids and drill holes in the aphids back. The adults usually feed on nectar or honeydew.

CHALCIDS

These are very tiny wasp parasites that are found all over North America that attack and kill caterpillars, scale, aphids, whiteflies, mealybugs, leafhoppers and the larvae of many beetles.

When you order them through mail order they will be shipped as adult wasps and will then lay their eggs on the pest as soon as they are released. The adults require flowers for nectar.

Recently, a new chalcid wasp is being sold called the "golden chalcid" **Aphytis melinus**. This parasitic wasp will be used to control California red citrus scale, San Jose scale and ivy scale. In cold climates they should be released in the spring.

ENCARSIA FORMOSA PARASITE

This wasp parasite prefers whiteflies and will lay its eggs on the scales of immature whiteflies. Then as the wasp gets bigger it will feed on the whitefly and kill it. If you see a whitefly with a black spec on its scales it is a wasp egg. These parasites are often used in greenhouses and will be at their best at temperatures over 70^{0}F. When they run out of whiteflies to eat they will reduce their population.

If you place a rose geranium plant in the greenhouse the plant gives off a chemical substance that reduces the metabolic rate of the wasp and places it into a state of suspended animation. Remove the plant when you need the wasps again to clear out the whiteflies.

ICHNEUMON WASP

These are unusual-looking wasps that have very long tubes that look like stingers but are really tubes to deposit their eggs with. They can use these tubes to bore through bark and lay their eggs on hiding caterpillars. They can locate their victims by sensing their vibrations.

They are dark-colored wasps that have clear wings and very long antennae. The adults will eat the host larvae and also consume honeydew and pollen. They are found in all areas of North America.

MUD DAUBERS

These wasps will attack their prey and paralyze them to death with their stinger. They prey on spiders, caterpillars and most other insects in the neighborhood. The adults will return to the colony with a portion of the prey and share it.

They will sting humans if bothered while they are at work. You will notice a loud buzzing sound before they sting you.

TRICHOGRAMMA WASP

These wasps will not sting either humans or animals. This species can kill hundreds of pests and prefer armyworms, cutworms, gypsy moths, hornworms, corn earworms, leafworms and even bollworms. One wasp is can parasitize as many as 100 pests in its lifetime. When the wasp eggs hatch they live off the host and eventually kill them from within. They can easily be purchased through the mail and need to be kept in a warm, humid location. They must be released at the time when the moths are laying their eggs or when you first notice them in your garden.

PRAYING MANTIS

Identification:
One of the best insects to have around your garden is the praying mantis. They are large, about 5 inches long and usually green but may be found in brown. They have enlarged front legs, which work great for grasping prey.

PRAY FOR THESE INSECTS

The praying mantis eats its meals of insects while they are still alive then proceeds to groom afterwards. It is capable of consuming large numbers of insects including aphids, bees, wasps, beetles, caterpillars, grasshoppers and even a small frog, salamander or other small lizard.

However, it is not too fussy and sometimes and may eat a beneficial insect for dessert. Another problem is that the praying mantis may also eat its own kind.

You can purchase praying mantis egg cases by mail order. They need to be attached to a low-growing twig in the fall. They will hatch in the early spring and disappear into the foliage immediately. They are very delicate when they first hatch resulting in a large number being eaten by ants and lizards.

If you place the eggs in a brown paper bag and allow them to sit on a windowsill, they will hatch. Be sure the area is not too hot or you will have **"fried mantis."** It takes about 8 weeks for them to hatch then release them as soon as their skin dries and hardens.

Praying Mantis is found throughout the United States and Canada. They can easily be tempted into your garden if you plant raspberry canes.

TACHINID FLY

General Information:

This fly looks like an ordinary black housefly, however, they may be seen in yellow, red or brown colors. They feed on nectar and honeydew secreted by other insects. These are a potent pest control parasite. Their larvae are deposited on the host and feeds on European corn borers, cutworms, armyworms, Mexican bean beetles and Japanese beetles. They love buckwheat and will be drawn to the grain.

WHEELBUG

General Information:

This is a real ugly bug that makes his home in your shrubbery. He is one of the good guys but not one you want to mess with. He has a wheel shape on his back to identify him, however, I don't think that you want to be that close. They eat other insects that do not have a hard shell and just sit and wait for a bug to go by. They do have a temper and will give you a stinging bite if bothered.

CHAPTER 15

SNAILS & SLUGS

SNAILS & SLUGS

SOLUTIONS TO THE PROBLEM

SLUGGING IT OUT WITH SNAILS

The preferred meal for a slug is a succulent plant, especially their favorite, pansies. They feed different from any other insect in that they eat the leaf from the middle to the end, leaving you half a leaf. They do not like dry, cold weather and daylight and will hide under boards or debris. They feed at night and they are easy to track since they leave a trail of slime.

Snails are hermaphrodites; which means that they contain both the male and female sex organs and do not need another snail to mate. Snails are capable of producing over 300 eggs per day, which can lie dormant in the soil for up to 10 years.

Their breeding seasons are spring and fall. They love moisture and the dark, which is where they will nest. Plain "cheap" beer seems to attract them and when they consume it, it has the ability to dry them out thus killing them.

JUNGLE RAIN WORKS GREAT
The following ingredients will be needed:

1¼	Tablespoons of brewer's yeast
1	Quart of very cheap beer
1	Quart of apple cider vinegar
1	Tablespoon of Jungle Rain™
1	Cup of warm tap water
2	Tablespoons of granulated sugar
1	One-gallon bottle

Place the cheap beer and vinegar in the gallon bottle and shake. Add the brewers yeast and the water with the sugar dissolved, to the beer and vinegar solution and mix. Add the Jungle Rain™, mix well and pour into small lids or holders that can easily be placed where the snails frequent. This will attract every snail in the neighborhood and do them all in.

Snails and slugs prefer a near beer and go crazy for Kingsbury Malt Beverage®

HAVE A SNAIL-PICKING PARTY

One of the best methods of eliminating or at least reducing the snail population in your garden is to pay a neighbors kid anywhere from a penny to a nickel per snail. They need a flashlight and prowl your garden after dark and pick the snails up by hand. Have rubber gloves available for the pickers and a bucket with salt, soapy water to drop them into.

ESCARGO FOR CHICKENS

If you don't want to kill the snails immediately and you or your neighbor has chickens, just feed the snails to the chickens. Chickens love to feast on snails.

HAPPY HOUR FOR SNAILS & SLUGS

Place a mixture of 1 quart of cheap beer, 1 teaspoon of powdered sugar and 1 teaspoon of white vinegar into wide jar lids or other similar container and leave out in the garden. Baker's yeast may be substituted for the vinegar if you prefer. This mixture will kill off hundreds of snails and slugs in short order. The slugs will really appreciate it if you place a small tent over the beer so that they will have some shade while they are dining.

SEASONING YOUR SNAILS
Use a saltshaker and mix together 1 part iodized salt and 1 part cayenne pepper. Shake the mixture on the snails and slugs to cause them to dehydrate and quietly pass away.

SLIPPERY GUNK FOR SNAILS
The following ingredients will be needed:

7	Ounces Vaseline®
8	Ounces castor oil
1	Ounce cayenne pepper
1	Ounce Tabasco Sauce™

Place the Vaseline® and the castor oil in a medium plastic container and mix. Add the pepper and Tabasco Sauce™ to give it a real boost. This mixture works great if placed on the trunk of a plant.

SHOWER THEM WITH AMMONIA
Fill a 1-quart spray bottle with warm tap water and add 1 tablespoon of household ammonia them shake and spray the snails and slugs.

USE SALAD DRESSING ON THEM
Mix up 2 tablespoons of white vinegar, 2 tablespoons of Ivory liquid soap and 1 tablespoon of red Tabasco Sauce™. Place the mixture in a spray bottle and spray the dressing on them. You can also just place 8-10 drops of Tabasco Sauce™ in 1 quart of water and spray them with this mixture. Actually any hot sauce will do, it doesn't have to be Tabasco Sauce™.

POWDER THEIR NOSE
Snails and slugs will not cross baby powder, flour or rock dust. Placing these powders around your plant beds will discourage them from entering.

PROTECT YOUR TREES
Place Tanglefoot™ around the base of trees to keep snails off the tree. Tanglefoot™ is made from castor oil and wax and works great as a natural barrier.

If you want to increase the effectiveness add a small amount of cayenne pepper to it. The barrier should be about 1-foot wide to have maximum effectiveness.

CACKLEBERRY SHELLS WORK GREAT
Snails and slugs will not cross an area that is covered with eggshells. It is too difficult for them to navigate across and they will avoid the area.

CLOG THOSE PORES
If you sprinkle diatomaceous earth (DE) around it will clog the pores and the snails and slugs will suffocate. You can mix a solution of DE, a small amount of Ivory Liquid Soap™ and water and spray your plants in areas that are frequented by snails and slugs. **DE will irritate your lungs so try not to breathe it in.** DE also prevents snails from laying eggs, which will reduce the population over the years.

GOOD FOR PLANTS, BAD FOR SNAILS
Alfalfa meal is a high nitrogen plant food that if sprinkled around plants will supply the plant with nutrients and will provide a barrier against snails and slugs. If you do use alfalfa meal, make sure that you do not water the plants for 24 hours after the treatment.

SNAIL BARRIER FROM THE SEA
Kelp or dried seaweed will provide a barrier for snails and slugs while providing your plants with an excellent source of trace minerals. Kelp is high in salt content, which the snails try to avoid at all costs.

HORSE POO, POO

Horse manure added to mulch and spread around the garden when you are fertilizing is another natural barrier for snails and slugs. There are also other ingredients that can be added to mulch such as pine needles, kelp and rock dust that will keep the little critters at bay.

Formula to paint on tree trunks:

1	**Bucket of old horse manure**
2	**Pounds of all-purpose flour**
4	**Ounces of cayenne pepper**
2	**Pounds powdered seaweed**

Add enough water to prepare a paste that can be used as paint, ask a neighbors kid to do the chore.

BAKE THEM A HOT CAKE
Mix together 1 cup of all-purpose flour, 1 tablespoon of cayenne pepper and just enough water to prepare a mixture that can be used in a spray bottle. Spray around tree trunks or the base of plants.

CALL FOR THE COPPER
Copper bands can be purchased from a gardening supply house or hardware store and provide a non-lethal method of keeping the snails and slugs from damaging your trees and plants.

SKINNED SLUGS ANYONE?
If you mix 1½ cups of household ammonia with 1½ cups of water you can prepare a mixture that will literally fry the skin off a slug and kill them. Just place the mixture in a spray bottle and when you see the very small slugs, just spray them and ZAP!

CALL IN THE WORMS

A common snail and slug deterrent is to use Nc nematodes to kill the pests. Nc nematodes can be purchased through most garden shops or agricultural supply houses. They will track down and infect the snail or slug causing them to develop a swollen mantle and they quietly pass away within 2-3 days.

FORMULA FOR STICKY STUFF

Place the following mixture around the base or on the stems of plants and trees to keep off the snails and slugs.

8	**Ounces of Vaseline®**
1	**Tablespoon of cayenne pepper**
10	**Ounces of castor oil**
½	**Ounce of any red-hot sauce**

LIKE BEES TO HONEY

If you don't mind picking up the little creatures, just attract them with any kind of citrus fruit into any container you have that they can easily climb into.

GIVE THEM A TREAT

Snails and slugs prefer cabbage before any other vegetable or plant. If you don't like cabbage, just plant a few in your garden and that is where you will always find them hanging out.

CHILI PODS WILL FIX THEM

Grind up 8 ounces of ripe chili pods then soak them in 1 quart of water for 24 hours. Mix well and strain then add 3 quarts of water and ½ teaspoon of liquid soap. Use as a spray; wherever the snails and slugs hideout.

GRIND UP YOUR OLD MARBLES

There are a number of barriers that can be placed in the garden to keep snails and slugs at bay. The barrier must be at least 3 inches wide to be effective. You can use marble dust, hydrated lime, ammonium sulfate, crushed oyster shells or wood ash.

SPECIAL MULCH
If your mulch is high in oak leaves or seaweed it will stop the snails and slugs from coming into the garden.

SNAIL-RESISTANT PLANTS
The following are plants that snails do not like and tend to shy away from: corn, grape, bean, basil, azalea, sage ginger, hibiscus, parsley, rose, poppy, sunflower, fuschia and rhododendrum.

REPELLENT PLANTS
There are two plants that will actually repel snails and slugs. These are prostrate rosemary *Rosemarinus officionalis* and wormwood *Artemisia absinthium*. If you prepare a tea with either of these herbs and use it as a spray it will deter the snails and slugs as well.

THE KILLER HAIR
Hair can be used very effectively to kill snails. Either human or horse works great, the coarser the better. Just scatter the hair around areas that the snails or slugs frequent and you can eliminate most of them. The horse hair especially will irritate their soft, moist skin to such a degree that they dehydrate themselves trying to get rid of the hairs that cling to them.

TURTLES ON THE LOOKOUT
Turtles like snails and slugs and will go after them every chance they get. If you place a turtle in your yard you will never see another snail or slug.

PROTECTIVE BARRIER
If you border an area with sand, lime or ashes it will protect the area from snails.

NEVER USE ANY POISONS TO GET RID OF SNAILS AND SLUGS. MOST OF THE COMMERCIAL POISONS MADE TO KILL THEM WILL KILL THE BIRDS IF THE BIRDS EAT THEM.

CHAPTER 16

WORMS

ARMYWORM

Identification:

This is a 2-inch long caterpillar that is green with yellow-orange stripes down its back. It is a type of cutworm and usually feeds close to the ground, usually on plant stalks. They lay their eggs on leaves and their larvae eat grass stems. They tend to travel in mass like an army and will invade your garden with extreme prejudice. They will feed at night and lay low during the day. The females may lay as many as 700 eggs.

SPRAY THEM OR TRAP THEM

Prepare a mixture of a soapy solution with ¼ cup of lime and spray the caterpillars. If you want to trap them use a commercial pheromone trap. Nc nematodes and Bt also work very well.

SOUTH OF THE BORDER, DOWN MEXICO WAY

To get rid of armyworms, just remove the seeds from Mexican poppies and grind them into a powder. Us the powder to dust the plants you are having a worm problem with. This is an excellent method of control.

BAGWORM

Identification:

These are real pests that hide inside a rolled up leaf and eat away from the inside out. It is very hard to find the worm inside their spindle-shaped bags.

They are a brownish color and seal up their bag they live in with silk. They will drag the bag along to different locations and stay hidden as they eat. A large number of bagworms can defoliate and kill a tree in short order.

Their eggs are laid in the winter months and hatch in the early spring. Most of the bagworms are found on the east coast.

SNEAKY LITTLE EAST COAST BUGS
If you have a bad infestation the best method of eliminating the problem is to spray Bt on all the foliage. If the infestation is light, just handpick the little devils.

GIVE THEM A SQUIRT OR TWO
The soap and lime spray works great. Just mix together ¼ cup of lime and 4 drops of liquid soap in 1 gallon of water. If you prefer, you can use garlic, onion juice or hot pepper sauce in place of the lime.

MEALWORM

General Information:

These little creatures reside in your flour or other grains and can survive in all conditions from very dry to moist. They love areas with poor sanitation, especially if grains or flour has fallen to the floor. Pet stores sell mealworms for people to feed to their pets such as turtles, fish and birds.

DOUBLE YOU'RE PLEASURE

Mealworms will avoid your grain products (macaroni, spaghetti, etc) if you keep a wrapped slice of spearmint gum near or in the products. The bugs do not like spearmint gum but love Juicy Fruit.

NEMATODES

Identification:

 The small worms are only $1/125^{th}$ of an inch and you will need a microscope to see them. They are tapered on both ends and their egg masses look like small, pearly lumps.

General Information:

These roundworms are the bad relative of the good Nc nematode and can cause wilting, yellowing and stunting of plants. The root-knot nematode causes galls or swellings on the roots of plants. They lay their eggs near the roots so that their offspring does not have far to go for a meal and can live their whole life underground. They can damage 2,000 different plants, which include almost any vegetable you can think of. They can be found everywhere in the United States, but like coarse soil the best.

Nematodes prefer soil that is lacking in organic matter. If you use mulch that is high in organic matter you should not have a problem with nematodes. There are over 500,000 species of this worm. They go from microscopic in size to a 20 footer that is found in whales.

LEMON CONTROL

There are beneficial nematodes that destroy other bug eggs as well as the bad nematodes. If you have the bad ones and you want to get rid of them, just grow lemon grass in the areas where you want to reduce or eliminate a population. This is one of the most effective methods of control.

HOW SWEET IT IS

2	Cup of granulated sugar
2	Cups of boiling water
1	Gallon of cool tap water

Dissolve the sugar into the boiling water, remove from the heat and add the cool water, then pour on the soil area that is infested. Sugar has the ability to draw moisture from the worms and dries them out.

TURN UP THE HEAT
If the weather is hot you can get rid of the nematode pests by giving them a steam bath. Make sure that there is no chance of rain and prepare the soil for cultivation first. Water the area thoroughly until the ground is well saturated, then cover the ground with a heavy-duty clear plastic sheet.

Secure the plastic sheet to the ground on all sides. If the temperature is hot it will make the ground about 140^0F and kill off the nematodes. This process will take about 5 weeks to accomplish. You will also eliminate many other pests as well as weed seeds.

GO FOR THE GOLD
There are two varieties of marigolds that when planted in an area that harbors nematodes will get rid of them. The French or African marigold releases a chemical from their roots that can kill nematodes. After the marigolds have finished blooming grind them into the soil or add them to your compost. Other plants that will repel nematodes are mustard, watercress, rutabaga and radishes.

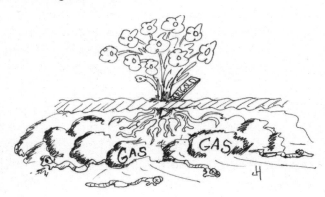

THE GREEN KILLER
Next time you cook asparagus, save the cooking water. The water will contain a chemical that will kill nematodes.

Pour or spray the cooking water in areas that are infested. Other plants that will repel nematodes include garlic, calendula, salvia, dahlias and velvet beans.

SEAWEED COMPOST
If you are able to acquire some seaweed, either place it on the soil or add it to your compost for a great nematode killer.

SUFFOCATE THEM
If you prepare a solution of corn oil mixed with water and sprinkle the solution near the roots it will kill off the nematodes. To make it easier to mix oil and water add 2 ampoules of lecithin to the mixture.

FERTILIZE THEM TO DEATH
If you use a fertilizer composed of 70% fish emulsion and 30% yucca extract (Pent-A-Vate™) nematodes will leave the plants alone.

GLUB, GLUB
If you flood an area where you are having a serious nematode problem, it will have to be under water for two years to get rid of the pest and all the egg masses.

ROOT-KNOT NEMATODE

General Information:

This is not the good Nc nematode. This one thrives on infecting plants causing cell decay and root galls to form. It will release toxins and bacteria as it feeds on the plant roots. The galls are large, round formations on the roots. The galls will split open and cause the plant tissue to decay. The plants will wilt and be stunted.

THE FRENCH CONNECTION
Root-knot nematodes will not go near a garden or plants in an area where there are French marigolds *Tagetes patula*. If you plant a whole area with the marigolds foe a season and then plow them under you will never have these destructive nematodes. The marigolds actually release a toxin that is very poisonous to the nematodes.

PICKLEWORM AKA MELONWORM

General Information:

The moths lay their eggs on the underneath sides of leaves on cucumbers, melons, pumpkins and squash. Squash is their number one favorite if it is available and will feed on the flowers and leaf buds. The caterpillars will feed on vegetation but a large number tend to find fruit and bore holes in them. The pickleworm is usually only found east of the Rockies and may also be found in New York State. The south is where the worst infestations are found, mainly in Florida and Texas.

SMELL THEM OUT

If you plant strong smelling herbs within your garden it will keep these pests out. They do not like onion and garlic plants.

WIREWORMS (CLICK BEETLES)

Identification:

The adults are called **"click beetles,"** which is the name they were given since when they right themselves after being turned over they hit the ground and it sounds like a "click." The larvae are very thin worms that have a leathery skin and three pairs of legs close to their head. They are yellow to dark red in color and can grow to 1½-inches long. They lay their eggs in the soil and will live for 3-4 years.

General Information:

The beetle got the name click beetle since it makes a clicking sound when it rights itself after being placed on its back. It loves to consume corn, peas, potato tubers, sweet potatoes, carrots and rutabaga. It also likes to munch on the roots of cabbage, onions, watermelon, cucumber and tomatoes.

SKEWER THEM

To trap wireworms you will need some wooden skewers, carrots and apples. Cut the apples and carrots into small pieces and place the skewer through a piece. Bury the food leaving the skewer where you can see it.

The wireworms will eat the fruit or vegetable since it an easier meal and then you can remove the skewer and destroy them with extreme prejudice. They also love potatoes and they can be used to trap them as well by just placing pieces of potatoes into the soil and digging them up in a few days.

WORMS WILL KILL WORMS
If you apply Nc nematodes about two months before you plant, it should eliminate the problem. This is one of the best methods of control.

THEY DON'T LIKE BUCKWHEAT
Wireworms do not like to be around buckwheat or white mustard. If you plant these around the plants that they do like they will stay far away. Natural plants used as repellants work very well with a number of insects.

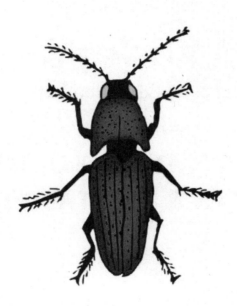

CHAPTER 17

PROBLEMS AND SOLUTIONS
FRUITS & VEGETABLES

PROBLEMS AND SOLUTIONS

FRUITS & VEGETABLES

GET THE LEAD OUT
If your garden is near a road and you are worried about auto emissions getting on your plants, just spray them with a solution of 2½ teaspoons of white vinegar in 1-gallon of tap water.

ARTICHOKES

ARTICHOKE PEST PROBLEM SOLVERS

THE PROBLEM	CAUSED BY
Holes bored in stems, discoloration of choke	Artichoke plume moth
Sticky substance on chokes or black mold	Aphids
Holes in leaves and stem, blackening of choke	Snails & slugs
Curled leaves, small plants, misshapen chokes	Curly dwarf virus
Grey or brown fungus growth	Botrytis fungus

ASPARAGUS

ASPARAGUS PEST PROBLEM SOLVERS

THE PROBLEM	CAUSED BY
New spears are chewed on	Snails & slugs
Growing tips chewed with black blemishes	Asparagus beetle
Rust-colored spots on spears	Fungus damage
Weak spears with discoloration	Fusarium wilt
Whitish or yellowish stippling on shoots	Spider mites
Plants stunted and rosetted	European asparagus aphid
Small holes eaten out of new spears	Cutworms

AVOCADO

AVOCADO PEST PROBLEM SOLVERS

THE PROBLEM	CAUSED BY
Leaves skeletonized and sometimes webbed...........	Amorbia caterpillar
Leaves skeletonized, no webbing, scars on fruit........	Omnivorous looper
Leaves smaller than normal, yellowish, feeder root blackened..	Avocado root rot
Purple discoloration around leaf veins.....................	Six-spotted mite
Leaves spotted, yellow mites with webbing...............	Persea mite
Leaves turn brown..	Avocado brown mite
Brown discoloration on fruit, tiny brown varnish spots...	Greenhouse thrips

BEANS

THE EARLY BIRD GETS THE BEAN

If you want your snap beans to produce over a longer period of time, just pick them when the beans are about pencil width. Make sure that the seeds are just visible. If you wait too long the plant will make the seeds larger instead of the meat of the bean and use up all its energy.

IS IT A BEANSTALK OR A CORNSTALK?

If you plant pole beans next to corn stalks, the beans will use the corn stalk and wind its way up making it easier to grow them without putting up pole for them.

BEAN PEST PROBLEM SOLVERS

THE PROBLEM	CAUSED BY
Seedlings collapse after they come up.....................	Seedcorn maggot
Plants weak, leaves yellow or dying........................	Stem rot
Plants wilt and turn yellow, fine webbing on underneath side of leaves......................................	Spider mite
Leaves curled and deformed, may have shiny appearance from honeydew and blackened..............	Aphids

White strippling on upper surface of leaves............... Leafhoppers
Leaves turn yellow, slightly curled, cloud of
tiny white insects fly up when plant disturbed............ Whiteflies
Stunted seedlings with misshapen leaves................. Thrips
Holes or leaves skeletonized................................. Cucumber beetle
Buds and flowers drop off. Beans pitted................... Lygus bug
Blossoms drop off.. Low soil moisture, smog
Stunted plants, roots have knots or beads............... Nematodes
Tiny white grubs inside pod, round holes.................. Bean weevil
Holes in pods, seed hollow and eaten...................... Lycaenid pod borer
Chewing damage on pods or flowers....................... Corn earworm

BEETS

IF YOU LIKE THEM YOUNG AND TENDER
Try sowing the beets in a short row about every two
weeks and begin four weeks before the last frost during
spring.

HOW SWEET IT IS
Beets grown in the spring and fall are usually sweeter than the beets grown
in the summer. The cool temperatures tend to cause the beet to store more
sugar. If you must grow beets in the summer and would like them sweet,
then mulch them to keep the ground as cool as possible.

BERRIES

PLANT THEM OR CHILL THEM
Strawberries need to be planted as soon as possible after being
purchased. If you can't plant them, then you need to store them in a
refrigerator at 40^0F to keep them dormant. When you remove them, they
must be planted immediately or the yield will be reduced.

THE SOUTH WINS THIS ONE
If you plant strawberries on a south-facing slope instead of a north-facing
slope, they will bear fruit at least a week earlier.

DON'T WANT THOSE SUNSHADES

If you plant strawberries in narrow rows you will produce more berries. When you plant in wide rows, the plants in the middle of the rows will receive too much shade.

BRRRRRRRRRRRRRRRRRRRR

Place about a 2-inch layer of straw over strawberry plants to protect them during the winter. More than 2 inches tends to allow water to percolate through the straw and suffocate the plants. This results in the soil being unable to breathe and allowing carbon dioxide to build up and kill the roots.

MATURE STRAWBERRIES IN 8 WEEKS??????????

The secret to harvesting mature strawberries in only 8 weeks will depend on the following:

- ♦ Plants should be spaced 4 inches apart in rows of 12 inches wide and allow enough room to walk between rows.
- ♦ Make sure you mulch the plants and allow them to flower.
- ♦ Remove all runners.
- ♦ The first year's crop will ripen about 2 months later. The second year's crop will be larger and will come in earlier.
- ♦ Forget the old matted row system of planting.

DON'T GET BLUE OVER BLUEBERRIES

Blueberries are one of the berry families that do not need a lot of feeding. If you have mature bushes, you should only feed them about 1 pound of a quality cottonseed meal every year to provide you with an excellent yield.

SOME BERRIES DON'T NEED AN OLD CANE

Blackberries, dewberries and most raspberry varieties produce the fruit on "canes" that grew the year before. After harvest pruning is essential in order to grow a good crop the following year. Cut the canes at ground level and do not allow them to remain in the garden. Take care not to damage the new canes that are growing since these will provide you with next year's crop.

BERRY PEST PROBLEM SOLVERS

THE PROBLEM	CAUSED BY
Blackberries don't turn black enough, become red and sour	Redberry mite
Leaves stippled and yellow, dried out and brown, underside of leaves with strands of webbing	Spider mites
Tips of young shoots wilt in sprung, thick white worm in cane	Raspberry horntail
New shoots wilt in spring, grub burrowing in cane	Raspberry cane borer
Plants stunted, cane dies, worm tunneling in cane	Crown borers
White winding trails on canes in spring or summer	Bushberry cane miner
Young stems wilt, partially chewed canes	Cutworm
Buds and new growth eaten in spring	Leafroller, orange tortrix
Tiny holes in leaves and skeletonized	Raspberry sawfly
Canes covered with white crust or brownish bumps	Scale
Tiny green insects along stems or on new growth	Raspberry aphid
Tiny white spots on leaves in spring, underneath sides of leaves inhabited by whitish bugs	Rose leafhopper
Berries deformed or scarred, thin insects on berries	Flower thrips

CARROTS

ARE YOU SUFFERING FROM CRUSTY SOIL?

Crust tends to form on the ground and causes patchy carrot growth. The seedlings are not strong enough to break through in some areas. Never cover carrot seeds with soil, instead use peat, compost or vermiculite.

CARROT PEST PROBLEM SOLVERS

THE PROBLEM	CAUSED BY
Carrots do not break soil	Seedling pest
Roots hairy or misshapen	Root knot nematode

Carrots curled around each other............................Planted too close together
Roots have surface tunnels with rusty excrement.......Carrot rust fly
White growth on leaves.......................................Powdery mildew

RADISHES TO THE RESCUE
Radishes have stronger sprouts and can break through
the soil easier than carrot sprouts. If you plant radishes
with the carrots they will break through the soil crust and
allow the carrots to sprout more easily.

CAULIFLOWER

BROWN OUT
It is a common practice to tie the leaves up around a cauliflower plant as it
grows to bleach the heads. Instead of the old method, try gathering up the
leaves and then place a brown bag over the head. The air will still be able
to circulate and will prevent rotting that is common when the leaves are
tied.

COLE CROP PEST PROBLEM SOLVERS
(Broccoli, Brussels sprouts, Cabbage, Cauliflower)

THE PROBLEM	CAUSED BY
Irregular holes in leaves, seedlings damaged............	Caterpillars
Small holes in leaves, stunted plant growth...............	Diamondback moth caterpillar
Deformed, curled leaves, gray-green insects on leaves, possibly honeydew................................	Aphids
Plants wilted, with misshapen leaves, browning.........	Harlequin bug
Tunnels through roots of seedlings, wilting................	Cabbage maggot
Stunted plants, wilting, yellowish leaves...................	Cyst nematode
Heads split prematurely.......................................	Heavy watering after dry spell

CHIVES

A WARM CHIVE IS A HEALTHY CHIVE
If you start seeds in the late summer and keep them inside where they can
get adequate sun, you will have a nice supply of chives during the winter
months.

CORN

DON'T HURT THOSE LITTLE SUCKERS

Corn suckers are the small shoots that grow out from the stalk at ground level. Many people remove them, but the latest research shows that they will not reduce yield and if there is a drought they will send nutrients to the main stalk. If you do remove them and don't remove them properly you may cause diseases to enter the stalk.

CORN PEST PROBLEM SOLVERS

THE PROBLEM	CAUSED BY
Worms eating kernels or tassels	Corn earworm
Holes in leaves	Armyworm, corn earworm, beetles
Ears only partially developed	Earwigs
Sticky or shiny leaves, small plants stunted	Aphids

FIGS

PUT A PLASTIC BAG ON JACK FROST

Figs do not like frost and the best method to protect them is to cover the branches that will bear fruit with a plastic bag before a frost appears. If you tie small cans filled with a few stones each to the bottom of the bags they cannot blow off.

GRAPES

GRAPE PEST PROBLEM SOLVERS

THE PROBLEM	CAUSED BY
Pale-colored stippling on top of leaves, leaf may die and turn brown, older leaves die first	Grape leafhopper
Yellow stippling on top of leaves spreading through main veins, webbing-underside of leaf	Spider mites
Pale reddish swelling on young leaves upper surfaces, underneath has plant hairs	Grape erineum mite
Honeydew and black sooty mold, black speckling of grapes, flies fly up when disturbed	Grape whitefly

Honeydew drips from clusters, black mold................ Grape mealybug
Scarring and reduced growth of new shoots,
grapes have dark scarring surrounded by halo...........Western flower thrips
Brown bumps on new growth, honeydew present.......European fruit lecanium
Whitish bumps on trunks and canes........................ Grape scale
Lower leaves folded together early in season,
berries webbed together and eaten......................... Omnivorous leafroller
Pencil-sized leaf rolls, berries eaten later in
summer, reduced foliage...................................... Grape leaffolder
Leaves and berries webbed together....................... Orange tortrix
Underneath side of leaf eaten, then skeletonized....... Western grapeleaf skeletonizer
Buds eaten away, new shoots chewed.....................Cutworms
Tiny round holes in leaves, whole leaves eaten......... Achemon sphinx moth
Large amount of leaf tissue eaten.......................... Grasshoppers
Young leaves and new shoots eaten when
shoots are 12-14 inches high................................ Hoplia beetle
New shoots wilt or break off in wind, holes in
crotch, tunnels filled with sawdust.......................... Branch & twig borer
Premature yellowing of leaves/stunted growth........... Grape phylloxera
Slower than normal growth, galls on roots................ Nematodes

LETTUCE

LETTUCE PEST PROBLEM SOLVERS

THE PROBLEM	CAUSED BY
Curled, distorted leaves, honeydew present...............Aphids	
Damaged seedlings, crowns chewed...................... Armyworms, corn earworms	
Ragged holes in leaves, holes in head.....................Loopers	
Skeletonized leaves... Armyworms	
Small holes in leaves or skeletonization.................. Vegetable weevil	
Black areas on borders of inner leaves................... Hot weather	
Torn areas on leaves, small pieces missing.............. Birds, rabbits, kids	

OKRA

GET OUT THE HAMMER AND CHISEL

Okra seeds have a very hard outer coat, which can hamper germination
resulting in an uneven patchy garden. There are a number of ways to avoid
the potential problem:

♦ Barely nick the seed coating with a sharp knife.
♦ Place the seeds on a piece of fine sandpaper and rub them with
another sheet.

- The seeds can be soaked in tepid water at room temperature for 24 hours.
- The seeds can be placed in the freezer for about 12 hours, and then soaked in hot tap water for 30 minutes just before planting.

ONIONS

ONION & GARLIC PEST PROBLEM SOLVERS

THE PROBLEM	CAUSED BY
Tunnels and cavities in bulbs & stems, wilting and yellowing	Onion maggot
Leaves turning silvery	Onion thrips
Seedlings are pale, thickened, deformed, bulbs swollen at base, leaftips dying	Stem & bulb nematode

PEAS

PEA PEST PROBLEM SOLVERS

THE PROBLEM	CAUSED BY
Surface scarring of pods or deformed pods	Thrips
Leaves and stems covered with honeydew and black sooty mold	Aphids
Holes in leaves, greenish-yellow beetle	Cucumber beetle
Leaves are skeletonized	Armyworm
Off white stippling on upper leaf surface and fine webbing on underneath side of leaf	Spider mite
Curving white trails in leaves, stems or pods	Leafminers
Half-moon chewed notches on edges of leaves	Pea leaf weevil adults
Pods partially damaged or removed	Birds, rabbits, kids
White grubs with brown heads in peas and round holes on pods	Pea weevil

PEPPERS

GIVE THEM SOMETHING TO READ

Next time you plant peppers, try wrapping each plant stem in 6X6-inch square of newspaper. Dip the newspaper in cool tap water before wrapping each pepper plant. When the roots are kept moist it keep away the cutworms.

PEPPERS & EGGPLANT

PEPPERS & EGGPLANT PEST PROBLEM SOLVERS

THE PROBLEM	CAUSED BY
Buds or fruit turns yellow or drop from plant, pods that remain may turn yellow or be misshapen	Pepper weevil
Curled and distorted leaves or stunted plants	Aphids
Small holes in leaves worse at lower levels	Flea beetle
White frothy foam on eggplant stems	Spittle beetle
Peppers have small worm, holes	Corn earworm or leafroller
Leaves wilt and turn yellow	Whiteflies

POTATOES

POTATO PEST PROBLEM SOLVERS

THE PROBLEM	CAUSED BY
Tunneling in tubers, pink eyes with silk	Potato tuberworm
Curled and distorted leaves, stunted plant	Aphids
Leaves curled upward, older leaves yellow, edges of younger leaves turn purple	Potato psyllid
White stippling on upper leaf surface, leaf edges yellow or brown	Leafhopper
Leaves have many holes, tubers have bumps, shallow winding trails on upper surface of leaf	Flea beetle
Bumps on tubers, swelling on roots, brown spots	Nematodes
Leaves missing, yellow-striped beetle visible	Colorado potato beetle

PUMPKIN

BOARD UP YOUR PUMPKINS

When your pumpkins or squash start to mature, try placing a small board under each fruit. This will protect the fruit from soil-borne bacteria and fungus.

CUCURBIT CROP PEST PROBLEM SOLVERS
(Cantaloupe, Cucumber, Pumpkin, Squash, Watermelon)

THE PROBLEM	CAUSED BY
Deformed or curled leaves, tiny, soft bodied insects on underneath side of leaves. Honeydew or black sooty mold present	Aphids
Fine strippling on leaves, yellowing or browning of leaves, orange or red dots	Spider mites
Yellowish leaves, honeydew present, clouds of tiny white bugs	Whiteflies
White strippling on upper leaf surface	Leafhopper
Holes in leaves, wilting, scarred runners	Cucumber beetle
Leaves have small yellow specs that turn brown, vines wilt	Squash bug
Swelling or beads on roots, low yield	Nematodes

RADISHES

FRIENDS FOREVER

Radish seeds develop strong sprouts that are capable of breaking through the ground. Parsnips do not have very strong sprouts and need the radish sprouts to open up the soil for them.

RADISH PEST PROBLEM SOLVERS

THE PROBLEM	CAUSED BY
Small plants wilt and die, grooves on root surfaces, tunnels in roots	Cabbage maggot
Foliage deformed with whitish-yellow spots	Harlequin bug
Tiny holes in leaves	Flea beetle

SPINACH

THE PROBLEM	CAUSED BY
Leaves partially eaten and green caterpillar hanging around	Loopers
Leaves yellowing	Aphids
Leaves have green or yellow spots with maggots in them	Leafminers

STRAWBERRIES

STRAWBERRY PEST PROBLEM SOLVERS

THE PROBLEM	CAUSED BY
New growth becomes stunted and crinkled, flowers wither and die	Cyclamen mite
Dry brown areas on lower leaf surface in spring, leaves get brown and die	Spider mites
Leaves rolled up and webbed together with silk, small holes, look for tiny caterpillar	Leafroller
Ripe fruit has large holes, some leaves eaten	Cutworms
Deep holes in berries with dried slime around	Snails & slugs
Holes in fruit with oval bugs in them	Sowbugs
Tiny holes in ripening fruit, no slime around	Earwigs
Plant wilting and dying in spring or fall, whitish caterpillar in crowns	Strawberry crown moth
Leaves have scalloped look, smaller roots eaten	Otiorhynchus root weevil
Honeydew and black sooty mold	Strawberry aphid
Berries have deep furrows or twisted shape, deformed areas, large hollowed seeds	Lygus bug
Plants wilt in warm weather even when watered, cottony deposit on roots	Ground mealybug

TOMATOES

TO FLOWER OR NOT TO FLOWER

 If you would like early tomatoes, purchase plants with flowers. Don't be upset if the flowers fall off while you are planting them. They are in their reproductive stage and more flowers will appear shortly. If the plants are young and without flowers they will bear fruit later but will give a better harvest,

SPEEDY PLANTING

The easiest method of planting tomatoes plants is to use a bulb planter. It will result in a deep hole and will not take a lot of work.

MOOOOOOO

Dry cow manure is the best fertilizer for tomato plants. It will give you a higher yield. Use about 100 pounds per square feet in plants that are spaced about 3 feet apart.

TOMATO PEST PROBLEM SOLVERS

THE PROBLEM	CAUSED BY
Worms in ripe tomatoes	Tomato fruitworm
Worms tunneling in fruit	Potato tuberworm
Leaves mined and folded, tiny worms tunneling	Tomato pinworm
Leaves eaten and only stems remain, fruit small	Hornworms
Fruit surface eaten or hollowed out	Snails & slugs
Yellowish cloudy spots on ripe tomatoes, soft spots	Stink bugs
Leaves totally eaten off young plants	Vegetable weevil
Lower leaves and stems are bronze color, plants losing leaves	Tomato russet mite
Leaves yellow and slightly curled, insects fly when disturbed, greenish scales on underneath side of leaves	Whiteflies
Leaves curled downward, fruit with shiny spots	Aphids
Seedlings or transplants with holes in leaves	Flea beetle
Poor yield plants, yellow leaves, swelling or beads on roots	Root knot nematodes
Irregular yellow blotches on leaves	Powdery mildew

TURNIPS

TURNIP PEST PROBLEMS

THE PROBLEM	CAUSED BY
Distorted plants, curling, wilting, insects on underneath sides of leaves	Aphids
Holes in leaves, chewing on buds and roots	Vegetable weevil
Irregular holes in leaves, seedlings destroyed	Caterpillars
Deformed leaves with yellow spotting, possible wilting	Harlequin bug
Tunneling in roots of seedlings, wilting	Cabbage maggot

FIGHTING PLANT DISEASES

HELP! MY BLOSSOMS ARE ROTTING
Blossom-end rotting; is usually caused by too little water or too much water. This problem is common on tomato, peppers and melon plants. If drought is the problem the plants will need at least 1-inch of water per week and keep the plants well mulched. The other cause of blossom-end rot is lack of calcium in the soil. The soil Ph should be about 6-6.5, which can be controlled by using limestone.

MY POTATOES ARE SCABING
To stop potatoes from developing scab, you will need to plant a new breed of potato called the scab-free potato or rotate your crop. If you rotate your crop, do not plant them in a field that has been growing turnips, carrots or beets since these vegetables tend to develop scab as well.

FIRE BLIGHT - CALL THE FIRE DEPARTMENT
Blight in an apple orchard is not uncommon. The best method to combat the problem is to spray with a 50:50 solution of apple cider vinegar and water. Make sure you spray after each rainfall, especially if you see burnt leaves.

BLIGHT PREVENTION

Celery is very susceptible to blight and the best method of avoiding the problem is to soak the seeds in very warm (120^{0}F) water for about 20-25 minutes before you plant the seeds.

GENERAL VEGETABLE SEEDLING PEST PROBLEMS

THE PROBLEM	CAUSED BY
Seeds will not germinate or emerge	Birds, seedcorn maggots, wireworms, garden symphylan, seedrot,
New seedlings emerge dead or fall over	Damping-off disease, summer high Heat
Seedling stems chewed off at soil line	Cutworms
Both seedling leaves & stem chewed off	Earwigs, snails and slugs, sowbugs, pillbugs, caterpillars, darkling beetles, vegetable weevils, rabbits
Roots of seedlings chewed off	Wireworms, maggots, gophers
Leaves have small round holes	Flea beetles
Yellow spots on leaves with tiny black spots	Thrips
Twisting white lines in leaves	Leafminers
Pear-shaped insects on leaves	Aphids
Plant has disappeared	Gopher or rabbit
Thin, spindly plants	Competition from weeds or other plants too close

CHAPTER 18

PLANTS FOR PEST CONTROL

PLANTS FOR PEST CONTROL

AGAVE

Crush the plant leaves and stems in water and use 1 part of the crushed up plant material to 5 parts water. Allow the mixture to sit for 1 hour before straining and placing in a sprayer. This is a general insect killer. If you prefer the plant parts can be dried and ground into a powder to dust the plants.

ANISE

This herb is best made into an infusion, which should remain for about 1 hour before adding a dash of hot sauce and ½ teaspoon of Dr. Bronner's Peppermint Soap™. This solution works on most caterpillars and leaf-eating insects. It will, however, remove many beneficial insects as well. Start with anise oil from a health food store.

AZALEA

Dry azalea flowers and crush them into a dust. This will kill many harmful insects by poisoning them, however, it is best not to use it on vegetable gardens.

BALM

Balm oil is the form to use. It will repel aphids, all ants and many other insects. Only use one capful to 1 quart of tap water. Balm should be available in most drug stores.

BASIL

It is best to purchase it as sweet basil oil. It is more effective when added to pyrethrum or tobacco leaves. The basil extracts are very powerful and it doesn't take much to eliminate mosquitoes, their larvae and even houseflies. Use only 1 ounce per gallon of water in a sprayer.

Basil has also been shown effective on a number of fungi. If you do use tobacco, remember it is a poison and keep it away from roses and fishes.

BEETS & JUICE

Flying insects hate beet juice especially if you add a small amount of Tabasco Sauce™ or other hot sauce to it. Effective as a spray, that will control a variety of plant diseases. Easy and inexpensive to make providing you have a juicer.

BLACK PEPPER

If you sprinkle a small amount of black pepper around squash vines it will repel squash vine borers.

BORAGE OIL

Prepare as an infusion to control most leaf-eating insects. Borage oil is very effective in repelling them as well.

CABBAGE LEAVES

These leaves are very attractive to aphids and are used to attract the bug into aphid traps. If you want to make an infusion for a spray, just allow some cabbage leaves to simmer in boiling water and add a dash of Tabasco Sauce™. Allow it to remain overnight before using it in the sprayer.

CHAMOMILE

Prepare as a tea and allow the tea to cool before spraying on plants. Commonly used by landscape supply houses, sprayed on flats and flowerpots. Also commonly used on cucumber seedlings to prevent mildew.

CHIVES

Use very fresh chives and prepare a tea that has steeped for about 15 minutes. Cool before using on plants and spray gooseberries and cucumbers to prevent mildew.

CAMPHOR

This is a whitish, crystalline substance that is produced from the gum of an Asian tree. The odor is very pungent and it will repel a number of insect pests. Moths, especially hate camphor. Dilution with alcohol is recommended if you plan on using it for a spray.

The natural sources for camphor include sage, tansy, feverfew and plants from the artemesia family.

COCONUT OIL

The oil can be diluted depending on the strength needed and will kill most soft-bodied insects. Coconut oil can kill beneficial insects, so you need to use sparingly. The leaves can also be used as well as the sap. Always make sure the label reads 100% pure coconut oil. It will work great against most hard-shelled insects.

CARAWAY

Caraway will work great on chewing insects when prepared as an infusion with a small amount of Ivory Liquid Soap™ added. You can also add a dash or two of Tabasco Sauce™ to give it a kick.

CASTOR OIL

Made from the castor bean it works better when added to pyrethrum or any other natural insecticide. Best to purchase the concentrated oil and use 1 ounce per gallon of water with pyrethrum added. It is not recommended for use on vegetables or fruit.

CATNIP

When a solution of catnip is sprayed on plants it will prevent insects from setting up housekeeping and it will even work on caterpillars and some worms. Best to make a tea that is not too strong so that you don't damage the plant while killing the bugs. Don't use if you have a cat or one visits your garden.

CAYENNE PEPPER

Tabasco Sauce™ is a good source of cayenne pepper; however, you can use the ground pepper with an equally good result. A weak tea can be prepared from the powder, which will kill most insect pests. Don't make the tea too strong or it may kill all the insects that are sprayed. Make sure you purchase only cayenne or hot sauce that does not contain any preservatives.

CITRONELLA OIL

Famous for its role as a mosquito repellant: as well as a base for many insect sprays. Do not use on oil-based trees such as a pine tree. It is best to use the essential oil from a health food store.

CITRUS OIL

Contains an extract derived for citrus peels called "limonene." Very effective: when combined with any number of natural pest remedies. Do not use more than 10 drops per gallon of water, if using the extract. The weak strength is very effective against most soft-bodied insects. The spray can be used on most plants and vegetable gardens. The spray will control flies, larvae and many chewing insects. The oil may kill some of the beneficial insects as well. It can be purchased as Citra Solv™ in most garden stores.

CORIANDER

The seeds are powdered and made into an infusion, then used in a sprayer to repel many chewing insects.

CUCUMBER

Cucumber and cucumber peelings have been used for hundreds of years as an insect repellant. The seeds are the most potent part and should be ground into a powder and used to make an infusion. They will repel worms, fleas, ants and some beetles.

CURRY

In some countries curry is made into a paste and painted on the trunk of plants and trees. When made into a liquid it is used in a sprayer.

Place the curry into a blender to liquefy then use 1 tablespoon to 1 gallon of water.

DILL

Purchase dill oil for the best results and mix it with water to be used in a sprayer to repel flying insects.

EUCALYPTUS OIL

It is best to add a small amount to almost any infusion to be used in a sprayer. It is capable of killing numerous soft-bodied insects on contact or will at least repel them. Works best when used with Dr. Bronner's Peppermint Soap™.

FENNEL

Purchase as an extract and make a spray adding 1 drop of fennel, a dash of a very hot sauce into 1 gallon of water. Effective: on almost all chewing insects.

FIREMIST SPRAY

This is a spray composed of a very hot sauce and is very effective on many insects. It is sold in many garden supply houses.

GARLIC

All parts of the plants can be juiced and used as a concentrate to be added to water. For a potent spray use 1 cup of garlic juice to 1 gallon of water and allow it to remain for about 45 minutes before using, then use immediately and discard the balance.

If you are purchasing the extract only use 1 ounce per 1 gallon of water. Garlic pellets can be purchase and placed in the ground around plants and trees to keep animals from damaging them.

HORSERADISH

This is one plant that very few insects or burrowing animals will eat. If you can purchase an extract made from the roots, place 1 ounce in 1 gallon of water and use as a spray against most insects.

HYSSOP

Hyssop has been used for centuries and is about as powerful as pyrethrum. It is best to try using it as an infusion to get rid of most insect pests.

LETTUCE LEAVES

It is best to simmer them and make an infusion to repel aphids and especially whiteflies. If you add a dash of a very hot sauce to the infusion it will be more effective.

MUSTARD SEED

The seeds need to be crushed and made into an infusion. Best to just purchase a strong Chinese mustard and place 1 tablespoon into 1 gallon of water. Allow the mixture to settle then strain well and add a drop or two of Ivory Liquid Soap™ to the mixture before placing it into a sprayer. This mixture can also be painted on tree trunks to keep critters and insects away.

NEEM TREE TEA OIL

This is one of the best anti-fungal oils that will also repel a number of insects. It tends to kill many insects on contact including the beneficial ones. This is one of the more commonly used natural pesticides.

ONION

Very effective in controlling many insects and critters! It is best to use strong onions and juice them. Use ½ cup of onion juice in 1 gallon of water.

PEANUT SAUCE
Produced in Thailand and is sold as Hot Peanut Sauce™ in many garden shops. To be used mainly to repel deer, rabbits and raccoons.

PENNYROYAL
Purchase as an extract and add only 1-2 drops per gallon of water that has already been made into a spray. Has the ability to kill most insects and when used in herbal powder form will repel spiders. Pennyroyal will works synergistically with almost all other herbs to make them more effective.

PEPPERMINT OIL
Mix 5 tablespoons in 1 gallon of water for the best results. It will kill most insects on contact.

PEPPERS
This is one of the best methods of natural pest control. It will repel the insects as well as the critters. Chili peppers are the best source of insect repellant and can be used as a powder; however, concentrates are available in health food stores. Chili pepper oil can be purchased in Asian markets and only 5 drops are needed in 1 gallon of water to be effective.

PEPPERCORNS
Peppercorns from India are usually the hottest and can repel most critters that will frequent your garden. Grind them into a dust and dust you garden to keep most insects and pest away.

PINE OIL
It is best used only on ants and will kill on contact by just placing 1 drop of the concentrate into 1 quart of water.

POTATO SOUP
Make up a pot of potato soup, strain it well and add 3-4 drops of Tabasco Sauce™ to it. Spray the plants to control chewing insects and beetles.

PYRETHRUM

Produced from the pyrethrum flower and considered a very strong insecticide. However, it will kill all insects even the beneficial ones. Try and find natural insecticides that will not kill all bugs. When small amounts are added as a synergistic it improves the effectiveness.

QUASSIA

The bark and chips have an excellent level of insecticidal properties when used as an extract. Do not use on fruits and vegetables. The chips need to simmer for about 3-4 hours then add a small amount of a very hot sauce and place in a sprayer.

RADISH

Use the leaves and make an infusion adding a small amount of a very hot sauce like Tabasco Sauce™. This will repel most chewing insects, ant and whiteflies when sprayed on the plants and may also keep rabbits away.

SABADILLA

A plant related to the lily family. The seeds need to be ground up and made into a tea. After the tea cools, strain the mixture and add a dash of Tabasco Sauce™, mix thoroughly and use in a spray. The powder can be used and is very toxic to insects since it affects their nervous systems.

SUGAR APPLE

The roots and seeds can be made into a very effective toxin to many insects. The roots especially are more effective than the seeds and can be dried and powdered.

Place ½ cup of the dried preparation into 4 cups of boiling water, then allow the mixture to remain standing for about 8 hours before using it.

TOMATO LEAVES

The leaves are dried and made into a tea that can be placed in a sprayer and is very effective in controlling most chewing insects.

CHAPTER 19

CARNIVOROUS PLANTS

CARNIVOROUS PLANTS

GENERAL INFORMATION:

Carnivorous plants should not be used to keep the insect population down in your garden or around the house or barn. They require a lot of tender care and plenty of water. While some will catch houseflies they do not have a big enough appetite to do a big job. They will eat flies, moths, butterflies and most small insects by attracting them with a sugary substance. To be called a carnivorous plant, the plant has to be able to attract, capture and kill life forms. It must also have the ability to digest and absorb the nutrients.

GOURMET BUGS FOR THE DISCRIMINATING PLANT

Your animals and small children are safe, the plants are harmless to people and animals and only produce a very weak digestive enzyme. These enzymes are not the acids we are aware of in the human stomach and are just weak enzymes that will digest small insect juices and soft tissue.

Many of the plants utilize bacteria to do the work of breaking down the bugs into a **"bug-soup"** so that they can utilize the nutrients. While others wait until the bug meal rots and then absorbs the food molecules.

The assassin bugs like the sweet substance excreted by the carnivorous plants and will eat the substance without being bothered by the plants and leave a pile of excrement for the plant to consume.

The largest carnivorous plant is the **Nepenthes**, which may occasionally catch a small frog and has large vines that will extend10-20 feet from the plant base.

THE MORE COMMON CARNIVOROUS PLANTS FOUND IN THE UNITED STATES

BLADDERWORTS (Utricularia)

There are over 210 species of this plant worldwide and the species is found in every state, even Hawaii, where it is considered a non-native weed. The largest number can be found in Florida and New Jersey. It lives above and below water; however, the carnivorous action only takes place under water.

Each plant develops a number of bladders, which are the mouths of the plant.

When a bug bumps into long hair-like organs, a trapdoor catches the bug and they are sucked in when a vacuum is formed. The trapdoor shuts in 1/30th of a second and the plant digests the bug.

BUTTERWORTS (Pinguicula)

These plants are only found in the lower 48 states and there are only eight species. The plant has leaves similar to the artichoke plant. The leaves have small glands that capture tiny insects like gnats and even have limited movement capabilities. The flowers look very much like a violet but there is no relation to the violet plant. The plant is grown mainly on trees in Mexico.

PITCHER PLANTS (Darlingtonia & Sarracenia)

The **Darlingtonia** species is found on the far west coast usually California and Oregon and is usually located near serpentine outcrops. The **Sarracenia** species are found in the southeastern United States with the largest plant population around Mobile, Alabama and are trumpet-shaped plants.

The pitcher plant secretes a number of chemicals to attract and digest their prey. Some use an insect narcotic, wetting agents or sweet substances to attract the bug and then use bacterial action to digest it. This plant will eliminate a number of insects but does not discriminate between good and bad bugs.

SUNDEWS (Drosera)

These plants are worldwide with only seven species found in the United States.

The plant has long whip-like leaves that are covered with short tentacles that contain an adhesive substance, which allows the plant to hold on to its bug prey. The prey is covered with a mucous coating and the more it struggles the more it is trapped and eventually drowns in the mucous coating. In some species the entire leaf will encircle the bug.

VENUS FLYTRAP (Dionaea)

Only found in specific areas of North and South Carolina with the colonies in South Carolina about gone. Human activity has all but eliminated this species in the United States. The plant captures insects by attracting the insect with nectar to bilobed leaves, which then snap shut trapping the bug. The plants are green with areas of red on the inside surfaces of the leaves.

CHAPTER 20

FRUIT, VEGETABLES, FLOWERS & SHRUBS AND THEIR MOST COMMON PESTS

FRUITS, VEGETABLES, FLOWERS & SHRUBS AND THEIR MOST COMMON PESTS

FRUIT/VEGETABLE/FLOWERS/SHRUBS	DAMAGING INSECTS
Apples	Coddling moth, tent caterpillars, cankerworm, apple maggot, European red mite
Artichoke, globe	Aphids
Artichoke, Jeruselum	None
Apricot	Pear borer, Oriental fruit moth
Asparagus	Asparagus beetles
Aster	Root aphids, flea beetles
Beans, fava	Black fly
Beans, green & pole	Been weevil, Mexican bean beetle
Beans, Lima	Mexican bean beetle, black fly
Beets	Leaf miner
Blackberries	Aphids, cutworms, Japanese beetles, cane borer, galls
Blueberries	Blueberry maggot, Japanese beetles, galls
Broccoli	Cabbage worm, aphids
Brussels Sprouts	Cutworm, slugs, cabbage worm, root maggot, harlequin bug
Cabbage	Cabbage root maggot, slugs, cutworm
Calendula	Cutworm, climbing cutworm
Cantaloupe	Squash bug, striped cucumber beetle
Carrots	Root aphids, carrot worm, root fly, wire worm, harlequin bug
Cauliflower	Cutworm, cabbage worm, root maggot
Celeriac	Celery hopper
Celery	Tarnished plant bug, celery hopper
Cherries	Plum curculio, tent caterpillar

FRUIT/VEGETABLE/FLOWERS/SHRUBS	DAMAGING INSECTS
Chicory	None
Chinese Cabbage	Cabbage root maggot, slugs, cutworm
Chives	Almost none
Chrysanthemum	Cabbage loopers, flea beetle, gall
Collard Greens	Cutworm, slugs, root maggots
Columbine	Columbine leaf miner
Corn, sweet	European corn borer, corn earworm
Cucumber	Cucumber beetle, aphids, root maggot fly
Current	Current aphid, current worm, gooseberry caterpillar
Dahlia	Corn ear worms, burdock borer, earwigs
Dandelion	None
Dill	Carrot worm
Eggplant	Flea beetle, Colorado potato beetle, cutworm
Elderberry	None or very few
Endive	None
Garlic	Onion maggot, gray fly larvae
Geranium	Cabbage loopers, leaf tier, fall web worm, tussock moth caterpillar
Gooseberry	Aphids, gooseberry caterpillar
Grapes	Leaf hoppers, Japanese beetles, rose chafer, grape curculio, leaf tier, mealybug
Hollyhock	Burdock borer, slugs, iris borer
Horseradish	Flea beetle
Hydrangea	Woolly bear caterpillar
Kale	Cutworm, slugs, cabbage worm, cabbage root maggot, harlequin bug
Kohlrabi	Same as for kale
Larkspur	Burdock borer, leaf miner

FRUIT/VEGETABLE/FLOWERS/SHRUBS	DAMAGING INSECTS
Laurel	European leaf roller
Leek	Onion maggot, gray fly larvae
Lilac	European leaf roller, greenhouse whitefly, leaf miner
Marigold	Greenhouse whitefly, Japanese beetle, earwigs
Muskmelon	Striped cucumber beetle, squash bug, squash vine borer
Mustard greens	Cutworm, harlequin bug, cabbage worm, slugs, cabbage root maggot
Nasturtium	Aphids
Okra	Green stink bug, cabbage loopers
Onion	Onion fly, onion maggot, thrips
Pansy	Leaf miner, cutworm
Parsley	Carrot worm
Peach	Peach borer, Oriental fruit moth
Peanut	None
Pear	Plum curculio, pear psylla, coddling moth, rose slug
Peas	Pea aphid, red spider mite, bean weevil
Peony	Leaf roller
Peppermint	Greenhouse whitefly
Peppers, hot	Cutworms
Peppers, sweet	Cutworms
Petunia	Flea beetle
Potato	Potato beetle, flea beetle, Colorado potato beetle, wireworm, potato stem borer
Pumpkin	Squash bug, squash vine borer
Radish	Radish root maggot, flea beetle, harlequin beetle

FRUIT/VEGETABLE/FLOWERS/SHRUBS	DAMAGING INSECTS
Rose	European leaf roller, leaf tier, burdock borer, tent caterpillar, rose flea beetle, June bugs, earwigs, leaf gall
Quince	Coddling moth
Raspberries	Raspberry fruit worm, cane borer, white grub, red spider mite, grasshopper
Rhubarb	None, leaves are poisonous
Rutabaga	Same as cabbage
Sage	Hawk moth caterpillar
Salsify	Carrot worm
Snapdragons	Stink bugs
Soybeans	None or very few
Spearmint	Hawk moth caterpillar
Spinach	Leaf miner, flea beetle
Squash, summer	Squash bug, squash vine borer
Squash, winter	Squash bug, squash vine borer
Strawberry	Cane borer, cutworm, crown borer, sawfly, strawberry weevil
Sweet basil	Asiatic garden beetle
Sweet peas	Pea aphids, corn ear worm, red spider mite
Sweet potato	None or very few
Swiss chard	Leaf miner, grasshoppers
Tomato	Cutworm, flea beetle, tomato horn worm
Watercress	None
Watermelon	Cucumber beetle, squash bug, squash vine borer
White daisy	Thrips, earwigs
Zinnia	Tarnished plant bug, Japanese beetle

CHAPTER 21

INSECT-RESISTANT VEGETABLES & FRUITS

INSECT-RESISTANT: VEGETABLES & FRUITS

The following fruits and vegetables will provide additional information regarding which fruits and vegetables are more or less resistant to insect infestations and subsequent damage by them. Remember, even the resistant varieties may not be 100% resistant in some areas of the world. If you plant the following fruits and vegetables it would be wise to plant the most resistant varieties for the best results.

FRUIT OR VEGETABLE	BUG		VARIETY
Alfalfa	*Aphid*	Resistant:	Cody, Lahontan, Zia
		Susceptible:	Buffalo
Barley	*Greenbug*	Resistant:	Omugi, Dictoo, Will
		Susceptible	Rogers, Reno
Bean	*Cutworm*	Resistant	Snap Beans: Wade, Idaho, Refugee, Gold Crop, Regal
		Resistant	Limas: Black Valentine, Baby Fordhook, Baby White
	Mexican Bean Beetle	Resistant:	Wade, Logan, Black Valentine (Limas)
		Susceptible:	State, Bountiful, Dwarf Horticultural
Broccoli	*Diamondback Moth*	Resistant:	Coastal, Italian Green Atlantic
		Susceptible:	De Cicco
	Harlequin Bug	Resistant:	Grande, Atlantic, Coastal
		Susceptible:	Gem
	Striped Flea Beetle	Resistant:	De Cicco, Coastal, Italian Green
		Susceptible:	Gem
Cabbage	*Cabbage Looper Cabbageworm*	Resistant:	Mammoth, Red Rock, Savory Chieftain, Savory Perfection, Drumhead
		Moderately Resistant:	Penn State BallHead. Early Flat Dutch, Badger Ball, Globe, Bugner, All Seasons, Wisconsin Ball Head
		Susceptible:	Golden Acre, Elite

FRUIT OR VEGETABLE	BUG		VARIETY
			Copenhagen Market 86, Stein's Flat Dutch
	Diamondback Moth	Resistant:	Michihli Chinese, Mammoth Red Rock
		Moderately Resistant:	Stein's Early Flat Dutch, Savory Perfection Drumhead, Early Jersey Wakefield
		Susceptible:	Copenhagen Market 86
	Harlequin Bug	Resistant:	Copenhagen Market 86, Headstart, Savory Perfection Drumhead, Stein's Flat Dutch
		Susceptible:	Michihli Chinese
Cantaloupe	*Mexican Bean Beetle*		All cantaloupe is resistant to this bug
	Spotted Cucumber Beetle	Resistant: (foliage)	Edisto 47, Edisto, Harper Hybrid
		Susceptible: (seedlings)	Edisto 47, Edisto, Harper Hybrid,
Honey dew		Susceptible: (foliage)	Honey Dew
Cauliflower	*Diamondback Moth*	Moderately Resistant:	Snowball A
	Harlequin Bug	Resistant:	Early Snowball X, Snowball Y
	Striped Flea Beetle	Resistant:	Snowball A & X
Collard	*Diamondback Moth*	Resistant:	Green Glaze
		Moderately Resistant:	Morris Heading,Vates Georgia Southern
	Harlequin Bug	Resistant:	Vates, Morris Improved Heading, Green Glaze
		Moderately Resistant:	Georgia LS, Georgia
Sweet Corn	*Corn Earworm*	Resistant:	Dixie 18, Calumet, Country Gentleman, Staygold, Victory Golden, Silvergent, Aristogold, Ioana
		Susceptible:	Spancross, Seneca Chief, North Star, Evertender

FRUIT OR VEGETABLE	BUG		VARIETY
	Fall Armyworm	Resistant:	Golden Market, Ioana Golden Beauty, Silver & Golden Cross Bantam, Triplegold, Deep Gold
	Sap Beetle	Resistant:	Country Gentleman, Deligold, Gold Pack, Tender Joy, Victory Golden, Tucker's Favorite
		Moderately Resistant:	Atlas, Duet, Eastern Market, Gold Strike, Golden Grain, Merit, Spring Gold, Merit
		Susceptible:	Aristogold, Gold Mine, Corona, Sixty Pak, Spring Bounty, Northern Belle, Titan
Cucumber	*Mexican Bean Beetle*	Susceptible:	Arkansas Hybrid 4, Colorado, Crispy, Hokus, Nappa 63, Piccadilly, Packer, Table Green
	Pickleworm	Resistant:	Arkansas Hybrid 4, Cubit, Gemini, Nappa 63, Princess Spartan Dawn, Stono, Ashley, Colorado, Hokus, Long Ashley, Packer, Table Green
	Spotted Cucumber Beetle	Resistant: (seedlings)	Ashley, Chipper, Crispy, Explorer, Jet, Gemini, Frontier, White Wonder
		Resistant: (foliage)	Ashley, Chipper, Cherokee, Gemini, High Mark II, Stono, Southern Cross, Pontsett
		Susceptible: (seedlings)	Cherokee, Coolgreen, Model, Nappa 61, Packer, Pioneer, Southern Cross, Table Green
		Susceptible: (foliage)	Coolgreen, Cubit, Hokus, Jet, Model, Nappa 63, Packer, Pioneer, Spartan Dawn, SMR 58

FRUIT OR VEGETABLE	BUG	VARIETY	
Kale	Diamond Back Moth	Resistant:	Vates
		Susceptible:	Early and Dwarf Siberian
	Harlequin Bug	Resistant:	Vale
		Susceptible:	Dwarf Siberian
	Mexican Bean Beetle	Resistant:	Dwarf Siberian
	Striped Flea Beetle	Resistant:	Vates, Dwarf Siberian Dwarf Green, Curled Scotch Lettuce
	Lettuce Root Aphid	Resistant:	Avondefiance, Avon Crisp
Muskmelon	Striped & Spotted Cucumber Beetle	Resistant:	Hearts of Gold
		Susceptible:	Crenshaw, Smith Perfect
Potato	Aphids	Resistant:	British Queen, DeSota, Houma, Early Pinkeye, Irish Daisy, LaSalle
		Susceptible:	Katahdin, Irish, Cobbler, Idaho Russet, Sebago Sequoia
	Colorado Potato Beetle	Resistant:	Sequoia, Katahdin
		Susceptible:	Fundy, Plymouth, Catoosa
	Potato Leafhopper	Resistant:	Delus
		Susceptible:	Cobbler, Plymouth
Pumpkin	Serpentine Leafminer	Resistant:	Mammoth Chili, Small Sugar
		Susceptible:	Green Striped Cushaw, King of the Mammoth
	Spotted Cucumber Beetle	Resistant: (foliage)	King of the Mammoth Mammoth Chili, Dickenson Field
		Susceptible: (seedlings)	Green Striped, Cushaw, King of the Mammoth, Mammoth Chili, Small Sugar
		Susceptible: (foliage)	Connecticut Field, Green Striped Cushaw, Small Sugar
Radish	Cabbage Webworm	Resistant:	Cherry Belle
		Moderately Resistant:	Globemaster
		Susceptible:	White Icicle, Red Devil, Champion

FRUIT OR VEGETABLE	BUG		VARIETY
	Diamondback Moth	Resistant:	Cherry Belle, White Icicle, Globemaster, Champion
	Harlequin Bug	Resistant:	Red Devil, White Icicle, Globemaster, Cherry Belle, Red Prince, Champion
		Moderately Resistant:	Crimson Sweet
	Mexican Bean Beetle	Susceptible:	Sparkler, Champion, White Icicle
	Striped Flea Beetle	Moderately Resistant:	Champion, Sparkler
		Susceptible:	Globemaster, Cherry Belle, White Icicle
Squash	*Mexican Bean Beetle*	Susceptible:	White Bush Scallop
	Pickleworm	Resistant:	Summer Crookneck, Butternut 23, Boston Marrow, Buttercup, Blue Hubbard
		Susceptible:	Black Beauty, Seneca Zucchini, Zucchini, Cozini, Cozella Hybrid, U Conn
	Serpentine Leafminer	Resistant:	Butternut 23, Cozella
		Moderately Resistant:	Blue Hubbard, Pink Banana, Zucchini, Boston Marrow,
		Susceptible:	Seneca Prolific, Long Cozella, Summer Crookneck, Green Hubbard, Zucchini
	Spotted Cucumber Beetle	Resistant: (seedlings)	Blue Hubbard, Green Hubbard, Summer Crookneck, Long Cozella, Seneca Prolific
		Resistant: (foliage)	Black Zucchini, Blue Hubbard, Royal Acorn, Early Golden Bush Scallop
		Susceptible: (seedlings)	Black Zucchini, Cozella, Cozini, Seneca Zucchini
		Susceptible: (foliage)	Boston Marrow, Buttercup, Cozini, Zucchini, Seneca Prolific

FRUIT OR VEGETABLE	BUG		VARIETY
	Squash Bug	Resistant:	Butternut, Table Queen, Royal Acorn, Early Summer Crookneck, Straightneck, Improved Green Hubbard
		Susceptible:	Striped Green Cushaw, Pink Banana, Black Zucchini
	Squash Vine Borer	Resistant:	Butternut, Butternut23
	Striped Cucumber Beetle	Resistant:	U Conn, Early Prolific Straightneck, White Bush Scallop, Cozella Hybrid, Black Zucchini
		Susceptible:	Cozini, Caserta, Black Beauty
Sweet Potato	*Southern Potato Wireworm*	Resistant:	Nugget, All Gold
		Moderately Resistant:	Centennial, Georgia Red, Porto Rico, Gem
		Susceptible:	Red Jewel, Georgia 41 Nemagold, Jullian
Tomato	*Twospotted Mite*	Resistant:	Campbell 135 & 146
		Susceptible:	Homestead 24
Watermelon	*Spotted Cucumber Beetle*	Resistant: (foliage)	Crimson Sweet, Sweet Princess
		Susceptible: (seedlings)	Blue Ribbon
		Susceptible: (foliage)	Charleston Gray, Blue Ribbon, Sugar Baby
Wheat	*Hessian Fly*	Resistant:	Ottawa, Ponca, Big Club 43, Pawnee, Rus, Dual

CHAPTER 22

NATURAL MICROBIAL CONTROLS

COMMERCIALLY AVAILABLE

Natural Microbial Control

NATURAL MICROBIAL CONTROL	BEST PRODUCT	GARDEN PEST	HOW APPLIED
Bt – San Diego	Ringer Colorado Potato Beetle Attack	Elmleaf beetle Potato beetle	Eaten by insect
Bacillus thuringiensis (Bt)	Ringer Caterpillar or Insect Attack	Caterpillars	Sprayed, dusted Eaten by insect
Bacillus popilliae (milky spore disease)	Ringer Grub Attack	Japanese Beetle grubs	Apply to soil
Nematodes (Nc)	Scanmask	Boring insects	Will seek out pests
Nosema locustae	Ringer Grasshopper Attack	Crickets, grasshoppers	Bait and consumed by insects
Granulosis virus	Decyd™	Codling Moth, Grasshoppers	Eaten by insect
Nuclear polyhedrosis Virus (NPV)	Gypchek™	Gypsy moth caterpillar	Eaten by insect

Information Regarding Controls

Bacillus Thuringiensis (Bt)

Bt is viewed as a rod-shaped bacterium and is sold as a mixture of the resting spore stage and as protein crystals that are diamond-shaped. The crystals will form close to the spores. However, it only affects caterpillars that eat it. The crystals cause the insect to stop feeding as the spores germinate and the insect dies. Bt should not be stored in direct sunlight or it will deactivate.

Its safety has been proven with humans and animals as well as plants and trees. The names it is marketed under include Dipel™, Thuricide™ Biotrol™. You can purchase it as a wettable dust or as an emulsion. While it is stable when stored it will lose potency in sunlight.

It is available in most garden supply stores or through mail order. Pellet bait is also available and marketed under the names Soilserv™ and Bacillus Bait™. It is approved for use in California and is widely used on an assortment of vegetables and fruits.

GARDEN PESTS CONTROLLED BY Bt

CROP	GARDEN PEST
Almond	Peachtree Borer
Alfalfa	Alfalfa Caterpillar
Apple Tree	Codling Moth Worm, Tent Caterpillar Fall Webworm, Eyespotted Bud Moth, Apple rust mite, Tentiform Leafminer, Winter Moth and Redbanded Leafroller
Artichoke	Artichoke Plume Moth
Castor Bean	Castor Semi-Looper
Celery	Celery Looper, Cabbage Looper
Citrus	Anise Swallowtail
Corn	Corn Earworm, European Corn Borer
Cotton	Cotton Leafworm, Cotton Leaf, Perforator, Bollworm
Crucifers	Cabbageworm, Diamondback Moth, Cabbage Looper
Grape	Grape Leafroller, Western Grapeleaf Skeletonizer
Lettuce	Corn Earworm, Tobacco Budworm
Orange	Fruit Tree Leafroller, Orangedog

CROP	GARDEN PEST
Peach..	Peachtree Borer
Stored Grain Crops...	Variety of Insects
Tomatoes...	Tomato Hornworm, Tobacco Hornworm, Cabbage Looper, Tomato Fruitworm
Trees (General)...	Fall Cankerworm, Spring Cankerworm, California Oakworm, Fruit Tree Leafroller,Gypsy Moth, Linden Loopers,Spruce Budworm, Winter Moth. Etc.

Bacillus Popilliae (BP)

This is a bacterium that inhabits the soil and infects only grubs of the Japanese and June beetle. The blood of these beetles is normally clear; however, it will turn a milky color and is known as "milky spore disease." It will not kill all types of grubs so it is best to check with your local supplier to be sure it will work on grubs in your area.

The BP is applied to grassy areas and around orchards, which is where the adult beetles lay their eggs. One application of milky spores will last 15-20 years.

Nematodes (Nc)

These are microscopic wormlike relatives of the worm family and attack and parasitize a number of insect pests. There are over 200 pests that can be controlled with Nc including vine borers and cucumber beetles. They seek and destroy very efficiently. Nematodes will enter the insect through their mouth or through spiracles, which are the insects breathing tubes.

When they feed on the insect they release bacteria causing the mummification of the insect. The insect will usually die within 24 hours. Nematodes; are usually shipped in peat moss or soil and is then easily applied to the infected areas. When applying nematodes the soil needs to be moist and never apply in direct sunlight.

Nosema locustae

This is a one-celled parasite that is prepared using cereal bait, usually wheat bran and is very effective in killing grasshoppers and crickets. However, it takes a year for the maximum effect.

Codling Moth Granulosis Virus (CMGV)

This is an active virus that will affect certain insects and not others. It is most affective for controlling codling moths.

APPENDIX A

GENERAL INFORMATION REGARDING
PREPARATION OF PLANT SPRAYS

Almost all sprays should be re-applied after it rains.

Soap is often recommended to help the spray stick to the plants or the insects.

The majority of plant oil extracts will act as a contact poison on all insects, however, the insects must be covered by the spray.

When preparing the sprays be sure that direct sunlight does not hit the liquid since sunlight will break down the spray and reduce its effectiveness.

Be sure and test a small area of any plant you are going to spray to be sure that the spray will not damage the plant.

The preferred time of day to spray is the evening hours, the later the better.

APPENDIX B

PLANTS THAT REPEL PESTS

PEST	PLANT
Ants & Aphids	Pennyroyal, spearmint, tansy, southernwood
Aphids	All of the above as well as garlic, chives, onions, coriander, anise,
Armyworm	Bear hops, mescal, coral bean Nasturtium, petunia
Asparagus Beetle	Tomato
Bean leafroller	Larkspur, Spanish dagger
Borer	Garlic, tansy, onion
Cabbage Maggot	Mint, tomato, rosemary, hemp, sage
Cabbage Moth	Mint, hyssop, rosemary, thyme, sage southernwood, hemp, wormwood, celery, catnip, nasturtium
Cabbageworms	Turkey mullein
Carrot Fly	Rosemary, sage, wormwood, black salsify, alliums, coriander
Chinch Bug	Soy beans, false indigo
Codling Moth	American wisteria, common oleander
Codling Moth (larvae)	Black Indian hemp
Colorado Potato Beetle	Green beans, horseradish, dead nettle, flax, catnip, coriander, nasturtium, tansy
Corn Borer (larvae)	Manroot, wild cucumber
Cucumber Beetle (spotted or striped)	Tansy, radish, buffalo gourd, false indigo
Cutworm	Tansy
Diamondback Moth	Rayless chamomile
Flea Beetle	Wormwood, mint, catnip
Fruit Tree Moth	Southernwood
Gopher	Castor bean
Grasshoppers	Chinaberry tea

Japanese Beetle	Garlic, larkspur, tansy, rue, Germanium, dwarf or red buckeye
Leafhopper	Petunia, geranium
Melonworm	Canadian fleabane
Mexican Bean Beetle	Marigold, potato, rosemary, petunia, summer savory, California buckeye Chinese wingnut
Mice	Mint
Mites	Onion, garlic, chives
Mole	Spurge, castor bean, mole plant,
Nematode (eelworm)	Marigold (African & French), salvis, dahlia, calendula, asparagus
Pea Aphids	Balsamroot, Sour sop
Plum Curculio	Garlic
Rabbit	Allium family
Rose Chafer	Geranium, petunia, onion
Slug (snail)	Prostrate rosemary, wormwood
Squash Bug	Tansy, nasturtium, catnip
Striped Pumpkin Beetle	Nasturtium
Tomato Hornworm	Borage, marigold, opal basil
Whitefly	Nasturtium, marigold, nicandra
Wireworm	White mustard, buckwheat, woard
Woolly Aphid	Tung-oil tree

APPENDIX C

SUPPLIERS OF BENEFICIAL INSECTS

AND MICROBIALS AS OF 2011

Havahart
(800) 800-1819
www.havahart.com
Deer-Off

Natural Pest Control Co.
8864 Little Creek Rd.
Orangevale, CA 95662
Mosquito fish

BioChem Products
Box 4090
Kansas City, MO 64101
Bt and Bti

Tanglefoot Co.
314 Straight Ave.
Grand Rapids, MI 49504

Exotic Hibiscus
www.exotic-hibiscus.com
Jungle Rain

Bugological
P.O. Box 32046
Tucson, AZ 85751
(520) 298-4400
Natural Insect Preditors

Bronner's Pure
Box 28
Escondido, CA 92025
Peppermint soap

If a company is no longer in business, try looking up the product on the Internet for another source. Many companies tend to in and out of business, however, as of

CATALOGS OF PEST CONTROL PRODUCTS

Gardener's Supply
128 Intervale Road
Burlington, VT 05401

Gurney's
110 Capital St.
Yankton, SD 57079

Harmony Farm Supply
3244 Gravenstein Hwy North
Sebastopol, CA 95472

Mellinger's
2310 W. South Range Rd.
North Lima, OH 44452-9731

Solutions
P.O. Box 6878
Portland, OR 97228-6878

Unique Insect Control
5504 Sperry Dr.
Citrus Heights, CA 95621

Maag Agrochemicals Inc.
5699 Kings Hwy.
Vero Beach, FL 32961-6430
Fire ant baits

Bat Conservation Intern.
P.O. Box 162603
Austin, TX 78716-2603
Bat house plans

GOPHER TRAPS
Guardian Trap Co.
P.O. Box 1935
San Leandro, CA 94577

Joseph B. Cook
11508 Keith Dr.
Whittier, CA 90606

PLANT NETTING
Orchard Supply Co.
P.O. Box 956
Sacramento, CA 95805

Animal Repellants Inc.
P.O. Box 999
Griffin, GA 30224

SLUG & SNAIL TRAPS
Cedar Pete Inc.
P.O. Box 969
Mt. Shasta, CA 96067

Brucker Snail Barrier Co.
9369 Wilshire Blvd.
Beverly Hills, CA 90210

SCARY BALLOONS
Rid-A-Bird Inc.
P.O. Box 436
Wilton, IA 52778

GLUE BOARDS
J.T. Eaton & Co.
1393 Highland Rd.
Twinsburg, OH 44087

FERRET SCENT
Bio-Pest Control
Box 401347
Brooklyn, NY 11240

ULTRASOUND
The Monadnock Co.
P.O. Box 189
Dedham, MA 02026

MOLE TRAPS
Nash Mole Trap Co.
5716 East "S" Ave.
Vicksburg, MI 49097-9990

SECRET BUG REPELLANT

When you are out-of-doors and the bugs are sure to bother you there is an herb that works to repel insects and even some animals. This herb solution has been around for hundreds of years and is easy to use.

The herb is anise, which you have probably heard about when making licorice. However, anise has chemical properties that make it one of the best natural bug deterrents that anyone has found.

Anise oil is available in all health food stores and you may also be able to purchase it through your local pharmacy, agricultural or garden supply house. Fisherman and hunters swear by anise oil and those in the know will not go on a hunting or camping trip without it.

One of the best ways to use the anise oil is to add a small amount to the clothes you will be wearing on the camping trip. Place the oil into the wash cycle so that it mixes with the soapsuds. This will place the oil into the clothing.

Anise will repel almost all bugs, especially houseflies, gnats, mosquitoes, green bottle flies and black blowflies.

To make a commercial bug repellant more effective and make it last longer: just add a few drops to the bottle and shake it up. Many people prefer this since many of the bug repellants have a more pleasant scent.

If anise seed is given to dogs it will make them more affectionate and may be used by breeding kennels. Anise is a love potion for dogs. If you encounter a dog and the dog licks your clothing that has been washed in anise oil, they will not be aggressive and be very affectionate.

GLOSSARY

Bacillus Thuringiensis (Bt)
The most widely used bacterial pesticide. ***Bacillus thuringiensis*** is a microbe that will infect most species of caterpillar. It may be purchased under the names of Biotrol™, Dipel™ or Thuricide™. Bt will not harm plants, animals or humans and most beneficial insects. Bt is very selective and for the most part only affects the bad bugs.

Bti
This is a special strain of Bt that only affects the larvae of mosquitoes and black flies.

BORIC ACID
Formulated from boron and is similar to borax. Boric Acid is one of the safest methods of killing cockroaches and other insect pests. **Poisonous if ingested by humans.**

COMPOST
It is composed of decaying plant matter, which has decomposed sufficiently to be a good source of plant food and may be used as a fertilizer. It is also a major component of forest soil. Other names may be humus or leaf mold.

DIATOMACEOUS EARTH (DE)
A mined mineral product; consisting of fossilized one-celled diatoms. Its sharp silica edges puncture the bug's outer shell and cause death by dehydration. The product will not affect birds when they eat the insects. DE will not kill earthworms.

HERBICIDE
These are usually petroleum-based products that stop plant growth and are used for weed and grass abatement. There is a new group of herbicides that are plant specific.

LARVAE
It is a stage in the life cycle of some insects that occurs between the egg and pupae stages. Normally, it takes the form of a soft-bodied caterpillar, grub or maggot and sometimes referred to as the worm stage.

LIME
Substance: that can supply calcium to the soil and plants while neutralizing acidic conditions. Very effective in sprays to control or kill many pests. It can be used to change the pH of the soil to make it more alkaline. Other forms include quicklime or hydrated lime. Lime draws water out of insects and causes them to dehydrate.

MICROBIALS
These are natural occurring microscopic organisms that can be found in the environment and can be produced on a large scale.

MILKY SPORE DISEASE
This is the common name for *Bacillus popilliae*, which is a naturally occurring bacterium that kills the Japanese beetles and other beetle pests. It is placed into the soil and the grubs eat the bacterium, which turns their clear blood milky and kills them. **It may be harmful to fish so it would be best to keep it away from fish ponds md lakes.**

Nc NEMATODE
An organism: that lives in the soil and is microscopic in size. It is worm-like and comes in several strains. They will feed and reproduce inside insects and eventually kill them. There are bad nematodes that attack and kill plants.

NEEM
Neem™ is produced from the margosa tree, which is an evergreen tropical tree that has insecticidal properties.In the United States the tree only grows in Florida and California. This is one wood termites will not eat. There are about 150 insects that are repelled by the extracts of this tree. It can be purchased under the name Margosan-O™ in most garden shops.

NPV
Nuclear polyhedrosis virus is an insect pathogen that has been registered for a limited number of pests and causes a disease process to occur. It is a microscopic organism or microbe.

NYMPH
This is a stage in the life cycle of a number of insects between the egg stage and adult. The life cycle of insects with a nymph stage is called incomplete metamorphosis since there is no pupae or cocoon stage.

ORGANIC
The most natural method of insect control: utilizing the least dangerous methods or chemicals to control insects. This method may employ many homemade sprays and remedies.

PUPAE

This is a stage in the life cycle of a number of insects between the larvae and adult stages. It is usually inactive in the cocoon or a hard shell found in the soil.

PYRETHRUM

It is produced from the dried flowers of the daisy plant *Chrysanthemum cinerariifolium*, which is mainly grown in Africa and is the only chrysanthemum plant with the effective pest control affects. It was used against body lice for hundreds of years. Do not purchase pyrethrum if it is combined with any other pesticide. The plant has been known to cause allergic reactions in susceptible individuals.

This is a potent stomach poison that affects insects and is prepared from the extracts of the tropical plants derris and cube.

RYANIA

A natural insecticide that is safe to use around humans and pets. Produced from the ryania plant that is native to Trinidad and is a relative of the tobacco plant. Has the effect of incapacitating the insect's ability to eat and they starve to death. Best used on caterpillars, codling moths, spiders Japanese beetles, thrips, moths and fleas.

SABADILLA

Produced from the South American lily it is an organic pesticide dust that has been in use since the sixteenth century. The plant has also been used to lower blood pressure. It does kill a wide range of pests; however, it is toxic to toads and bees. **This is the most toxic pesticide to humans and animals.** It is effective against grasshoppers, codling moth larvae, armyworms, European corn borer, silkworms, aphids, cabbage loopers, melonworm, chinch bugs, webworm, greenhouse leaftier and the harlequin bug.

SILICA AEROGEL

Has the ability to dehydrate the bugs by absorbing moisture from the bug's outer surface. The particles in the gel have the ability to absorb hundreds of times their weight in moisture.

SULFUR

This is one of the oldest known pesticides: even the Egyptians used it to fumigate their granaries. It should be used when the temperature is over 70^0F and under 90^0F for the best results. A powder form is now available for dusting plants. It should not be used within 2 months of spraying horticultural oils.

TANGLFOOT

Sticky substance produced from castor oil gum residues and vegetable waxes.

TRICHOGRAMMA

This is a very small insect that lays its eggs inside other insect's eggs and causing the host egg to die.

INDEX

403